PREMONITIONS:
A LEAP INTO THE FUTURE

PREMONITIONS:

A LEAP INTO THE FUTURE

by Herbert B. Greenhouse

Published by
BERNARD GEIS ASSOCIATES

To
Ralph L. Woods
Who Is Always Ready
With a Helping Hand

The author is grateful to William Sloane Company for
permission to paraphrase two incidents from *Hidden
Channels of the Mind* by Louisa Rhine © 1961 and to
Harper & Row for permission to quote from *The Imprisoned
Splendour* by Raynor Johnson © 1953.

CONTENTS

ACKNOWLEDGMENTS

The author is grateful to the following for their contributions to this book: psychics Lorna Middleton, Eva Hellstrom, Jeanne Gardner, Adrienne Coulter, Ann Jensen, Martha Lynne Johnson, Alan Vaughan, Malcolm Bessent, Paul Neary, and the late Arthur Ford; parapsychologists E. Douglas Dean, Dr. Stanley Krippner, Dr. Jule Eisenbud, and Professor Hans Bender; Robert and Nanci Nelson of the Central Premonitions Registry, and Jennifer Preston of the British Premonitions Bureau. Valuable material was culled from the professional papers of Dr. Ian Stevenson and the late Dr. J. C. Barker, and from publications of the Society for Psychical Research. Extensive use was made of the libraries of the American Society for Psychical Research and the Parapsychology Foundation.

CHAPTER ONE

"Something Terrible Is Going to Happen"

On October 14, 1966, Mr. Alexander Venn, a retired employee of the oceanliner *Queen Mary,* began to feel uneasy, but he didn't know why. Mr. Venn, who lived in the southwestern part of England, said to his wife, "Something terrible is going to happen, and it won't be far from here, either." The sense of imminent disaster was so strong that Venn, an amateur artist, went to his room and sketched his emotions on paper. He kept thinking about coal dust and drew a human head surrounded by an ominous black background.

Three days later, on the evening of Tuesday, October 17, a thirty-one-year-old man living in Kent, southeast of London, was resting in bed when he suddenly knew that on Friday there would be a frightful catastrophe. The next day, Wednesday, he remarked to a girl in his office, "On Friday something terrible connected with death is going to happen." What it would be he didn't know, but he felt depressed for the rest of the week.

"SOMETHING BLACK . . . DEEP BLACKNESS"

Early in the morning of Thursday, October 20, a middleaged Englishwoman woke up in a state of panic, unable to catch her breath. She had had a horrible nightmare of being smothered in "deep blackness." During the same night several other persons in England dreamed about "blackness." In her dream one woman saw a mountain flowing downward and a small child running and screaming.

Later that morning a nine-year-old girl named Eryl Mai Jones, who lived in a South Wales mining village, woke up and said to her mother, "Mummy, let me tell you about my dream last night." Her mother answered, "Darling, I have no time now. Tell me later." The child replied, "No, Mummy, you must listen. I dreamed I went to school and there was no school there. Something black had come down all over it!"

Eryl Mai's mother recalled that two weeks before the child had made a very strange remark: "Mummy, I'm not afraid to die." Her mother had said, "Why do you talk of dying, and you so young?" Eryl Mai had repeated, "I'm not afraid to die. I shall be with Peter and June." Peter and June were her classmates.

A SCREAMING CHILD . . . A BLACK,
BILLOWING MASS

On Thursday afternoon, October 20, a London television performer suddenly cancelled a pretaped comedy show set for a Saturday broadcast. The show was about a Welsh mining village, and the actor had a "feeling" that it shouldn't be on the air.

At 9 P.M. that evening Mrs. C. Milden was in Plymouth, England, at a meeting of spiritualists. Suddenly a vision appeared before her as if on film, showing an old schoolhouse in a valley and an avalanche of coal rushing down a mountainside. At the bottom of the mountain she saw a terrified little boy with a long fringe of hair. All around him rescue workers were digging into the coal slag looking for bodies. One of the workers wore an odd-looking peaked cap.

Friday, at 4 A.M., a London woman woke up gasping for air and thought the walls of her bedroom were caving in. At almost the same moment a Mrs. Sybil Brown in Brighton, south of London, had a terrifying nightmare of a screaming child in a telephone booth. Another child was walking toward the dreamer, and following him was a "black, billowing mass." Mrs. Brown woke her husband and said, "Something terrible has happened." He reassured her that they had heard no bad news, but she couldn't sleep the rest of the night. The child's screams rang in her ears.

About the same time, in the early morning hours of Friday, October 21, an elderly man living in northwestern England had an unusual dream. He saw, spelled out in a brilliant light, A-B-E-R-F-A-N. The word meant nothing to him—until he heard a radio broadcast later that day.

"TODAY IT IS GOING TO HAPPEN"

The tiny village of Aberfan, South Wales, lay in a valley at the base of a mountain. The top of the mountain was a dumping ground for huge amounts of coal waste from the nearby mines. Six hundred feet below stood the Pantglas Junior School. One of its students was Eryl Mai Jones.

At 9 A.M. on Friday, Eryl Mai went off to school. As she left, the clock in her house stopped ticking. Also at 9 A.M., the thirty-one-year-old man from Kent came into his office and said to his co-worker, "Today is the day it is going to happen."

A few minutes later Eryl Mai joined her classmates in school. Morning prayers were over in the assembly hall, and the classrooms were filling up. The children, talking and laughing, sat in their seats while their teachers got ready to call the roll. About half a block away, at the senior high school, three older boys were sitting on a wall, waiting for their classes to begin at 9:30.

At 9:14 a secretary in an aircraft plant, Mrs. Monica McBean, had a sudden feeling that "something drastic" was going to happen. In a vision she saw a "black mountain moving and children buried under it." Terror-stricken, she left her desk and went into the ladies' lounge, where she sat down, trembling.

THE PREMONITIONS COME TRUE

A few moments later it happened—a disaster that had been seen in dreams and visions weeks in advance. Half a million tons of coal waste, loosened by two days of heavy rain, began to rumble, then roared down over the village in a "black, billowing mass" forty feet high. Trees were uprooted, houses and cottages crumbled to the ground. The three boys sitting on the wall at the senior school disappeared. Pantglas Junior School was buried beneath the moving mountain, and with it over a hundred small children.

Most of those who had had premonitions of the Aberfan disaster lived in other parts of England and didn't know about the tragedy until they heard the news on radio and television or saw the next morning's edition of the London *Times*:

200 LOST AS COLLIERY TIP
ENGULFS SCHOOL

Mothers Join in Night Search
For Their Buried Children

85 Bodies Recovered, 36 Injured

A death toll of about 200 is feared in the disaster at the mining village of Aberfan, Glamorgan, where yesterday morning a rain-soaked 800-foot slag tip slipped and engulfed a school, a row of terraced houses, and a farm. Early today known deaths totalled 85.

The slag was part of a colliery tip.

The final death toll was 144, 28 adults and 116 children, most of them from the Pantglas Junior School. Rescue workers dug in the rubble all day and all night to recover the bodies. On Sunday Mrs. Milden was watching a television broadcast of the rescue operations when on the screen appeared the terrified little boy with the long fringe of hair she had seen in her vision. One of the workers nearby wore an odd-looking peaked cap.

A mass funeral was held on October 25, and the small bodies of 116 children were buried in a common grave. Among them was little Eryl Mai Jones, who was "not afraid to die." She was buried between her classmates, Peter and June.

AN APPEAL TO DREAMERS

Among those watching the rescue operations on Saturday, October 22, was J. C. Barker, a London psychiatrist who was interested in premonitions. Dr. Barker was writing a book called *Scared to Death*, in which he discussed cases he had come across of persons dying at the exact time predicted by fortune tellers and other psychics. Some of those who died, he reasoned, probably succumbed because they had literally frightened themselves to death as the fatal day approached. He suggested that psychics should not make such predictions because they could become self-fulfilling.

He was less certain about premonitions in general. For two thousand years and more there had been prophecies of death and disaster that had come true. Such cases had been reported in classical Greece and Rome, Babylon, China, and other ancient civilizations. Plagues, fires, tornadoes, earthquakes, and volcanic eruptions had been seen beforehand in visions and dreams by such prophets as Nostradamus, William Lilly, Madame de Ferriëm, and others in many countries and different eras.

Yet if so many premonitions had proved accurate, why hadn't this foreknowledge been used to prevent disasters, or at least warn those who later perished? Suppose, Dr. Barker mused, there had been psychic warnings of the Aberfan tragedy. Would it have been possible to save the adults and children who died? At this time Dr. Barker did not know about the many premonitions of the coal slide, but he was determined to find out by doing a scientific survey.

Barker telephoned Peter Fairley, science editor of the London *Evening Standard,* and asked him to send out a newspaper appeal to those who had had such premonitions. In two weeks 76 replies were received, most of them from the London area. The Psychophysical Research Unit at Oxford University launched a similar appeal through a London newspaper, the *Sun.* A third newspaper, *News of the World,* also did an investigation including interviews with Alexander Venn and Monica McBean. There was a total of 200 replies to the three surveys.

Dr. Barker discarded 16 of his 76 replies and did a follow-up of the other 60. Using criteria that had been established by parapsychologist G. W. Lambert, he evaluated each premonition on the basis of five questions:

1 Had the dream, vision, feeling, etc. been put down in writing or reported to other persons *before* the event?
2 Was the time interval between the premonition and its fulfillment short enough to indicate a close relationship between the two?
3 Was the event, at the time of the dream, something that did not seem likely to happen?
4 Was the description in the dream of an event that would be literally fulfilled and not just vaguely foreshadowed in symbols?
5 Were the details of the dream or vision identical with those of the disaster?

Another question Dr. Barker asked, one that is of paramount importance to those who investigate psychic phenomena, was, what kind of person had the premonition? Was he emotionally stable? Was he sincere? Were his statements believable? Did he allow bias and fantasy to creep into his story?

Granted that a premonition meets one or more of these criteria, other questions must be asked. Why do people have premonitions? Why do they come to one person in a dream, to another in a vision, while a third hears a voice? Finally, if we can know the future, what are the implications for our conception of time and space?

ARE SOME PEOPLE "HUMAN SEISMOGRAPHS"?

Of the sixty premonitions carefully studied by Dr. Barker, twenty-two were confirmed by from one to four other persons who had been told about them before the coal slide. Two more were recorded before the event: a London woman stated in a letter that she had dreamed about a little boy buried up to his neck in the ground; another woman wrote in a dream notebook about uprooted trees and hurtling logs. Except for little Eryl Mai Jones who died in the tragedy, the dreamers and visionaries did not live in the Aberfan area and had no interest in the mining village. There had been agitation in the village for several years about the danger from the coal wastes, but this was an issue well removed from the lives of those having the premonitions.

Most of the dreams gave literal details of the tragedy. A few pictured the event symbolically, but in symbols easily identified with the disaster. Mrs. Sybil Brown, who dreamed about the screaming child in the telephone booth, was herself a telephone operator—a case that illustrates how a dreamer uses materials from his own life to dramatize the content of a dream, precognitive or not. Another more symbolic dream, two weeks before the coal slide, was of "hundreds of black horses thundering down a hillside dragging hearses." In a vision twelve hours before the slide, a woman saw a school and children going to heaven dressed in the Welsh national costume.

The precognitive dreams could be differentiated from ordinary dreams by their vividness, the here-and-now quality of the future taking place in the present. Mrs. Brown, for example, felt that the tragedy had already happened—and perhaps in another dimension it had. Many of the dreams were so frightening they were in the form of nightmares. A week before the tragedy, a woman dreamed of "screaming children buried by an avalanche of coal in a mining village." She woke up screaming herself. Most of the psychics experienced strong emotions during their dreams and visions, from vague feelings of depression to outright terror.

Many common themes ran through the sixty premonitions examined by Dr. Barker: children, school, screams, Aberfan, valleys, blackness, avalanche, digging, buried houses, graves, descending mountains. Each dreamer saw the tragedy from a slightly different angle, as he would if he had actually been watching it, with some details more prominent than others.

The premonitions occurred in what are called "altered states of consciousness," when awareness of present time and place fades out slightly or altogether, as in dreams, visions, the twilight state between sleeping and waking, or hypnotic trances. Thirty-six of the premonitions studied by Dr. Barker came in dreams. Other persons interviewed had visions, either stationary or in the form of moving pictures. Mrs. Milden actually pre-viewed the scene that would appear two days later on television.

To many the premonitions came as vague feelings of uneasiness but with the certain knowledge of something very unpleasant in the immediate future. Such was the experience of Mr. Venn, who drew a picture of how he felt, and of the thirty-one-year-old Kent man who knew that "something terrible" was going to happen.

Four men and three women suffered acute mental and physical unease from four days to a few hours before the coal slide. Three more had what is known medically as dyspnoea—choking sensations and a feeling of suffocation. Dr. Barker theorized that such feelings of distress before a tragic event might be part of a "pre-disaster syndrome." Persons having this syndrome might act as "human seismographs" and might sense forthcoming disasters just as a seismograph records an earthquake.

Some of the Aberfan seismographs claimed that in the past they had had the same symptoms prior to a disaster. Mrs. Pamela Healey, a woman interviewed by *News of the World,* said: "What I experience is a period of absolute black depression for several days beforehand. Later this disappears and is followed by a peculiar feeling of relief as the awareness of disaster lifts from me. Once that has happened I always know that within a day or two the world will be shattered by news of some tremendous tragedy. . . ."

Could these human seismographs be found and used to forecast future tragedies? Could another Aberfan be averted this way? Writing in the London *Medical News-Tribune* of January 20, 1967, Dr. Barker said: "While analyzing the letters, I realized that the time had surely come to call a halt to attempts to prove or disprove precognition. We should instead set about trying to harness and utilize it with a view to preventing future disasters."

COMPUTERIZED PREMONITIONS

Dr. Barker's plan was to set up a kind of central clearing house where people might write or telephone if their "seismic sense" told them "something terrible" was about to occur: danger to a public official; a natural disaster such as a fire or an earthquake; an accident to a ship, plane, or train, and so forth. A computer could be used to exclude "trivial, misleading, or false information," and to detect "peaks or patterns" in the flow of pre-disaster data. If the computer signaled an unusually large number of premonitions pointing to a disaster at a specific time and place, an "early warning" system could go into effect, and the proper officials could be alerted.

In the Aberfan case, for example, the early warning alert would not have been sounded until two weeks before the coal slide. Since most of the premonitions came during that period, there would have been a clear indication that a disaster would occur very soon, involving a Welsh mining village, a school with children, something black such as coal, a mountain moving downward, etc. Add Eryl Mai's feeling that she would die in the disaster and the dream of the word ABERFAN in a bright light, and all the pieces would have fit together as in a puzzle. An early warning alert would have been indicated.

In December, 1966, Dr. Barker called Peter Fairley, who had launched the original appeal for letters, and suggested setting up a premonitions bureau in connection with his newspaper, the London *Evening Standard*. Fairley agreed to operate the Premonitions Bureau for a period of one year and to invite the public through press, radio, and television to send in their premonitions. Barker then contacted the sixty persons who had sensed the Aberfan tragedy, and asked them to communicate with the Bureau immediately if they had similar visions, dreams, or feelings of distress that foretold another disaster.

Dr. Barker hoped that in the experimental year the Bureau operated, two kinds of psychics would emerge. Individuals might be found who had a talent for "seeing" future events in altered states of consciousness. And among the general public there might be a far larger number of human seismographs who would experience the pre-disaster syndrome of worry and fear, depression and distress, with the knowledge that "something terrible" was going to happen.

SIX PSYCHICS ARE BORN

The British Premonitions Bureau began operations in January, 1967. In its first year it received about 500 premonitions of natural disasters, disasters involving planes and other vehicles, political events, deaths and assassinations, etc. Most predictions in 1967 were of air crashes, with earthquakes second. The great majority of letters and phone calls came from London and other parts of Great Britain.

In 1967 and 1968 there was no natural disaster in England equal in severity to the 1966 Aberfan tragedy, and no early warning alert was sounded. Disasters were sensed for other areas of the world by unusually psychic individuals, not by the more common human seismographs. It may be that those in the latter group are more sensitive to forthcoming disasters in their immediate area.

Dr. Barker's second goal, however, was realized in the Bureau's first year of operation—to find psychics consistently tuned in to all kinds of disasters. At the end of the first year at least six persons had been sending in, on a regular basis, predictions of events good and bad around the world. Four unusually accurate predictions were received before the Robert Kennedy assassination. (See Chapter Seven.)

In February, 1969, the Bureau moved its operation from the *Evening Standard* to the *T.V. Times,* a London publication. Up to May, 1970, about 1,000 predictions had been received, the most accurate coming from the six psychics who seemed to have an inborn sensitivity to future events. Some of their "hits," covering the years 1967–71, are described later.

Following the sudden death of Dr. Barker in 1968, the Bureau has been operated by Peter Fairley, now science editor of the *T.V. Times,* and Mrs. Jennifer Preston, his secretary. The Bureau's latest psychic protégée is a woman journalist, who, in Mrs. Preston's words, "shuns publicity, so I cannot give her name." Writing about this psychic, Mrs. Preston says: "She has had this gift since childhood and takes it for granted. Pictures flash across her mind, as opposed to conscious projection. She doesn't hear sounds or voices—the words come without thinking to fit the picture."

On July 11, 1970, the woman journalist sent this note to the Bureau: "Have strong impression of crowds, many children and much panic associated with animals not native to this country. Animals roaming free." On August 25, almost seven weeks later, a child was mauled by a lion in the wild animal reservation at the Duke of Bedford's Woburn Park estate.

On June 5, 1970, the psychic sent another note: "News re Queen Mother—may be connected with dog." Two days later the Queen's favorite corgi was severely injured during a dog fight at Windsor Castle and had to have a leg amputated.

Almost two weeks earlier, on May 25, the same psychic had a strong feeling about Jeremy Thorpe, the leader of England's Liberal Party. "I saw him on television and looking at him, front view, in my mind's eye I saw him back view and a current of shock seemed to go through him from his heels upward, rather like an electric shock would, I imagine. The premonition flashed through me that he would suffer shock, real and deep shock. It had nothing to do with politics. It was personal."

The psychic added that she thought Thorpe's wife would be killed but decided that she was "just imagining this to fit the depth of shock that registered." At the end of June Thorpe's wife was killed in an accident.

Since its inception, the Bureau has registered the premonitions it receives in the following categories: Air and Space; Rail; Sea; War and Riots; Royalty; Personalities; Natural Disasters; Collapse of Buildings; Politics; Racing; Fire; Economy; Explosions; Non-Specified Disasters.

Concerning the aims of the British Premonitions Bureau, Mrs. Preston writes: "Every effort is made to keep track of the events foretold and to retain an unbiased attitude to the evidence. We neither believe nor disbelieve in premonition as a possibility. We are simply curious."

CHAPTER TWO

The Central Premonitions Registry Is Formed

Early in 1968 Dr. Barker visited America and spoke at a meeting of the American Society for Psychical Research about the formation of the British Premonitions Bureau and the search for psychics. As Robert Nelson, a young executive with a metropolitan newspaper, listened to Dr. Barker, the idea of starting a similar agency came into his mind.

Nelson had been assisting Dr. Stanley Krippner in his Dream Laboratory experiments at the Maimonides Medical Center in Brooklyn. The object of these experiments was to see if telepathic messages could influence dreams. While the dreamer slept in one room, a "sender" in another room studied the print of a famous painting and tried to "beam" details of the painting to the sleeper.

Nelson was a volunteer worker on the project, editing the dream reports and sometimes taking the role of sender. Both he and Krippner noticed that often the sleeper would dream not about the target painting for that night but of a picture that would be used on the following or a later night—a clear example of precognition. This awakened Nelson's interest in the subject of premonitions and when he heard Dr. Barker's speech he decided, with Krippner's help, to establish a premonitions bureau in New York City.

Nelson was in many ways well suited to run a bureau of this kind.

Besides his interest and research in parapsychology, his newspaper contacts gave him access to news services that could be checked daily to see if the prophecies received were being fulfilled. The Central Premonitions Registry was activated in New York City in June, 1968, with Nanci, Nelson's wife, as his assistant.

Similar in structure and purpose to the London Bureau, the Registry had two requirements for an authentic premonition: It must be recorded in writing and given to someone before the actual event, and it should be sufficiently detailed and unusual enough to make coincidence unlikely. The first requirement would be met when the premonition was mailed to the Registry. The second would wait upon the event itself. Nelson also asked each person submitting a premonition to send a newspaper clipping later that might validate the forecast.

Each message would be filed under the date received and cross-filed under the sender's name, the kind of premonition, and the verification, if any. Premonitions of personal situations were not encouraged, only those newsworthy items relating to public events and figures. As in the case of the London Bureau, an alert would be sounded if enough human seismographs wrote in at the same time predicting the same disaster, with matching details.

An alert would also be considered if three proven psychics sent in the same prediction. Added weight would be given to premonitions made by patients in a psychiatric setting and mailed to the Registry by the doctor. In case of an alert, public officials or other persons affected by the predicted disaster would be notified by the Registry.

The categories first used by the Registry were roughly similar to those of the London Bureau, although there was no conscious duplication. In addition, because of the strong psychic link between the Kennedy family and the American public, a special category was set up just for premonitions about the family.

Actually, the Registry's initial impetus came from a letter relating to the Kennedys received from Germany and written by an American psychic, Alan Vaughan, who was studying there. The letter arrived in May, 1968, and predicted the assassination of Robert Kennedy. (This letter is discussed in detail in Chapter Seven.) Kennedy was shot on June 5, 1968, and the Central Premonitions Registry was activated shortly thereafter.

Whenever a subject in the Miscellaneous file generated enough interest, a new category would be added. By the end of 1970 this list of categories was in effect:

PROMINENT PERSONS–DEATH OR INJURY
PROMINENT PERSONS–MISCELLANEOUS ITEMS
TRANSPORTATION ACCIDENTS–AIR, LAND, AND SEA
NATURAL DISASTERS–FIRES, PLAGUES, NONTRANSPORTA-
  TION ACCIDENTS (BUILDINGS BLOWING UP, ETC.)
POLITICS
ECONOMICS
WAR AND INTERNATIONAL RELATIONS
CRIME
CIVIL UNREST–LAW AND ORDER
THE SPACE RACE
THE KENNEDYS
SPORTS AND RACES
SCIENCE AND HEALTH
SPECIFIC DATES PREDICTED
MISCELLANEOUS (RELIGION, ETC.)

In its first year of operation the Registry received about 600 premonitions. As of May, 1971, about 2,000 predictions were on file. The majority of letters came from California and the Middle West, with most of the predictions coming in dreams. Women letter-writers comprised about 70 percent of the total. Most of the men who had written in were more than 65 years old.

Most predictions were in the Prominent Personalities–Death or Injury category, with many relating specifically to the Kennedys. The second most popular category was Natural Disasters, followed by War and International Relations, The Space Race, Politics, Civil Unrest, and Airplane and Ship Disasters. Trailing all other categories in predictive interest was Economics. Later it will be demonstrated why categories suggestive of emotional ties generate more premonitions than the others.

Apart from forecasts made by psychics who have been developed by the Registry, most of the predictions have been of disasters in the geographical area where the amateur psychic or human seismograph lives. This is in line with the experience of the London Bureau and certainly applies to the Aberfan case, when nearly every premonition came from someone in Great Britain. (There was one known premonition in America.) No predictions were received for the two devastating natural disasters in 1970, the earthquake in Peru and the floods in Pakistan. Yet chances are that if there had been premonitions bureaus in these two countries, they would have been deluged with warnings.

There have been many startling predictions received from both established psychics and human seismographs since the Registry was activated: spectacular visions of railroad wrecks and plane crashes; forecasts of what would happen during the Apollo moon shots; a dream about one of the outstanding events of 1970—the troop movement into Cambodia; another dream accurately picturing the alleged murderers of United Mine Workers official Joseph Yablonski; a sports item which, at least to New Yorkers, was a happy rather than an ominous prophecy—the Mets would win the National League pennant and World Series in 1969; and many more. Several of these are discussed in later chapters.

The Central Premonitions Registry has performed a valuable function in acting as a clearing house for home and office psychics who receive little sympathy from their friends and relatives. According to Nelson, "Most of the people who write to the Registry are ordinary people who are puzzled by their strange dreams. Their family and friends often regard them as 'kooks' and pay no attention to their premonitions. Yet it is the scientific study of such people that may lead to significant breakthroughs in understanding the mystery of the precognitive process."

Some of these amateur psychics have responded by coming up with astonishing forecasts. On June 23, 1969, a Pennsylvania woman sent in a prediction for the Kennedy file: ". . . there is to be an explosion and fire on the water . . . Ted Kennedy appears to be involved . . . an accident brought about by carelessness . . ." A month later Senator Kennedy was involved in the accident at Chappaquiddick.

A woman in Bridgeport, Connecticut, had a feeling on August 17, 1970, that President Nasser of Egypt would die of a heart attack. As the time approached when the prediction would be realized, she began to get stronger and stronger impressions. On September 21, she sent her forecast to the Registry. Nasser died suddenly on September 28. The Bridgeport psychic wrote that she would get her premonitions while reading the newspapers—they came as answers to questions posed in the news articles.

In addition to watching for human seismographs who en masse may alert the Registry to impending disaster, Nelson and Krippner plan to test psychics at the Maimonides Medical Center who show a talent for prophecy. In the Registry's first year a few new psychics emerged, including Alan Vaughan of New York and Mrs. Katharine Sabin of San Diego. Two English psychics who have contributed regularly to the London Bureau also send their predictions to the Registry—Lorna Middleton and Alan Hencher.

Mrs. Sabin has a unique system of reading the future by shuffling a pack of cards. She assigns symbols to the cards, lays them out, and sends herself a telegram with the prediction. On October 5, 1968, she sent the Premonitions Registry the following message: "I see San Diego involved in a big fight or battle. This may occur in the October-November period. It seems to be the start of an attack by a foreign power."

In November, 1968, a Mexican vessel began firing at an American tuna boat off the coast of San Diego. Fortunately, we were not about to go to war with our southern neighbor, but the card-reading prophecy was accurate.

Miss Middleton, a London dance instructor who was discovered by Dr. Barker, sent the Registry this note in July, 1969: "I think a building will collapse, a building that is being demolished, or not strongly built. Perhaps in England or America." She included a sketch showing a vacant lot for the building. The door of the building in the sketch was green.

Two days later a building in London collapsed and of the four workmen killed, one was from Hall Green. Symbolic details of this kind (the green door) often appear in dreams, along with realistic details, as they did in the Aberfan dream of children going to heaven dressed in the Welsh national costume.

Another young psychic from overseas, Malcolm Bessent of London, is now sending predictions to the Registry. In December, 1969, he mailed several short- and long-term forecasts. Here are a few of them:

A Greek tanker, black in color, will be involved in a disaster having international significance within 4-6 months time. (Onassis-connected—

perhaps the danger is symbolic, but I feel that the ship may represent him personally.)

In February, 1970, an oil tanker belonging to Onassis, the *Arrow,* was wrecked off the coast of Nova Scotia, spilling out its cargo of oil when a tug tried to get it loose. This became an "international" incident because of the oil slick and the contaminated beaches.

General de Gaulle will die within one year.

De Gaulle died on November 10, 1970, eleven months after the prediction.

Prime Minister Wilson in change of government next summer (1970).

This was, of course, a direct "hit," especially because up to the moment the first ballot was cast, the political experts in England thought that the Conservative candidate, Edward Heath, didn't have a chance. All the polls had shown Wilson an easy winner, by as much as a 15 percent majority. In addition, it had been planned to call for the elections some time in November, and the June date had been chosen only a short time before.

Nixon will not serve another term as President.
Senator Muskie will be the next President.

The above two predictions must wait upon the 1972 elections, of course. However, since Bessent first sent them to the Registry, Senator Muskie has come into greater prominence and at this writing is the leading candidate for the Democratic nomination. Bessent claims that he rarely reads newspapers and had only a vague idea who Muskie was at the time of the prediction.

The Greek military regime will be overthrown from within during the next eighteen months. The changes brought about will be in leadership only.

This has not happened yet.

Starting with 1972–73 it will be a crucial year for the U.S.A. Water everywhere, resulting in social upheaval, anarchy, and political confusion. The people will be looking for a new leader, but none forthcoming. A new political structure will come into being.

This ominous prophecy ties in with predictions by other psychics and is discussed later in connection with their forecasts.

In addition to its "star" performers and potential human seismographs, the Registry keeps on file all known predictions made by popular psychics such as Daniel Logan and Jeane Dixon. To date Maurice Woodruff and other well-known prophets have not sent their forecasts to the Registry or the London Bureau.

A few more years of operation and continuous publicity will be necessary before the two bureaus can prove themselves to the satisfaction of skeptics. 600 premonitions in one year are relatively few; 6,000 would give a wider sampling of psychics in America and Great Britain; 60,000 would justify the installation of a computer to detect "peaks and patterns." Statistics aside, however, the emergence of psychics such as Lorna Middleton and Alan Vaughan alone would justify the work of the two bureaus.

The majority of amateur psychics have not yet learned how to separate a valid premonition from one that may be motivated by their fears or may be pure fantasy. After we have considered many interesting cases of prophecy that came true, both those recorded before the formation of the London Bureau and the New York Registry and those on file with the two organizations, there will be suggestions on how to become a better psychic and send accurate predictions to the Registry.

Meanwhile, until another Aberfan is about to occur in England or the United States and the first early warning alert is sounded, it may be productive to look closely at premonitions of natural and mechanical disasters in the past, along with predictions of such disasters that may occur in the future. Some of these cases are extremely well documented because they were thoroughly investigated by men like Dr. Barker.

One such case was the sinking of the *Titanic* in April, 1912. Recent studies by parapsychologists have shown that there were intimations of the disaster years in advance and that, as the time of sailing approached, the pre-disaster syndrome was very much in evidence, along with specific visions and dreams of many psychics. An early warning system in operation before April, 1912, might have helped prevent one of the most spectacular maritime accidents in history.

CHAPTER THREE

A Ship Sinks Twice—In Different Centuries

It was the year 1898. In a studio room on 24th Street in New York City, a man named Morgan Robertson was sitting on a straight-backed chair, staring at a typewriter on the table in front of him. Robertson, who had spent a good part of his life as a sailor, was a writer of stories about the sea. He already had several books to his credit, but now, for some reason, the words would not flow.

Robertson thought he knew what the trouble was. He was not yet in "the mood." An uneducated man, he had always astounded others and delighted himself with his tales of ships and the men who sailed on them, written with a power of description that made the reader feel the salt air and hear the roar of surging waves. But every time he sat down at the typewriter, it was as though he had never written a word before. It took hours, sometimes days, before the words would come. Finally "the mood" would creep over him, he would drift off into a trance, and soon the typewriter keys would be clicking away under his fingers.

Morgan looked around the room, which was fixed up like a ship's cabin, and thought about his life as a sailor. Directly ahead of him the window had been converted into a porthole, while in one corner there was a life preserver and in the other a ship's wheel. On his left

was a bunkbed with a ship's bell on either side of it, and on his right
a small bureau holding a compass and a ship's log. The table that
supported Robertson's portable typewriter was actually a bathtub
with a wooden board on top of it. Knotted ropes hung from the wall,
and overhead nautical lights shone down on the room.

Robertson leaned back in his chair and stared at the ceiling lights.
He was far out at sea now and he could hear the restless churning of
the waves. As if on film a scene began to move in his mind, showing
a broad expanse of water with the setting sun at the horizon. He felt
the cold April air of the mid-Atlantic ocean, and he heard the warning sound of foghorns in the distance. Now, as he sank more deeply
into his trance, he saw a ship appear in the fog. It was moving very
fast, too fast, at a speed of twenty-three knots.

It was a beauty of a boat, a luxury liner more than 800 feet long,
the largest he had ever seen, with three propellers and a horsepower
he reckoned at 75,000—top speed 25 knots. In his fantasy the ship
came closer, and through the mist he saw people moving about on the
long, broad decks—well over 2,000 persons, more than had ever
sailed on one ship.

The liner raced by and on her side he could see these words in
bold letters: THE TITAN. Another word came to him—"Unsinkable . . . unsinkable . . ." Fearfully he counted the lifeboats hanging
in the davits. There were twenty-four, far too few for the number of
passengers on board. And just ahead, barely visible in the thick fog,
part of an iceberg loomed above the surface of the water.

Morgan Robertson shook himself and began to type. The words
came freely now, as if written by another hand: "She was the largest
craft afloat and the greatest of the works of men . . . spacious cabins
. . . decks like broad promenades . . . Unsinkable, indestructible,
she carried as few boats as would satisfy the laws. . . .

"Seventy-five thousand tons—deadweight—rushing through the fog
at the rate of fifty feet a second . . . hurled itself at an iceberg . . .
nearly 3,000 human voices, raised in agonized screams . . ."

Bear in mind that Robertson wrote *The Wreck of the Titan* in
1898. A real ship, the *Titanic,* was not built until 1911. It was also
the "largest craft afloat" and it made its first and only voyage in 1912
—with between 2,000 and 3,000 passengers.

"THERE IS DANGER FROM WATER"

In the 1880s, some years before Robertson wrote his book, an article appeared in a magazine called the *Pall Mall Gazette*. It was an imaginative story about a ship equal in size to the *Titan,* and it also sank in mid-Atlantic. The writer, W. T. Stead, claimed that he wrote the story as a plea that ships take safety precautions before sailing. At the end of the article was this warning: "This is exactly what might take place and what will take place, if liners are sent to sea short of boats."

Throughout his life Stead, like Robertson, was preoccupied with the sea and ships. In 1892 he wrote another article in the *Review of Reviews,* of which he was editor, and added a few more details about the imaginary shipwreck. In this story a steamship collides with an iceberg in the Atlantic and its only surviving passenger is rescued by a White Star liner called the *Majestic.* At that time there was an actual ship named the *Majestic,* and its captain was Edward J. Smith, who later captained the *Titanic* (another White Star liner) in 1912.

Again, in 1910, Stead gave a lecture in London in which he pictured himself, in a shipwreck, floundering in the water and calling for help. Now the recurrent theme is no longer an impersonal tragedy at sea. Stead himself is the victim—at least in his own imagination.

Meanwhile, work had begun on the *Titanic.* This was to be the finest liner in the world, 882 feet in length (Robertson's *Titan* was 800 feet long), with a displacement tonnage of 66,000 (almost equal to the 70,000 of the *Titan*). The ship would be capable of the incredible speed of 25 knots (equal to that of the *Titan*), and would have a capacity of nearly 3,000 passengers (the number carried by the *Titan*). And there was an ominous note in one of its proud boasts —the *Titanic* would have watertight compartments and would be unsinkable.

W. T. Stead could feel his own fate coming nearer. While the *Titanic* was being assembled, something made him visit Count Louis Hamon, the palm-reading psychic who also made predictions of world events. Hamon warned him that there would be danger to him from water and to stay away from the sea. Hamon kept thinking about Stead as the months went by and on June 21, 1911, he hurried off a note to him warning that "travel would be dangerous in the month of April, 1912."

Now the *Titanic* was about half completed. Stead visited another psychic, W. de Kerlor, who told him that he would go to America. Stead was surprised, for he had no such plans. De Kerlor nodded emphatically and said, "I can see . . . the picture of a huge black ship . . . *but I can only see half of the ship* . . . when one will be able to see it in its whole length, it is perhaps then that you will go on your journey."

Later in the year de Kerlor had a dream which he recognized as applying to Stead. "I dreamed that I was in the midst of a catastrophe on the water; there were masses (more than a thousand) of bodies struggling in the water and I (Stead) was among them. I could hear their cries for help."

An American lady suddenly had an intuition that Stead would die. She wrote to *Light* magazine that a solemn voice had told her: "The time is soon coming when he will be called home. In the first half of 1912—in six months." A few months later Archdeacon Colley sent a letter to Stead in which he predicted that the *Titanic* would sink.

Now the ship was almost ready. Morgan Robertson's trance-vision, de Kerlor's dream, W. T. Stead's theme of death in the water were soon to reach a climax. As April, 1912, drew nearer a Mr. Colin Macdonald turned down an offer of a position as second engineer of the *Titanic* because he had a "hunch" that something was going to happen to the ship.

The stage was set. On April 10, 1912, the impregnable *Titanic* with its 20 lifeboats and its watertight bulkheads was ready to sail. Close to 2,500 persons had booked passage from London to New York. One of them was W. T. Stead.

TWICE THE SAME DREAM

Unaccountably, from April 3 to April 10, several persons, including banker J. Pierpont Morgan, cancelled their passage. Many gave the excuse that it was unlucky to sail on a ship's maiden voyage. Not everyone, however, is a human seismograph and most of the passengers had no such fears.

On March 23, 1912, seventeen days before the date of sailing, passage was booked by a gentleman named J. Connon Middleton, a London businessman. A week later Mr. Middleton had a disturbing dream, far more vivid than his usual dreams. He saw the *Titanic* "floating on the sea, keel upwards and her passengers and crew swimming around her." The next night he had the same dream. Middleton did not see himself struggling in the water. He "seemed to be floating in the air just above the wreck."

Middleton began to have the pre-disaster syndrome. He felt uneasy, then depressed. Yet because his business in America was urgent, he did not cancel passage. He was a practical man, not given to belief that dreams come true, and he tried to put his two dreams out of mind. Mercifully, his life was saved in another way. About four days after his first dream, he received a cable from New York urging him to postpone his trip for a few days. Before the ship sailed, he told members of his family and friends about the recurring dream, and they corroborated his story later.

Did the man who sent the cable have a premonition about the *Titanic?* As Dr. Barker noted, although knowledge of the future may not reach an individual's consciousness, the person finds himself compelled to act in a way that will avert disaster for himself and others. This may have been true of those who suddenly cancelled passage without knowing why they did so.

"DON'T LET THEM DROWN!"

On Wednesday, April 10, the day the *Titanic* was to embark on her maiden voyage, a psychic, V. N. Turvey, warned that "a great liner would be lost." He then sent a letter to a Madame I. de Steiger predicting that the ship would sink in two days. The letter was published in *Light* magazine on June 29, 1912.

Turvey's warning went unheeded. On a bright, sunlit morning thousands of passengers, among them Col. John Jacob Astor and his young wife, stood on the decks of the *Titanic* as it proudly steamed out of Southampton on its way to America. The time for premonitions was past, and if the passengers had uneasy feelings, they quickly put them out of mind. An exciting journey was about to begin on the world's greatest steamship, with its decks like "broad promenades," its "spacious cabins," and its three dining rooms. The *Titanic* even had a swimming pool and gym, and a hospital with an operating room.

Friends and relatives who came to see them off shared the festive mood as they waved goodbye. And families in their homes along the coast gathered on rooftops to watch the ship as it slowly plowed through the water. It was a calm day, with only a slight breeze blowing, and an accident was unthinkable.

As the ship passed near the Isle of Wight, members of the Jack Marshall family stood on the roof of their home, watching it in the distance. There was a slight fog, but the *Titanic* was clearly visible, and they waved their handkerchiefs enthusiastically. Never had they seen a more magnificent liner. But the mood was suddenly broken when Mrs. Marshall grabbed her husband's arm and screamed, "It's going to sink! That ship is going to sink before she reaches America!"

Her family tried to quiet her, but she became more hysterical. In a vision she saw the *Titanic* going down and its passengers dying far off in the Atlantic. "Don't stand there staring at me," she cried. "Do something! You fools, I can see hundreds of people struggling in the icy waters! Are you so blind that you are going to let them drown?"

As the ship slowly disappeared over the horizon, Mrs. Marshall kept yelling, "Save them! Save them!" The nightmarish film of the future was already unreeling in her mind.

The *Titanic* was to make two more stops for passengers—at Cherbourg and Queenstown—before it sailed out to open sea. A young fireman had a premonition that the ship would sink and deserted at Queenstown. W. T. Stead, invited to America by President Taft to speak at a peace conference, sent letters from Cherbourg and Queenstown in which he wrote: "Something is awaiting me, some important work the nature of which will be disclosed to me in good time."

"FOR THOSE IN PERIL ON THE SEA"

It is four days later—April 14, 1912. The *Titanic* is now well into the Atlantic, sailing faster, almost up to her capacity of twenty-five knots. It is a calm, cold night and the fog is thicker, but the sea is not as restless as the waters of the Atlantic usually are. New York City is still several days away, but no one is worried about getting there—at least not consciously. The passengers have just finished their supper and are leaving the sumptuous first-class and the less ornate but attractive second- and third-class dining rooms.

The food was plentiful and tasty, and now the travelers stroll about the decks or sit on the comfortable deck chairs and talk. Later in the evening a minister, the Rev. Carter, invites the more pious to go back to the second-class dining room and sing hymns.

In Winnipeg, Canada, another minister, the Rev. Charles Morgan of the Rosedale Methodist Church, is at home looking over a list of hymns from which he will choose those to be sung at the evening service. The Rev. Morgan is a bit fatigued and he lies down on the sofa for a short rest. Gradually he drifts off into a trance. The name of a hymn goes through his mind, and he wakes up with a start as he hears these words: "Hear, Father, while we pray to Thee, for those in peril on the sea."

The Rev. Morgan has never sung this hymn before and it is unfamiliar to him. Yet it keeps running through his mind and he feels compelled to put it on his list. He goes into his library, finds the music, and takes it to church with him. Later in the evening his congregation stands up and solemnly intones: "Hear, Father, while we pray to Thee, for those in peril on the sea."

At the same hour, in the second-class dining room of the *Titanic,* the Rev. Carter is leading a group of passengers in the hymn "For Those in Peril on the Sea." It is a strange song for passengers to sing on board ship in the middle of the Atlantic. Yet both the Rev. Carter and the Rev. Morgan had the same compulsion and at almost the same time. The passengers on the decks hear the gloomy strains floating out of the dining room.

It is now 9:30 P.M. The fog is very thick and it is almost impossible to see the ocean ahead. Do the singers unconsciously know that in just two hours the *Titanic* will hit an iceberg in the middle of the Atlantic and they will truly be "in peril on the sea"?

THE UNSINKABLE SHIP SINKS

It happened almost imperceptibly. The time was 11:40 P.M. First there was a slight impact, then a booming sound as the ship struck the iceberg, ripping open five of the *Titanic's* "watertight" compartments. Steam hissed out of the boilers, while the engines slowed and finally stopped. The passengers gathered on deck, wondering what had happened, but there was no panic. They watched the crew working but were not aware that there was any danger.

Finally the call came for the lifeboats, and flares were sent out to signal other ships. Slowly the liner tilted upward while the crew frantically worked to lower the lifeboats, which carried mostly women and children. A first-class passenger, Miss Edith Evans, remarked to a survivor that a fortune teller had once warned her to "beware of water." Impulsively she gave up her place in a lifeboat to another passenger and was later drowned.

The ship's stern rose as the bow sank. At 2:20 A.M. the *Titanic* slid at a sharp angle into the depths while, all around in the dark night, people were struggling in the water and screaming for help. One of them, Colonel Archibald Gracie, prayed that he could somehow reach out to his family in New York and send them an affectionate goodbye.

At the same moment, Gracie's wife in New York City woke up with a start and heard a voice say, "On your knees and pray." She got out of bed, opened a prayerbook and her eyes fell on the words, "For those in peril on the sea." Suddenly she realized that her husband was praying for her. She lay awake until 5 A.M., certain that something terrible had happened.

In another home in New York City a woman had a nightmare. There had been a shipwreck and her mother was in a crowded boat in the middle of the ocean. The woman woke up and told her husband about her dream, but he reassured her that since her mother was safe in London, there was nothing to worry about. But the dream had been so real, she couldn't get it out of her mind. It was as though she herself had been there in the water, the cold salt air whipping her face as she shivered in the boat with her terrified mother. Nearby a great liner disappeared into the icy waters, while all around she could hear the pitiful cries of the drowning.

The next day she heard about the disaster and saw her mother's name on the passenger list. The mother was one of the survivors. When she reached New York, she told her daughter that she had booked passage as a surprise. At the time of her daughter's dream, she was in an overcrowded lifeboat that swayed precariously in the sea, in imminent danger of turning over. All her thoughts had been concentrated on her daughter.

A SURVEY OF THE PREMONITIONS

Of the 2,207 passengers aboard the *Titanic,* 705 were rescued by the liner *Carpathia,* while 1,502 lost their lives. In at least one case, that of W. T. Stead, a premonition of the disaster did not prevent a personal tragedy. How many others who perished had had dreams, seen visions, felt depressed or worried, or heard voices telling them not to book passage on the ship? This is not known. If there were such forebodings, they were obviously ignored.

For more than fifty years since the *Titanic* disaster, analyses have been made of the known premonitions. One of the best of these is a paper by Dr. Ian Stevenson of the University of Virginia department of psychiatry, written for the American Society for Psychical Research. Stevenson points out the astonishing number of details common to the *Titanic* and the fictitious *Titan* of Morgan Robertson. There was the myth of unsinkability, the name of both ships, the month (April) in which the real and the imaginary ship sank, the length and displacement tonnage, the number of propellers and lifeboats, the number of passengers, the speed of both ships at impact with the iceberg, the iceberg itself, and the great loss of life, actual and imagined.

Dr. Stevenson describes nineteen cases of premonitions occurring within two weeks of the disaster, in England, the United States, Canada, and Brazil. The premonitions, similar in kind to those preceding the Aberfan coal slide, came in dreams, visions, trance-states, through voices, and in the form of the pre-disaster syndrome. As in the Aberfan case, some of the dreams and visions reproduced actual details of the tragedy; in others there were symbolic details. When Middleton saw himself "floating in the air just above the wreck," it was probably an indication that he was not going to be involved in the tragedy.

One woman dreamed that she saw a "high structure [with] people hanging on the outside of it, many in nightclothes, gradually losing hold and slipping down inclined sides of the structure." When an artist drew a sketch of the sinking, she declared that it was exactly what she had seen in the dream. Another symbol pointing indirectly to the tragedy was the hymn "For Those in Peril on the Sea," which came to the minds of three persons.

As in the Aberfan case, there were common themes running through the premonitions, but each person saw different details of the shipwreck. It may be that we see the future as we do the present, each of us observing from a different angle and mental viewpoint. What stands out for one may be in the background for another or may not be seen at all. In Middleton's dream, he saw one detail incorrectly. Instead of the ship's keel moving upward, the *Titanic* actually slid into the sea bow first.

Probably the most authentic quality of a premonition is the emotional tone, the impression of an actual experience taking place in the "now." Dr. Stevenson writes about the "vividness" of premonitory dreams and points out that such dreams "completely lack any vagueness and passivity of thought and emotion." This kind of dream may be "more real than reality." A parapsychologist, G. N. M. Tyrell, has written about the precognitive dream as having an "insistent, compelling character."

Middleton's dream made him feel despondent. Others who dreamed about the *Titanic* reacted so strongly that they woke up. The woman who saw people hanging onto a sloping structure said later: "They were all terrified, and I felt the terror so strongly that it wakened me." The emotional tone of visions in the waking state can be just as strong—Mrs. Marshall, who had her vision on the Isle of Wight, became hysterical.

Many persons felt uneasy without knowing why, and this was probably the reason tickets were cancelled at the last moment. Every person's psyche is structured differently. Some, to whom premonitions come in direct and undisguised form, may have the courage to face the future squarely, even if they know it holds great pain and suffering. Others are spared direct knowledge, but they act out their subconscious fears.

TWO LIFE-THEMES OF THE SEA

Let's take another look at Morgan Robertson and W. T. Stead and ask why each, in his own way, was allowed a glimpse of the future. What was there in the life-experience and personality of each man that linked him to the destiny of the ship?

Morgan Robertson saw the future of the *Titanic* while he was writing a story. More will be said later about a possible relationship between being "creative" and in a sense "creating the future," but there was an additional factor in Robertson's case—he knew he was something of a psychic. Awed by his ability as a writer, he theorized that the spirit of a literary person who had died took over his body and brain when he sat down to write his stories of the sea.

Robertson called his co-author his "astral writing-partner." When he tried to coax his conscious mind into producing a story, nothing would happen and he would sit for hours at a time staring at his typewriter. Then "the mood" would come on. He would go into a trance, the present would fade away, and he would find himself in another dimension of time and space. It was in this mental state that he saw his vision of the *Titanic* and wrote about the *Titan*.

Robertson had joined a vessel at the age of sixteen to become a sailor. All his stories were about the sea; this was his life-theme and it culminated in his vision of the *Titanic*. Psychics such as Gerard Croiset and Alan Vaughan claim that their most valid experiences come in their areas of interest. Robertson's vision of the *Titanic* was the more real because most of his thoughts, experiences, and associations centered about ships and water.

Late in life Robertson's "astral writing-partner" deserted him and nothing more would come out of his typewriter. Finally in 1915, three years after the *Titanic* sank, he went off to Atlantic City and took a room in a cheap hotel. In the morning he was found dead, sitting upright in a chair so that he could die as he watched the waves come in.

In the case of W. T. Stead the theme of death at sea kept returning, first as a purely intellectual idea, then gradually, as the years wore on, coming closer and closer to the man himself. The sense of inevitability that follows the life of Stead suggests, in a way, the unfolding drama of a Greek tragedy. Stead was not aware in his earlier years that his recurring thought pointed to his own fate. In his unconscious, however, or in the extrasensory dimension in which he divined the future, he probably knew what was going to happen.

As the day of reckoning came nearer, it must have dawned on Stead that he had been fearful all those years for himself. Why else would he visit Count Hamon and other psychics and ask for a reading of the future? His daughter Estelle writes that her father was getting subliminal messages of his fate in the winter months preceding the voyage of the *Titanic*.

Watch for recurring dreams or ideas that keep knocking ominously on the door of the mind. They may be significant, in many cases for present circumstances in one's life, in others for a future disaster that may be inevitable or may, if heed is taken, be averted.

COULD THE TITANIC HAVE BEEN SAVED?

Suppose the Central Premonitions Registry had been set up in New York before 1912, while its London counterpart, the Premonitions Bureau, had also been in operation at that time.

On the day the *Titanic* sailed, it will be recalled, Mr. V. N. Turvey had a feeling that "a great liner would be lost." He then posted a letter to Madame de Steiger with his prediction, but the letter was not received until April 15, just after the tragedy occurred. Had there been a Premonitions Bureau, Mr. Turvey might have gone to his wall telephone, turned the crank, and given the operator the number of the London Bureau.

"Hello, this is V. N. Turvey calling. I have a very strong feeling that the *Titanic* will sink in a few days. Can you stop the ship from sailing?"

Let us suppose that a Mr. Peter Farrington runs our imaginary Bureau in 1912. Mr. Farrington thanks Mr. Turvey and records the date of the premonition and its details. He sits down with his assistant, Miss Jeri Weston, and they study other premonitions about the *Titanic* that have been received. Are there enough to call an alert?

The warnings started coming in a few months back. At first there were only a handful, not enough to be taken seriously. Some of the letters and phone calls had only mentioned a "ship" and were vague about details and dates. Other persons sensed that a "disaster" would take place but had no idea when or where, or what might be involved. A few said that many people would die on the same day "sometime in 1912." And without identifying details, something that could be pinpointed, there was no way to warn about a disaster.

However, there were a few disquieting letters centering around a rather prominent gentleman, W. T. Stead, celebrated writer and editor. In June of 1911 Count Hamon phoned the Bureau and predicted that Mr. Stead would die at sea in 1912. A Mr. de Kerlor wrote a letter some time later stating that a ship disaster would take Mr. Stead's life. In America a lady had written to the Premonitions Registry that he would die in the first half of 1912. Other letters came in—all about Mr. Stead's death at sea—seen in visions, dreams, trances, told by disembodied voices.

Certain persons, Miss Weston points out, such as Madame Couédon in France and Madame de Ferriëm in Germany, have a high degree of success in predicting the future. Mr. Turvey, Mr. de Kerlor, and Count Hamon have all called numerous times with warnings about accidents and other unfortunate happenings that did occur, and often the three have warned about the same event. The Bureau takes two important factors into consideration before issuing an alert —the number of premonitions that seem to point to a specific disaster within a short time, and the reputation of known psychics who contact the Bureau.

The phone rings again. It is another caller predicting that the *Titanic* will sink. Then another call, and another, with hardly a pause in between. Miss Weston opens the mail, unusually heavy today, and almost every letter warns that the *Titanic* will go down. Is it mass hysteria, a superstitious fear about a ship going to sea for the first time? Or is it a genuine glimpse at a tragic event about to be unveiled in the near future? Have the dark vibrations of the *Titanic* somehow gotten through to the people in London who are "tuned in"?

The film of the future now begins to move faster, the photography is clearer, the characters can be seen in sharp focus. From all over England the letters are arriving and voices on the phone are begging: "Don't let the *Titanic* sail. I have had a dream . . . a vision . . . a feeling . . . I heard a voice . . . I know something terrible will happen. . . ." One letter from a minister tells of hearing a great chorus of voices singing "for those in peril on the sea . . . for those in peril on the sea. . . ."

The *Titanic* will sail in another hour. Mr. Farrington and Miss Weston debate what to do. Should they call an alert and get in contact immediately with the Ministry of Transport?

Meanwhile, in New York City, the office of the New York *Herald-Express* is buzzing with excitement. The desk of Mr. Robert Belson,

who founded the Central Premonitions Registry in 1909, is piled high
with letters and telegrams, all warning that the *Titanic* must not sail.
Several of the letters, including one from Canada, describe dreams
and visions in which a little-known hymn is sung—"For Those in Peril
on the Sea."

Mr. Belson and his assistant, Miss Lancey, want to cable the London Bureau immediately and, as an additional precaution, call the
State Department in Washington and ask that service to contact the
American Embassy in London. But the rest of the newspaper staff
ridicules them. The hard-headed city editor and reporters point out
that they will be the laughingstock of America and England if they try
to prevent the *Titanic* from sailing.

Mr. Belson explains that this is no ordinary case of premonition.
There has been an unusually heavy number of calls and letters about
the *Titanic* and he cannot, in all conscience, ignore these warnings. If
something does happen to the *Titanic,* he will never forgive himself
if he failed to call an alert. After all, this is why the Central Premonitions Registry was activated—to prevent a disaster.

A cocky young reporter says that if the *Titanic* doesn't sail, the
premonitions would not be premonitions in the true sense of the word
because nothing would have happened. How would he ever know
that the *Titanic* would have sunk if it had sailed? Mr. Belson patiently
explains that evidence from past cases suggests that the future can be
altered—it is not always fixed but is subject to changing conditions
and the actions of human beings. But this is a philosophical matter—
the age-old argument about determinism versus free will. There is no
time to lose if the *Titanic* is to be saved.

Belson goes to the telephone and sends a cable to London, then
puts through a call to the State Department in Washington, D.C. He
speaks with three secretaries and two public relations men, who are
polite but somehow give him the impression that they think he is out
of his mind. Distressed, Belson puts down the phone. Time is racing
ahead.

In London Farrington is finally successful in reaching the Ministry
of Transport, and he tells his story. The Ministry official chuckles.

"My dear chap, it's nice of you to phone, but we really cannot act
upon that sort of hunch, or whatever you call it."

Farrington pleads with him and explains that other premonitions sent to the Bureau have proved accurate. There was, for example, the fire at—

The official interrupts him rather brusquely, says he doesn't have time to listen, and hangs up. Mr. Farrington sits down in a state of dejection.

The *Titanic* sails on schedule.

Or perhaps it doesn't happen that way. Perhaps there have been a few early warning alerts before 1912 that were ignored—and now the Government treats the Premonitions Bureau with more respect. The Ministry of Transport quickly gets in touch with Southampton and says the *Titanic* must not sail.

The White Star Line officials are furious. What kind of nonsense is this? Thousands upon thousands of pounds, a year of work went into the building of the *Titanic*. Nearly three thousand persons are now coming aboard. Should all that be scrapped just because a few hysterics had crazy dreams?

"I repeat, sir," insists the White Star Line official, "that the *Titanic* is unsinkable, sir, unsinkable." He gives the statistics again—15 bulkheads, absolutely watertight, 20 lifeboats, length 882 feet, tonnage—

The Ministry of Transport is firm. The Premonitions Bureau has proved itself in the past. The *Titanic* is not to sail.

The *Titanic* stays in Southampton, thus altering the future. The disappointed passengers leave the boat with their luggage, their money is returned, they go home disgruntled and not a little angry. They have been put to very great inconvenience and many of them threaten lawsuits. The next day editorials appear in three London newspapers, castigating the government for reverting to medieval superstition.

Eventually, perhaps in six months or a year, the *Titanic* does sail, after having had some adjustments made in its construction to convince the authorities that it is indeed seaworthy. This time there are few or no premonitions and no early warning alert. When Mrs. Marshall sees the magnificent liner steam through the English Channel in the bright sunlight, she is as enthusiastic as the rest of her family, and she has a vision. She can see the ship sailing proudly past the Statue of Liberty into New York harbor, while Americans cheer and wave at the passengers.

Perhaps this time the *Titanic* has a safe voyage. Or on another trip it does hit an iceberg and go down. Or now, since the future has been changed, there is only slight damage, and the ship continues on its course.

The purpose of this imaginary jaunt is to suggest that when enough people know about the Central Premonitions Registry and the Premonitions Bureau, and when there are not hundreds but thousands of warnings sent in, disasters such as the Aberfan tragedy and the sinking of the *Titanic* may be prevented. Planes, trains, ships, even spacecraft will cancel trips that seem to be ill-fated. Fires, floods, explosions, the collapse of bridges and buildings may be averted if there is an early warning signal.

The tragedy of the *Titanic* may not have been in vain—if we become aware that the future may move alongside the present, ready to burst into human consciousness when a catastrophe threatens.

CHAPTER FOUR

Previsions of Nature on a Rampage

A child dreams that "something black" has come over her and she is going to be buried alive. A man has an uneasy feeling that he will perish at sea. In a vision a woman sees a steamship sinking and cries out that the passengers must be saved. Several persons sense that "something terrible is going to happen" and many people will be killed. The more a premonition is tied to human beings in danger, the more accurate it seems to be. Perhaps the dreamer or visionary himself is in jeopardy, or it may be a relative or a friend. Sometimes the emotion reaches out to strangers, often children, who are about to die, as in the Aberfan tragedy.

Never does danger threaten man more than when a great natural catastrophe is imminent. Life is sustained by the four elements—earth, air, fire, and water—yet we have uneasy memories stretching back for thousands of years of nature in her angry moods. These memories stir up the psychic centers and give rise to visions of a volcano about to erupt, flames that will fan out and destroy a city, a tornado soon to unleash its fury, a river that will overflow and devastate the surrounding land. There have been many spectacular visions and dreams of this kind, such as that of the eruption of Mt. Pelee in 1902 and of the 1967 floods in Alaska.

Ironically, however, the more earthshaking the cataclysm predicted, the less likely that it will happen. Many prophets accurately forecast relatively mild upheavals, but they frequently go wrong when their premonitions are impersonal and cosmic in character, presaging violent, large-scale movements in nature. The people in such visions are often a faceless mass, so many movie extras taking part in an extravaganza. Missing is the emotional link to human beings in peril that is the most important ingredient of premonitions.

For thousands of years prophets of gloom have been predicting that the world was about to end with a bang, and they would often gather with their flocks on mountaintops to await oblivion. Nor are they in the least embarrassed if the fatal day passes and the world is still going about its business. They merely get out their crystal balls and astrological charts and pick another date for the final curtain.

In the tenth century hundreds of pilgrims journeyed eastward to witness a last judgment scheduled for the year 999. (We'll hear more about similar predictions for 1999. The end of each millennium seems to hold a kind of fascination for certain prophets.) Then, in the sixteenth century word went around that a new Deluge was on the way, and many peasants stopped planting crops, got out their carpenter's tools, and set to work building arks. Today astrologers are studying the conjunction of planets and again predicting an early demise for the world. Scientists are more leisurely in their prognosis— they give the earth another billion years.

In this century Edgar Cayce foretold catastrophic earthquakes on the West Coast. California, warned Cayce, would break off like a piece of cake and expire in the Pacific Ocean. Since Cayce is the prophet's prophet, his forecast triggered a wave of premonitions throughout the country and particularly on the West Coast. California, sitting uneasily on the San Andreas Fault, has been trembling—at least psychically—on the brink of disaster. A group of nervous seers got together and picked the exact month and year that Hollywood would sink with its load of sin beneath the waves—April, 1969.

April came and went, however, and the state was still there, along with Governor Reagan, Disneyland, the Los Angeles Rams, and tall palms waving in the Southern California breeze. Meanwhile many of the psychics had been so frightened by their own visions that they packed their bags and moved to a safer part of the country. Some of these visions were in the Cecil B. DeMille tradition—freeways buckling, buildings coming apart as if struck down by King Kong, thousands of autos swallowed by the sea.

Hysteria is not a proper mood in which to make predictions, and the prophets were caught in a wave of fear vibrations that spread through California before April. There may have been another factor involved, however—time displacement. Dreams and visions of natural catastrophes may be activated by buried memories of the past rather than premonitions of the imminent future.

A controversial writer, Immanuel Velikovsky, claims that major earth changes have come about by sudden violent upheavals rather than by gradual change, the theory favored by most scientists. He also thinks that these catastrophes were so terrifying that memories of them have been suppressed in the human psyche and are responsible for our neuroses. If so, our more neurotic prophets may be responding to visions of past rather than future catastrophes. Sometime in the future, however, if Velikovsky is correct, there will be more great upheavals, not necessarily on any given date in the next few years but perhaps in two, five, even ten thousand years. The cosmic visions of prophets may be accurate but may be previsions of events in the far rather than near future, as well as playbacks of ancient disasters.

One doesn't have to be a psychic to predict an earthquake in California, as there are many minor quakes known only to seismologists. According to Louis C. Pakiser, Jr., chief scientist at the U.S. Geological Survey's National Center for Earthquake Research in Menlo Park, California, there are about 10 tremors a day in the state. He predicts that there will be 100,000 earthquakes in central California before the year 2000, of which only 100 will be strong enough to be noticed by the average person. 10 will cause damage—as did the February, 1971 quake in Los Angeles and environs—and only one will be close to cataclysmic.

The trick for the prophets will be to pick the really bad quake. Dr. William T. Pecora, director of the U.S. Geological Survey, believes it may come sometime before 1980 but, as a scientist, sets no specific date. It should be noted that many modern prophets—Jeane Dixon, Daniel Logan, Alan Vaughan, and Adrienne Coulter, to name a few

—did not foresee any major catastrophe for California in April, 1969. Prophecy is something of an art requiring training and mental discipline.

OF EARTH, AIR, AND WATER

Prophets are on firmer ground when they predict earthquakes, volcanic eruptions, tornadoes, and floods that may cause dislocation and suffering but do not turn the earth topsy-turvy. Although Edgar Cayce's trance-predictions touched off an unfortunate wave of false prophecies, Cayce was accurate in many of his forecasts. He was careful not to pinpoint a month and year but promised earth changes, gradual at first and cataclysmic later, over a forty-year span—from 1958 to 1998.

In 1932 Cayce forecast disturbances on the West Coast, in the South Pacific, and in the Mediterranean during the forty-year period, changes that would be a prelude to more dramatic catastrophes. The Alaskan quake in 1964, eruptions of Mt. Etna in the Mediterranean in 1960 and in 1971, and alterations of the coast of Morocco have to some extent borne out Cayce's predictions. He also warned about more sensational events, such as Europe's disappearing "in the twinkling of an eye," but was careful not to set the time.

Among Dr. Barker's human seismographs there are evidently some who literally sense vibrations in the earth before quakes are recorded. One of the men who had a premonition of the Aberfan disaster told Dr. Barker that on several previous occasions he would "feel the ground trembling" and this would be followed by a major earthquake within twenty-four hours. In November, 1969, another human seismograph, policeman Joe Morris of Hartford, Conn., was so sure there had been an earthquake in the Midwest that he walked into a radio station and asked for details. The next morning twenty-two states in the Middle West suffered a quake.

A natural-disaster barometer among modern prophets may be Lorna Middleton, who in one two-year period, 1966–68, had no fewer than ten premonitions of subsequent earthquakes, floods, and tornadoes. Many of these were verified by Dr. Barker, to whom she reported her predictions, and by the British Premonitions Bureau. Shirley Harrison, a psychic from West Buxton, Maine, had a vision of a later earthquake in Greece. Adrienne Coulter of Flushing, New York, foresaw the

Alaskan tidal waves of 1967. Alan Hencher, a regular contributor to the two premonitions bureaus, predicted floods in England.

Mrs. Elizabeth Steen, who had several frightening visions of the California disaster that never came, had had some remarkable premonitions a few years earlier. While living in Holland in 1952, she had a vision of the ocean overflowing the country and causing much damage and loss of life. Her own home, which she predicted would be in the path of the flood, was inundated three weeks later.

"4,000 PEOPLE WILL BE KILLED"

In 1902 a British engineer named J. W. Dunne was stationed with the British Mounted Infantry in South Africa. One night he dreamed that he was standing on the spur of a mountain watching jets of vapor shoot out of fissures in the rocks. He was terrified because he knew in his dream that he was on an island about to be devastated by a volcano. Yet his fear was not for himself but for the thousands of people who lived on the island.

Watching the gasses hiss out of the rocks, he cried out, "Good God! The whole thing is going to blow up!" In the dream he recalled the frightful catastrophe on the island of Krakatoa in 1883, when a volcanic explosion killed everyone on the island and caused waves to boil up on shores 8,000 miles away. Dunne was determined to save the 4,000 people on his island who would otherwise die when the volcano erupted. Instantly, as is the way in dreams, he found himself on another island, where he pleaded with the French authorities to send ships and save the natives. He ran from official to official, but they ignored him.

Throughout the dream he kept thinking: "4,000 people will be killed . . . 4,000 . . . 4,000. . . ." He woke up in a sweat shouting, "Listen! Four thousand people will be killed unless—"

Some time later a newspaper arrived at the army post with the news that Mount Pelée on the island of Martinique in the West Indies had erupted, with over 40,000 lives lost. When Dunne read the article, he saw the figure as 4,000, as it had been in his dream. Some months later he looked at the newspaper again and noticed his mistake.

Dunne, who had a scientific mind, worried about the incorrect figure. Did that one mistake mean that his dream was not a true premonition? He even wondered whether he had actually had the dream, but when he continued to have precognitive dreams and immediately wrote them down upon awakening, he concluded that he had had a valid premonition of the Mount Pelée eruption.

It is possible that Dunne foresaw not the actual catastrophe but the later scene in which he read the facts in the newspaper and mistook 40,000 for 4,000. Then, in his dream he dramatized the events at Martinique, assuming that 4,000 persons would die.

Premonitions move in mysterious ways, but they often perform wonders.

THE "CALAMITY SEERESS" PRE-VIEWS AN EXPLOSION

A German psychic of the early 1900s, Madame de Ferriëm, also foresaw the eruption on Martinique and said when it would occur—in 1902. Madame de Ferriëm was an unusual "calamity seeress" whose visions appeared to her well in advance of a catastrophe as if, in present-day terms, projected from a movie or television camera. In 1896 she had a frightening vision of a future mine explosion and described it in the style of a radio or film narrator (significant details are italicized):

> All these people here at the *mine entrance!* How white they are! Like corpses!—Ah! That is what they are, all corpses! Yes, they are coming out—all being now carried out. The whole region is so black, nothing but *small huts* all about. The people that I see speak a different language . . . Now they are bringing out one wearing a *belt with a shining buckle on it.* It will soon be Christmas—it is *so cold!* There is one who has a *lamp with a little wire grating about it.* Ah, this is a *coal-mine* . . . Now I understand what one of them is saying. He says, "The *doctors* are all coming from *Brüx!*" Oh! This is a *Bohemian place* . . . They are *Bohemians.* The women and children all wear *kerchiefs* . . . Are those *physicians,* applying friction? . . . Many of them have *bands with crosses on their arms* . . . Oh, that is a *rosary* . . . "*In the coal mines of Dux,*" he is saying. But what I read is *Brüx.* Why, I see it on his *arm-band*—Oh, they are from the *health department.*

Note the sense of immediacy of Madame de Ferriëm's vision. No fanciful picture of highways buckling and buildings toppling over, but specific here-and-now details about women and children with kerchiefs, the names "Dux" and "Brüx," the small huts, the cold weather, Bohemia. Note also that the scene is not instantly complete. This gradual filling in—often spaced out over months and years—is characteristic of many premonitions. Sometimes the one or two details that might have helped prevent a disaster—such as the actual location —have been cruelly omitted, or came into the vision when it was too late to avert a tragedy.

In 1899, three years after Madame de Ferriëm's vision, a description of it appeared in a German newspaper. A year later, in September, 1900, there was a mine explosion at Dux, near Brüx in Czechoslovakia. Hundreds were killed, and bodies were still being carried out a month later, during an unusually cold October. The only inaccurate item in the vision was about Christmas. Madame de Ferriëm felt the cold and thought it was the Christmas season.

PREVISIONS OF FIRE

No terror is greater than that of being trapped in a fire. Those who envision this kind of calamity can feel the flames heating up their cheeks, and can smell the odor of burning wood or human flesh. A high percentage of premonitions of nature on a rampage are of fire.

J. W. Dunne, who dreamed about the eruption of Mount Pelée, had a later dream about a fire that took many lives. He saw himself on a balcony, while from a fire engine below a hose was sending up a stream of water. There were many other persons on the balcony, but he could hardly see them through the smoke. They were collapsing all around him and he could hear their pitiful moans. Finally the smoke rolled over everything, obliterating the whole scene.

Dunne heard later about a fire in a rubber factory near Paris. Several of the girls working in the factory sought refuge on a balcony, while firemen below sent up streams of water to put out the flames around them. Unfortunately, as in Dunne's dream, smoke poured through broken windows behind the balcony, and the girls were suffocated.

As in his dream about Martinique, Dunne felt a strong emotional link to the persons who would die in the fire. He was no mere spectator but shared the distress of the girls on the balcony and felt the horror of death when the smoke came through from the rear.

Among the premonitions that have come down through history, those of fire rank among the most authentic. In 1759 Emanuel

Swedenborg, a renowned Swedish scientist and mystic, visited a friend in Göteborg, 300 miles from his home in Stockholm. During dinner Swedenborg suddenly paused and looked straight ahead as if seeing a vision. Then he said slowly that a terrible fire had broken out in Stockholm. He could see the flames clearly and he watched the fire as it moved from house to house.

Swedenborg's vision came to him at 6 P.M. In a restless mood, he went out of the house and returned several times to describe the progress of the fire. At eight o'clock he said with a sigh of relief that the fire had finally stopped—just three houses away from his own. Messengers arrived later from Stockholm and verified all the details he had seen in his vision. Ostensibly Swedenborg was watching the fire as it raged, yet so mysterious is the nature of time, that he could have anticipated the outbreak of flames or he might have been watching a rerun of the total scene.

GREAT CITIES SHALL BE DESTROYED

Stockholm was not the only city that has been psychically seen going up in flames. For some reason, perhaps wishful thinking, world capitals have been singled out for fiery destruction by many prophets. A great fire was predicted for London, and a few seers told the year —1666. Humphrey Smith foresaw the fire in 1660 and claimed that "the vision remained in me as a thing secretly shewed me of the Lord."

George Fox, founder of the Society of Friends, recorded his own prophecy in his *Journal* and also told about one Thomas Ibbott, who not only had a premonition of the fire but acted it out in the streets of London. Arriving in the city two days before the fire broke out, he jumped off his horse and ran around shouting that he was fleeing from the flames. Many Londoners may have thought he was out of his mind, but two days later they were rushing through the streets in the same way.

William Lilly, an astrologer of the seventeenth century, published a book in 1648 in which he predicted the 1666 fire: "It will be ominous to London, unto her merchants at sea, to her traffic on land, to her poor, to all sorts of people inhabiting in her or her liberties, by reason of sundry fires and a consuming plague." The plague was thrown in as a bonus.

Sure enough, the Great Plague hit London in 1665, and the fire broke out the next year. So astonished were members of a board of inquiry, that Lilly was hauled before the board and asked if he had had anything to do with setting the fire. Lilly patiently explained that he was a prophet and not a conspirator and that he didn't go out of his way to make predictions come true. He was exonerated, but not without some suspicious head-shaking by a few members of the board.

Nostradamus, who must rank at the very top of any all-star cast of prophets, went Lilly a hundred years better by announcing in 1566 that the same fire would occur a century later. Just as the visions of disaster of some present-day psychics may have been inspired by Edgar Cayce's trance-prophecies, Lilly may have been influenced somewhat by the words of the medieval master seer. Lilly did, however, have a high percentage of accurate predictions and was a star psychic in his own right.

The greatest conflagration of all has been predicted for the city of Paris. It hasn't happened yet, but seers promise that it will be the grand climax of all urban fires. Nostradamus, turning 1666 upside down, set the time for 1999, the pet year for twentieth-century prophets. Seers with a biblical bent have looked upon the coming destruction of Paris as evidence of Jehovah's wrath at her immoral ways, just as one prophet of Southern California's demise sees it as a punishment because of wickedness "with its hippies, homosexuals, and topless nightclubs."

A shepherdess named Marianne Gaultier predicted in the nineteenth century that "the great prostitute (Paris) will be destroyed by fire." Another prophetess said that "Paris will be extinguished like Sodom and Gomorrah," while a nun of the last century put it even more strongly: "Oh, Paris, execrable city, for how long have you deserved my indignation! Your inhabitants will one day curse you . . . because they will have found death in your bosom."

Meanwhile Paris goes her gay, insouciant, perhaps lascivious way. Just wait till 1999, say the prophets.

A PERSONAL PREMONITION OF FIRE

The author of this book is no psychic, yet I once had a premonition of a fire without being aware of it. At the time, I was living in a motel in New Jersey, where I made coffee every morning on a hot-plate that rested on a television set. One afternoon while typing, I smelled smoke. I searched my room, but nothing was burning. I went outside and walked completely around the motel, sniffing the air. I could still smell the acrid fumes but I didn't know where they came from.

I called the clerk. He smelled nothing but humored me as we prowled back and forth, opening doors to see if someone's carpet was burning or expecting to find an occupant who had fallen asleep while smoking in bed. Finally, I had to admit that it was only my heated-up imagination at work. Everything was in order.

A week later I took a trip to New York. When I returned, I saw firemen carrying out the charred remains of a television set, a coal-black hotplate, and a carton of ruined manuscripts that I mourn to this day. I had carelessly left a saucepan boiling on the hotplate and the flames had surged through, ruining the saucepan and destroying the television set. The flames had just reached the rug when the fire-men arrived.

If I had been writing about premonitions at the time, I would have realized that I had received a warning to take care. From that day on I have started no more fires.

"THE SMELL OF BURNING WAS HORRIBLE"

The case of the *Volturno* illustrates how vividly the vibrations of fire can reach across time and space, bringing a sense of horror to persons far removed from the scene. It was almost a total clairvoyant experience, involving the senses of seeing, hearing, touching, and smelling. It was, in addition, a collective vision, shared by many persons. The time-correlation between the actual event and the psychic knowledge of it is not certain. The vision could have been con-temporary with the fire, after the fire, or—in some elements of the scene—before the fire.

The *Volturno* was a British ship carrying emigrants from Holland to New York City. The year was 1913, eighteen months after the *Titanic* sank. There were hundreds of passengers in the steerage when the boat caught fire at 6:30 A.M. on October 9. At 2:30 that afternoon the liner *Carmania* (note the similarity of name to the

Carpathia, which went to the aid of the *Titanic*) arrived on a rescue mission. The *Carmania* tried for several hours to lower a lifeboat alongside the stricken ship, but a fierce gale and mountainous waves kept pushing it back. Other ships, summoned by SOS, joined in the rescue attempt, but the storm drove back their lifeboats.

At 9 P.M. there was an explosion in the boiler room. Flames shot up amidships and quickly spread from stem to stern. The men in the lifeboats and in the other ships could do nothing but helplessly watch the conflagration and listen to the screams of passengers who were being burned alive. Another explosion followed.

The fire went on all night long. As morning came, the storm gradually subsided, and finally the lifeboats were able to draw alongside the ship and take on the survivors. At about 11 A.M. on Friday, October 10, the rescue ships sailed away, leaving the *Volturno* floundering in the sea with its victims. The death toll was 136, 100 drowned and 36 burned alive.

On Thursday evening, October 9, a group of persons were holding a seance in a London living room. At this time they knew nothing about the fire, as the news did not reach the London papers until Saturday. One of the group, a young lady named Miss Scott, suddenly trembled and cried out that she could feel the heat of flames all around her. The others also smelled something burning and heard the sound of water dripping. They searched through the house but could find no fire. The faucets in the kitchen and bathroom were all tightly closed.

A vision began to unfold before Miss Scott's eyes. She saw a ship in flames and heard the passengers screaming. "The smell of burning in the room was horrible," Miss Scott said later. "I could smell charred wood and see many pairs of hands stretched out and imploring for help."

Now the vision spread out until it filled the room, and everyone present could witness the tragedy. In one voice they cried out that the smell was like burning flesh, and they were sickened by it. Then the sound of explosions was heard and streaks of light darted through the room. The group watched in horror as the people who were thrashing about in the water finally went under. Two women in the living room saw "the tips of fingers sticking out of the water."

Cold gusts of sea air swept through the room and made its occupants shiver.

Miss Scott said, "We shall hear of a disaster at sea." Two days later, on Saturday, October 11, the London afternoon newspapers told about the *Volturno* tragedy.

Whatever one may think of seances, the participants often lose consciousness of time and space and are highly susceptible to psychic experiences. Seances must be ranked with visions, dreams, trances, and other paraconscious states during which scenes from "out there" are vividly played in the "here-and-now." The *Volturno* fire linked the people on the boat in the Atlantic to those in the living room in London. The emotions generated by that age-old phobia of man—the fear of fire—bridged the time-space gap.

"THE DOCKS ARE BURNING"

"What a terrific fire! An appalling fire. So many ships. A ship is burning. Clouds of black smoke—coal-black smoke. How thick it is! The docks are burning. Oh, this is terrible . . . A conflagration in New York . . . I see a ship burning in New York harbor and I hear a terrible crash. So far as I can see, it is not an American ship. The city is New York; I know I am right . . ."

It is our old friend Madame de Ferriëm again, giving us a blow-by-blow description of a fire that hasn't flared up yet. Once again she has pre-viewed a disaster, which she "sees" in vivid detail.

On June 30, 1900, fire broke out in the Hoboken, New Jersey, docks, just across the river from New York City. Three German ocean liners were destroyed—the *Main,* the *Saale,* and the *Bremen.* About 200 persons lost their lives. As the calamity seeress had predicted, no American ship was touched by the flames.

A remarkable psychic was Madame de Ferriëm. We'll be hearing again about her premonitions and prophecies.

"THE MANY BODIES ROASTING, THE MANY
CHARRED REMAINS"

In the 1890s a group of society persons were gathered in the Paris home of a gentleman named Count de Maillé. A famous psychic of the time, Mademoiselle Couédon, had consented to give a reading.

Many eminent persons were present who could later verify what she had predicted, among them the editor of a Paris newspaper, *La Libre Parole,* and several noblemen and their ladies.

After doing personal readings for the one hundred or so guests, Mlle. Couédon suddenly leaned back in her chair and gazed thoughtfully at the ceiling. Then she began to chant:

> Near the Champs Élysées
> I see a place not very high
> Not to pious aims devoted
> But still it is approached
> For a charitable end,
> Which is only half the truth.
> I see the fire leaping,
> And the people screaming.
> The many bodies roasting,
> The many charred remains—
> What horrid masses of them!

Mlle. Couédon then explained to her guests that she had "seen" a fire that would take place some time in the future at a charity affair sponsored by Paris society. All of the Count's guests would attend the affair, but none would be affected by the tragedy. None, that is—she now turned slowly to her host—except Count de Maillé. But fortunately, he would escape personal injury. He would be affected only distantly, indirectly.

On May 4, 1896, one of Paris' worst fires broke out at the Charity Bazaar. More than a hundred society women perished, but those who had been present at Mlle. Couédon's reading escaped unhurt. Count de Maillé, who attended the Bazaar, was not injured, but a distant relative was burned to death.

A LETTER PREDICTS A FIRE

In December, 1969, while I was writing this section on predictions of fires, I received a letter from Lorna Middleton, which said in part:

> At 11:45 tonight I felt there may be a tremendous disaster, at first thought it appears to be an oil refinery. The location? Near a harbour. A tremendous fire, sheets of white flame . . .

A month later Miss Middleton sent me a clipping from the London *Sun* of December 29, 1969:

GIANT OIL PLANT BLAZE

More than 250 firemen raced to a giant oil refinery last night after an explosion turned the plant into an inferno . . . Huge clouds of billowing smoke poured from the fiercely blazing refinery—the second biggest in Europe . . .

The refinery is located at Fawley, near the "harbour" of Southampton, where the *Titanic* began her ill-fated voyage in 1912. When Miss Middleton first had her premonition, on December 6, she couldn't pinpoint the location. On December 27, two days before the fire, the name Southampton came to her.

CHAPTER FIVE

Premonitions of Jet-Age Disasters

In this age of automation—with more and more vehicles moving on the ground, in the air, and out in space—there is an uneasy feeling that man may be at the mercy of the machines he has created. Whenever a plane or train starts on its journey, a certain amount of anxiety seems to be generated, and many premonitions come through in dreams, visions, and hunches. There is an emotional link between the psychic and those about to board an airliner or take off on a space flight.

The Central Premonitions Registry and the British Premonitions Bureau constantly receive warnings of plane crashes, but many of them are unsupported by specific details. If, however, the psychic should give the name or type of plane that will crash, the time of takeoff, the location of the disaster, and other such information, the Registry and the Bureau will note the premonition with more than casual interest.

Although some letters have been received with one or two details matching the circumstances of a plane crash or a train wreck, the most accurate jet-age premonitions—involving planes, trains, and spacecraft—have come from psychics of long standing who have been developed by the two bureaus.

A DREAM-PLANE FROM SPAIN

Before his untimely death in 1968, Dr. Barker closely followed the dreams and visions of two London psychics—Lorna Middleton and Alan Hencher—and asked them to call him any time they had an unusual hunch about a disaster. Hencher, a man in his late forties, often gets a headache when he senses that "something terrible" is going to happen. One night he had a vision that was so disturbing he felt tight bands of pain around his head.

After tossing and turning all night, he phoned Dr. Barker in the morning and gave him the details. He had "seen" a plane crash on an island where there was a church surrounded by statuary. One hundred twenty-four persons would die. The location, said Hencher, must be Nicosia on the island of Cyprus.

Some weeks later a plane did crash in Nicosia, and 124 persons were killed. The psychic was off in one detail—another passenger died later, making the toll 125. Hencher envisioned only the time of the crash and omitted what led up to it or what happened later. Speaking photographically, his was a still or flash picture of the event, rather than the continuous film vision of a Madame de Ferriëm. The dramatic moment of the crash itself was what brought the future vividly to him.

In another vision, however, Hencher not only saw the climax of a disaster but observed the sequence of events that led up to it. In this vision the psychic himself played a role. Late in October, 1967, Hencher dreamed he was sitting in a plane with four very young girls. The dream-plane took off from Spain, soared over a mountain, then ran into a storm as it flew over England. One engine exploded and one wing of the plane crashed into a hill. There was a heavy death toll.

Hencher felt that this accident would occur about the beginning of November, two weeks after he reported his dream to Dr. Barker and the British Premonitions Bureau. On November 4 a Caravelle jetliner left the resort town of Malaga in southern Spain and headed for England. During a rainstorm the plane crashed into a hillside in Surrey, forty miles southwest of London, and thirty-seven persons were killed, including two little girls.

An interesting aspect of Hencher's vision was his link with the little girls. As in the Aberfan tragedy, small children, perhaps because they are generally open in their emotions, seem to penetrate the psyche of sensitive adults.

"SNOW AND FLASHES OF ORANGE LIGHT"

Lorna Middleton has sent many accurate predictions of plane crashes to both the London Premonitions Bureau and the Central Premonitions Registry. On January 11, 1968, she wrote to Dr. Barker that there would be a plane crash in the snow: ". . . lots of *snow* and *flashes of orange light*" (italics mine). She thought it would happen in either Canada or Switzerland.

On January 23, about two weeks later (most premonitions sent to the Bureau and the Registry seem to come about two weeks in advance), a B-52 bomber crashed through seven-foot thick ice in Greenland Bay, east of Canada. The resulting fire ("flashes of orange light") may have melted the ice, and the load of bombs sank to the sea bed.

One of Miss Middleton's most spectacular premonitions was sent to the Central Premonitions Registry on December 1, 1969:

Dear Mr. Nelson:
I have a premonition there will be a disaster connected with a mountain.
A plane may crash.
I see people climbing up a side of the mountain in mud mainly, but they are heavily clothed. They climb because of an accident. Plane or train—it is always difficult to distinguish . . .

With the letter she enclosed, as she so often does, a sketch she had drawn, this time of men and women pulling themselves up the side of a steep mountain.

On December 8, 1969, a news dispatch from Athens, Greece, reported that ninety persons were killed when an Olympic Airways DC-6B plane crashed into Mount Paneion during a storm. Rescue workers climbed up the side of the mountain for three quarters of an hour before they reached the scene of the wreckage.

PRELUDE TO A PREMONITION

What brings on a premonition? Generally it comes without warning as an abrupt invasion into a mind occupied with other thoughts.

Sometimes there is preparation, a slow buildup to the realization that "something terrible" is going to happen. The psychic may glance at an object, a random thought may occur to him, or a mood may be generated by a book or music. Then a train of associations is formed, leading the mind of the psychic through a series of ideas or images that culminate in a vision of the disaster.

Tholen, a Dutch psychic, was once looking at a music-book when the face of the Madonna floated over it. Then the face became that of Queen Juliana of Holland, and superimposed over it were the words *Ave Maria*. Now the image changed to that of an airplane with forty-one funeral cars, and one person walking away.

A week later the airplane *Queen Juliana* crashed in Frankfurt, Germany. Forty-one persons were killed. The only survivor was the stewardess, who walked away from the disaster scene. Music was probably the catalyst that brought on Tholen's premonition, starting with the music-book itself, then leading to the strains of *Ave Maria* and a vision of the funeral cars.

Sometimes the future setting of the disaster forges a bond between the psychic and those who will be killed. It is as if vibrations are already emanating from the scene of the tragedy, affecting sensitive persons who are there shortly before it happens. Raynor Johnson in his book *The Imprisoned Splendour* tells about one such premonition.

A young Australian lady, who later told the story to Johnson, had left her children in the care of a governess and gone off on a vacation by herself. One morning in October, 1948, she was walking through a forest in the Mount Macedon region when she noticed "smoke curling up the Mount on the Wood End side." The smoke was blowing in her direction.

"Not wishing to be involved in a bush fire," she wrote, "I decided to take the path leading directly to my home. I discovered that it crossed a firebreak, and once past that I entered the forest again and sat down under a tree to eat my lunch and to read Wordsworth. But for some reason I felt uneasy and was unable to concentrate . . . Telling myself not to be foolish, I found a hollow, where I crouched down so as to be hidden from the view of anyone approaching the firebreak, and waited.

"Then suddenly it happened. Over me flowed a wave of acute

terror, loneliness and pain, amounting almost to an agony. After a moment of paralyzing suspense, I turned and ran through the forest. Nor did I stop until I reached home, panting . . .

"I faced all the physical possibilities that could have induced fear, but decided that the overwhelming character of the sensation was not justified by any known physical cause. I rather tended to think that . . . it was associated with some event that had occurred in that place in the past. . . ."

On November 8, 1948, a week after the young lady's experience, the newspapers reported the crash of a Douglas DC-3 airliner. The plane had hit a firebreak close to the spot where the woman had been sitting. Both pilots were killed. One died right away, the other, rescuers said, suffered intense physical and mental torture before he died.

Johnson comments that instead of "memories of the past," this place held a "record of the future." He calls this experience a case of "pre-sentience." An emotional link between the young lady and the pilots of the plane had been created at the scene of the disaster. The fact that the plane hit the firebreak as it was coming down may have added to the strength of the premonition.

"I SAW YOU DIE LAST NIGHT"

Suppose you are about to take a plane trip, and you are invited to a cocktail party the night before to celebrate your departure. While you are sipping a drink, you overhear a man tell someone that you have just died in a plane crash. He had dreamed about it the previous night, and the dream was so striking that he was firmly convinced you were already dead.

You interrupt to tell the dreamer that you are very much alive. He doesn't deny your existence, but something about the look in his eyes disturbs you, and you ask him for details of the dream. He describes how your plane was caught in a snowstorm, circled around a mountain, and finally crashed into a village below. There were no survivors.

Now you are interested, and perhaps a bit worried, because you are inclined to believe in premonitions. You press the dreamer for further details. Who were the other passengers on the plane? A military crew, is the answer, and three civilians—two men and a woman.

Now you smile with relief. You are a military man yourself and so is the crew of your plane, but there will be no civilians aboard. Nothing to fear.

But the gods who have arranged this little sport are not going to let you off so easily. Your host, a civilian, asks if he may go along as a passenger. Uneasily you consent. Later in the evening another guest invites himself on the trip. All right, that makes two civilians, both of them men. No woman will be on the plane.

As the party is about to break up, a young girl asks to speak with you. A request for her services has come from another city. You freeze. . . .

Sounds like a melodrama concocted out of a playwright's imagination, but it did happen—to Air Marshal Sir Victor Goddard of the Royal New Zealand Air Force. At the end of World War II, in January, 1946, Goddard was in Shanghai on his way back to Australia. He was to leave next morning for a stopover in Tokyo, and the British consul-general, George Alwyne Ogden, gave a party in his honor. It was on this night that he overheard an English soldier, Dewing, describe his dream. "Too bad about Goddard," said Dewing. "He died last night in a crash."

When Dewing saw Goddard, he stared at him as if actually seeing a dead man. After an embarrassed silence, he apologized to the Air Marshal but urged him not to travel for a few days, so realistic had been his dream. Dewing had seen a "rocky, shingly shore." The plane had been flying in the evening and "there was a snowstorm . . . You had been over the mountains in a cloud . . . I watched it all happen."

Dewing described the plane as a Dakota, an ordinary transport plane. The craft Goddard was about to fly, the *Sister Ann,* was also a Dakota. On the dream-plane there had been three English civilians —two men and a girl—along with the military crew. The *Sister Ann,* however, would only carry military personnel.

Later in the evening, while Goddard was talking with his host, the Chinese butler brought an envelope on a tray. It was a radio message requesting the consul-general to leave for Tokyo as soon as possible. With some misgivings Goddard agreed to take him along. He couldn't do otherwise.

A short time later Seymour Berry, an English newspaperman,

asked if he could also be a passenger on the plane. Then, when Ogden's butler appeared again with another message, Goddard feared the worst—and he was right. An official in Tokyo needed a secretary and requested Ogden to bring one with him. The girl was Dorita Breakspear, an Englishwoman.

Goddard was worried but he didn't want to alarm his passengers, so he said nothing. The next morning, at 6:30, the plane took off. All day it moved through dark clouds and had to climb as high as 17,000 feet, where ice kept forming on the wings. But it was still morning, and in the dream the crash had occurred in the evening. Perhaps they could get to Tokyo before nightfall.

The storm grew worse, and the plane was caught in a fierce gale— high over cliffs that bordered the sea. At 3:30 Goddard noticed uneasily that it had begun to snow. Then, through the mist they saw a tiny fishing village below—on a "rocky, shingly shore." The pilot circled around for an hour and finally, after the plane had maneuvered through dark clouds with only occasional glimpses of the mountains below, the village came in view again. They were lost—and the plane was running out of gas.

There was only one thing to do—attempt a precarious landing on the beach bordering the village. Goddard gave his passengers blankets, coats, and mattresses to cushion the shock of impact. He tried to control his emotions. It was now evening, as in the dream, it was snowing, and there was the mountain. Was this to be the end?

The pilot was going to try landing wheels down until the plane could slow up on the beach, then retract the wheels to keep the plane from turning over. They were now close to the cliff as the plane swooped down, overshot its goal, climbed, swooped down again, again overshot, and climbed back up for its final try.

Goddard looked at his passengers—two Englishmen and an English girl. They were huddled in their seats, white-faced. Once more the pilot dove—and the plane hit the ground with a bang. Goddard felt excruciating pain and watched in horror as Ogden flew out of his seat.

Ogden, lying on the floor in a heap, suddenly looked up and said, "My chair came off!" The tension was broken, and everybody laughed. There were no injuries. As the plane came to a stop, the villagers gathered around to help.

Why was the premonition accurate in every detail but the most important one—Goddard did not die in the crash? If Dewing had been present at the actual crash but watching it from a distance, he might have jumped to the conclusion that Goddard and his passengers had perished. In his dream he saw the future in the same way, making a false assumption for which Goddard, today very much alive, has always been grateful.

The story of Goddard and Dewing's dream was first told in the *Saturday Evening Post* of May 26, 1951. In 1955 a film based on his experience was produced—*The Night My Number Came Up*, starring Michael Redgrave.

PREMONITION IN A COCKTAIL BAR

On the night of January 16, 1969, a gentleman named Joseph DeLouise walked into a cocktail lounge in Chicago and asked not for a drink but for a newspaper. He wanted to read about the head-on crash of two trains somewhere just south of Chicago. The men at the bar looked up with interest and concern. What crash? Where? No one had told them about any train wreck. There had been nothing about it in the newspapers.

"Somewhere south of here," said DeLouise slowly, "two trains hit each other in a fog. It was the worst train disaster we have had since World War II, twenty-five years ago. Many people were hurt and killed."

DeLouise spoke in a far-away voice, as if he were seeing a vision —but of an event that had already taken place. Interested, the bartender turned on the radio, but there was nothing about a train wreck. Some of the men wondered whether DeLouise had had one too many drinks.

Two hours later, at 1:00 A.M. on January 17, two Illinois Central trains met head-on in a fog just south of Chicago. Three persons were killed and forty-seven hurt, the worst train disaster in the area in twenty-five years.

How did DeLouise know? How does any psychic know? This premonition could easily be verified. The men who were in the tavern that night signed a statement that DeLouise had predicted the wreck. Even more impressive was DeLouise's appearance on a radio station in Gary, Indiana, in December, 1968, when he announced that the crash would occur in five or six weeks. He gave the same details then as he did later in the tavern.

An interesting aspect of this case is that DeLouise expected to read about the wreck in a newspaper before it happened. He may also have foreseen the newspaper article describing the accident, just as J. W. Dunne "saw" the news item about the eruption of Mount Pelée and Mrs. Milden pre-viewed a television broadcast of the Aberfan tragedy.

HOW TO AVOID AN ACCIDENT

Premonitions about train and plane disasters often come close to home, and the psychic herself is warned. Countess Lillimay Kobylanska, writing in Eileen Garrett's *Beyond the Five Senses,* told about being awakened one morning by a voice which instructed her to cancel her reservation on the one o'clock train. She took a later train, then found out that the first train had been wrecked.

Aniela Jaffé tells in *Apparitions and Precognition* about a woman getting ready for a ski-outing with her seven-year-old boy. Just as they were about to leave for the railroad station, a feeling came over her that they must not go. They stayed home and in the evening heard news of a terrible railway accident involving the train on which they would have returned home.

Shirley Harrison of West Buxton, Maine, is a well-known American psychic who has been called in many times to help the police solve crimes. During the 1950s, while she was living in Philadelphia, she took a trip with her husband to see relatives in Maine. On the return trip, after getting off the train at Boston, a transfer point, Mrs. Harrison suddenly felt uneasy. Although she did not like to travel by bus, she insisted that they must not take the second train. When they reached their destination, news came that the train they avoided taking had been wrecked in Rhode Island.

An even larger part of the population may be "accident-avoiders" without knowing it. Maurice Maeterlinck, the Belgian writer and psychic investigator, observed that "some strange chance keeps away a number of people who would otherwise be present at a catastrophe and perish"—as in the case of the cancellations before the sailing of the *Titanic.*

In the 1950s, a researcher in psychic phenomena, W. E. Cox, concluded as the result of a survey that there are fewer passengers on a train destined to be wrecked than on one that will have a normal run. Cox called this phenomenon "accident-avoidance" and conjectured that there are probably more cases of this kind than those in which the psychic has a conscious premonition of a disaster. Cox contacted American railroads to find out how many accidents there had been since 1950. Then he constructed a table to compare the number of passengers in a train on an accident-day with the number on each of the six previous days and on the corresponding day in each of the four preceding weeks—eleven days in all.

Many of the trains on their accident-days carried fewer passengers than on any of the other 10 days in the study. An outstanding example was the Georgian, a Chicago and Eastern Illinois train, which had an accident on June 15, 1952. Only 9 persons were on the train that day, compared with 68, 60, 53, 48, 62, and 70 on each of the preceding six days. A week earlier, on June 8, there had been 35 passengers. On June 1 there had been 55, on May 25 there were 53, and on May 18 there were 54 passengers.

For the 10 days, excluding the accident-day, the average number of passengers on the Georgian was 54. On the accident-day the figure went down to only 9, a 600 percent drop. The passengers who cancelled their reservations or who had second thoughts about taking the Georgian that day were probably experiencing what Cox calls the "subliminal premonition."

On another day—December 15, 1952—train #15 of the Chicago, Milwaukee, and St. Paul line was wrecked with fifty-five passengers aboard. On five of the previous seven days the train carried well over one hundred passengers, and on the other two days at least thirty more than on the accident-day. The average number of passengers for the ten accident-free days was over one hundred, 50 percent more than on the day of the wreck.

"HE'S GOING TO THE MOON . . . HE'S TERRIFIED

. . . HE'S BURNING"

Fortunately, as this book goes to press, there have been no tragedies involving U.S. astronauts in outer space, although *Apollo*

XIII was in deep trouble during its flight to the moon. There was, of course, the shocking flash fire in January, 1967, that took the lives of three astronauts on the ground. In his book *The Reluctant Prophet,* Daniel Logan says that a friend of his foresaw that tragedy. Logan himself has hinted that visitors from other planets will in some way hamper the space program, and that many astronauts will die under "mysterious circumstances."

So far, if interplanetary visitors are around, they have not bothered our spacecraft. As for astronauts meeting death, this may well happen as space travel becomes more common, just as there are fatal accidents in the air and on the ground. Those in the space program are well aware of the risks they take and know that tragedies are possible. Considering the phenomenal success of the program to date, however, such mishaps may be well in the future.

On file with the Central Premonitions Registry are several accurate predictions of problems that did develop during the earth orbits and moon shots. Prior to the *Apollo IX* countdown in March, 1969, a San Diego woman sent a telegram to the Central Premonitions Registry, predicting illness during the flight. She also foretold an argument between the astronauts and Mission Control, and an unusual splashdown.

She scored on all three predictions. The astronauts caught cold in deep space, there was an argument with Mission Control over whether to transmit television pictures, and when the return capsule splashed into the ocean, it was upside down. None of these predictions was remarkable in itself, but the combination of all three coming true points to a genuine premonition.

An unusual space prediction came in two parts and involved two psychics, Alan Vaughan in the United States and Mrs. M in Germany. When they finally met and compared notes, they discovered that their forecasts dovetailed. The first premonition came to Vaughan a week before Walter M. Schirra, Jr., and Thomas P. Stafford took *Gemini VI* into space in December, 1965. Vaughan sensed danger to the astronauts from a mechanical condition in the spaceship. He felt that an adjustment would have to be made before liftoff.

The trouble was found just before *Gemini VI* was launched. Someone had forgotten to remove a plastic cap from the fuel line, and the line was blocked. After the cap was removed, the ship shot off the launching pad and made a successful journey into orbit and back.

Three years later, in 1968, Vaughan was visiting in Germany and met a German actress and psychic, Mrs. M, whose paranormal abilities were being studied by Dr. Hans Bender of the University of Freiberg. She told Vaughan that she too had had a premonition of mechanical trouble in *Gemini VI,* coming in the form of dream symbols. In her dream Mrs. M's daughter was an astronaut and with her was a man who was choking to death from a plastic cap caught in his throat.

When she woke, she immediately thought of *Gemini VI* and realized that the plastic cap might spell trouble for the spaceship. The other part of the dream was a prevision of another situation. Mrs. M's daughter, who was also an actress, was later given a role in a program about astronauts and space. There had been no indication at the time of the dream that she would get such a part.

In the television drama Mrs. M's daughter played the role of a girl astronaut and did a countdown. On the night the show was produced, Mrs. M dreamed of another countdown but she felt "tragedy in the dream because of stupidity and carelessness." That same night—January 27, 1967—*Apollo VI* went up in flames with the three astronauts.

Lorna Middleton saw no disaster for our astronauts but foretold the death of a Russian cosmonaut. In April, 1967, she had a vision: "Someone is going to the moon. He's terrified. He's burning." The following day cosmonaut Vladimir Komarov died in the Russian spaceship *Soyuz I.* After the ship had orbited the earth for twenty-four hours, the re-entry parachute (cosmonauts return on land) became tangled and the ship crashed.

Whether Komarov was "burning" is uncertain, but there is evidence that something was wrong during the orbits, when there were no reports from *Tass,* the Soviet news agency. Also, Komarov was not wearing a spacesuit and was vulnerable to a change of conditions within the spacecraft.

"A CRY FOR HELP FROM OUTER SPACE"

In Chicago, New York, and London three psychics had a "feeling" about *Apollo XIII.*

On the morning of April 13, 1970, I received a letter from Lorna Middleton written five hours before the oxygen tank in the service module exploded. "I have what I call my 'flat feeling' about this . . . I feel no success about this venture, only grimness . . ." Since Miss Middleton had predicted the success of the three Apollo moon-landing projects (XI, XII, and XIV), her concern about *Apollo XIII* takes on added significance.

Four months earlier in January, 1970, a Chicago psychic named Ruth Zimmerman said that there would be a "cry for help from outer space." The cry came on April 13 when Mission Control heard astronaut John L. Swigert, Jr. call out, "Hey, we've got a problem!"

Alan Vaughan experienced what might be called the "telescoping effect" in precognition. Before the *Apollo XII* moon shot, Vaughan sent a letter to the Central Premonitions Registry in which he said, "Unless something in the fuel system or electrical system is corrected, there will be an explosion which could kill the astronauts . . . It may be that this flight will be aborted . . . I do not feel these astronauts will reach the moon. . . ."

What Vaughan was describing was the trouble that developed on *Apollo XIII,* when a short circuit ignited the electrical insulation in the oxygen tank, causing the explosion.

Dreams, precognitive or not, have a way of combining several elements in the dreamer's psyche into a neat little dramatic package with interpretations possible on several levels. This is true of the experiments with dreams at the Maimonides Medical Center. Along with the actual telepathic and precognitive material, the dreamer weaves in his own psychological problems. Two or more dramas, masquerading as one, are performed on the stage of the sleeping mind.

The psychic who dreams or has visions of the future must be careful not to let his own preoccupations get in the way of his predictions. In evaluating premonitions, the personality and background of the psychic should always be considered. What are his (or her) fears and biases, personal problems that may generate what appears to be a premonition? Suggestions will be given later on how the aspiring psychic may sharpen his prophetic sense and get a clearer picture of the future.

Hopefully, when every psychic reaches the level of Eileen Garrett, who was a volunteer subject in many scientific experiments, we may be able to know which planes and trains have accident-days and which will be safe to ride in. And if all the signs and portents tell us that California is about to break loose and float out to sea; if dreams, visions, voices, and human seismographs all point to the cataclysm; if subliminal premonitions cause a wholesale cancellation of train and plane reservations to the West Coast during the tourist season— then we may suspect that "something terrible" is going to happen, and we can calmly evacuate the residents of the area.

Until such an early warning alert can be seriously considered, we will continue to hope that most earth changes will be minor, and that our present age of planes, trains, and spacecraft will be relatively free of tragic accidents.

CHAPTER SIX

Dark Clouds Gather Over the White House

When the president of the United States is about to die, the tragedy is sensed by thousands, perhaps millions of Americans. As the nation's leader, symbol of the nation itself, the chief executive shares a psychic bond with the people he serves. If danger threatens him, a feeling of uneasiness spreads through the land, and there are countless dreams, visions, and other extrasensory warnings of what is to come.

It has been estimated that at least 50,000 persons had premonitions that President Kennedy would be shot. Although it is impossible to get statistical proof, there were probably many more who experienced the pre-disaster syndrome without knowing why. When a president's life is in jeopardy, a feeling of despair seems to grip the national psyche, as if there is subliminal knowledge that the tragedy is inevitable. Those psychics who are consciously aware that there will be an assassination attempt generally feel helpless to prevent it. Almost no one will listen to them, least of all the man who is threatened.

There have been dark clouds over Washington many times since the death of William Henry Harrison in 1841. Harrison died after just one month in office, and thus began the ominous "twenty-year cycle" of presidential deaths. Since 1840, every president elected in a year ending in a zero has either died while serving his term or was killed by an assassin's bullet. Abraham Lincoln, first elected in 1860, was shot to death in 1865—the second victim of the cycle. Garfield, elected in 1880, was assassinated in office, as was McKinley, re-elected in 1900. President Harding, elected twenty years later, died while serving his term. President Roosevelt, elected for the third time in 1940, died in 1945. The most recent victim of the twenty-year cycle was John F. Kennedy, president-elect in 1960.

There have been many premonitions of the deaths of presidents involved in the cycle. Nettie Colburn, a medium of the last century, warned Lincoln that "shadows" would hover over him during his second term. Lincoln's wife had a strong feeling that he would die in office. His stepmother, Sarah Bush Lincoln, said that she knew "something would befall Abe" and she would never see him again. When she learned of his death, she said, "I knowed they'd kill him." Lincoln remarked that mediums from all over the country had written to him warning that an attempt would be made on his life.

In December, 1864, *Broughton's Astronomical Journal* made this prediction for April, 1865, in its "Fate of Nations" section: "Some noted general or person in high office dies and is removed about the 17th or 18th day." A year earlier the famous psychic D. D. Home was asked by a Russian to gaze into a crystal ball. In the crystal he saw a crowd of people, and a man who was shot and falling off a chair. Home said, "That is Lincoln, and within the year it will take place."

Both Lincoln and Kennedy had premonitions of their own deaths. Garfield foresaw his death by assassination. McKinley sensed that he would be killed, and symbolic visions were seen in Washington just before he was shot. Shortly before Franklin D. Roosevelt's death, he was told by Jeane Dixon, a Washington psychic, that he had only a few months to live. Mrs. Dixon also knew that his successor, Harry Truman, would become president through an "act of God." While in a trance, Edgar Cayce foresaw the deaths of both Roosevelt and Kennedy.

"A BLUE-EYED MAN WILL DIE"

When John F. Kennedy was elected president in 1960, students of "recurring events" were apprehensive. Jeane Dixon had predicted in 1952 and again in 1956 (before she knew who Kennedy was) that a blue-eyed, youngish man, a Democrat, would be the victorious candidate in 1960 but that he would either die or be assassinated while serving.

The dark clouds gather slowly. Dreams, visions, and disembodied voices began well before 1963 to hint at what was coming. During the 1960 campaign Adrienne Coulter, a psychic living in Flushing, New York, heard a voice say, "Nix on Nixon. Kennedy will become president and will be assassinated." Another voice told Jeanne Gardner, a West Virginia housewife, that Kennedy would be killed. A New Jersey psychic, Mary Tallmadge, "saw" Kennedy facing a coffin, the flag at half-mast. In 1962 a psychologist, while under the influence of a hallucinogenic drug, had a vision of the president's death.

The late Arthur Ford, one of America's leading mediums, told the author about a prediction he made while in trance a year and a half before Kennedy's assassination. The trance reading was taped in Washington, D.C., in the presence of many politicians, including Senator McClellan of Arkansas. In Ford's vision, or rather that of the alleged spirit-control who came through, President Kennedy was "falling forward in a moving vehicle and dying." Ford believed that the anxiety those present felt for the safety of the president was an emotional factor that helped bring on the premonition.

Sometimes newspapers, magazines, or other printed matter carry an ominous message that only an observant person can decode—as if some unconscious force were directing the mind and hand of the editors. A 1963 calendar seemed to "know" that Kennedy would die. Because of a misprint, November 22, the day Kennedy was to be shot, was shown as a legal holiday. A replica of this calendar appeared in the October, 1969, issue of *Fate* magazine.

As the moment of truth drew nearer, Mrs. Dixon and other psychics became increasingly uneasy. What had been a hunch about an unknown politician in 1956 became something more personal and worrisome in 1963. The English psychic, Pendragon, feared an assassination and said so in June, 1963. In October he wrote a letter to the president suggesting that he double his bodyguard. In August, 1963, Jeanne Gardner heard the name "Oswald" but didn't know what it meant.

A few days before the assassination, Mrs. Dixon saw the symbolism of dark clouds forming over the White House. She tried to warn the president, as did many others, known psychics and ordinary Americans sensitized by their emotional bond to the head of government. Some sent letters, others came to Washington with their warnings. In an Ohio hospital, a young boy dying from leukemia woke up from a coma on the morning of November 22 and told his mother that the president had been killed.

THE GUN AT THE BLACK STATUE

Previsions are sometimes induced by drug-taking, when the perceptions are quickened and the sense of time and space is blurred. Dr. Stanley Krippner had a startling premonition of President Kennedy's assassination two years before it occurred while he was participating in a hallucinogenic drug experiment.

"It happened near the end of my first psychedelic session which took place at Cambridge, Mass., in 1962," he wrote. "Meeting that evening at a friend's apartment, we spent a great deal of time in selecting appropriate music. The selections ranged from Debussy and Beethoven to folk songs and Spanish flamenco music.

"At 5:30 that evening I took several tablets of the drug. We played Moussorgsky's 'Pictures at an Exhibition' and waited for the drug to take effect. I closed my eyes and saw a kaleidoscopic vision of colorful shapes and swirls. When I opened my eyes, the room was vibrating with brilliant colors. I remarked that the whole scene looked like a Vermeer painting.

"My fingers were tingling and my limbs were trembling. I closed my eyes again, reclined on the sofa, and visualized a mushroom spreading over me like a magic umbrella . . . My sense of hearing astounded me. I heard music as I had never heard it before. Visually, every item in the apartment was transformed. I felt a kinship with my companions that I was unable to express. . . ."

In this psychedelic state Krippner found himself in the court of Kubla Khan, then in an "immense hall" where a concert was being performed. In a flash he was at Versailles, observing Benjamin Franklin in conference with the King and Queen of France. As the background music became lively and gay, Krippner moved into Spain and was "caught in a frenzied whirl of flamenco dancers and gypsy guitars. One girl kept throwing roses in the air which exploded like firecrackers."

Forward and backward in time as the setting changes: "The scene shifted to the New World. I was with Thomas Jefferson at Monticello as he was explaining his newest invention to a friend—then with Edgar Allen Poe in Baltimore. He had just lost his young bride and was mourning her death. He mumbled something about 'Lenore' and 'Annabel Lee' between sobs."

Notice the change of mood as the themes of politics and death enter. As Krippner's psychedelic vision moves to its climax, each image is related to the next one as though they were part of a film sequence.

"From Baltimore I traveled to the nation's capital. I found myself gazing at a statue of Lincoln. It was entirely black and the head was bowed. There was a gun at the base of the statue, and someone murmured, 'He was shot. The President was shot.' A wisp of smoke rose in the air.

"Lincoln's features slowly faded and those of John F. Kennedy appeared. The scene was still Washington, D.C. The gun was still at the base of the statue, with the wisp of smoke seeping from the barrel and climbing in the air. The voice repeated, 'He was shot. The President was shot.' My eyes opened and they were filled with tears."

Krippner wrote down his premonition and sent it in a report to Harvard. "Nineteen months later," he continues, "on November 22, 1963 the visualization came back to me as I mourned Kennedy's assassination."

The same process that Krippner could observe and report on while in the psychedelic state may go on unconsciously in the minds of psychics whose visions seem to come out of the blue. The influence of music or another stimulus to the emotions may gradually lead the subliminal mind away in time and space to a point where the premonition suddenly flashes into awareness.

Krippner comments: "It is not at all surprising that I might have had a glimpse into the future. After all, are not the past, present, and future part of the same eternity?"

A HEARSE FOLLOWED BY SOLDIERS

In the town of Catskill, N.Y., a seventeen-year-old girl was asleep. In the middle of the night she heard noises and lights flashed in her closed eyes. She got out of bed and went to the window, but the scene below was an unfamiliar one. She saw a strange street in a strange city and a large, excited crowd gathered in front of her house. Now the body of a tall man was brought upstairs and laid upon the bed in her room. He was unconscious, and a stream of blood flowed from a bullet wound in his head.

Was she still asleep? Or was this an uncanny vision of something happening elsewhere, in another time and place? She had seen this man before, but she couldn't remember where. Doctors were standing around, probing the body with instruments, examining the wound. Many persons were crying, and she heard one of them ask in a trembling voice, "Is there no hope?" The doctors shook their heads. A lady who appeared to be the wife of the wounded man was weeping.

The girl fell asleep again, then awakened later in another city. She was standing on the pavement as a hearse went by, followed by a procession of soldiers. There were crowds of people around, watching silently, sadly. Once more the girl fell asleep. At breakfast the next morning she told her family about the strange double vision.

Could her premonition have been about John F. Kennedy? The details are striking. A tall man, wounded in the head, brought upstairs to what could have been a hospital room. The distraught wife . . . doctors examining a bullet wound in the head . . . the scene in Washington over the weekend, with the hearse and soldiers . . .

The girl, Maggie Plugh, had her vision in April, 1865. The following week news came that Abraham Lincoln had been shot. As she had foreseen, he was brought into a room in a private house, bleeding from a bullet wound in the head. On the weekend there was a funeral in Washington, with a hearse followed by soldiers.

Maggie's story appeared in *The Progressive Thinker*, a magazine of the early twentieth century. It was told by a lady for whom she had worked as a nurse. The writer described the mature Maggie Plugh as a woman of excellent and sober character and was sure that she told the truth about her two visions.

"THE PRESIDENT IS SHOT"

On Wednesday night, two days before the assassination, a little girl lay sleeping in a home for handicapped children. The child was a deaf mute and could communicate only by sign language. This night she slept restlessly because she was having a disturbing dream.

During the night the child rose from her bed, still asleep, and walked down the hall, turning into the room of a young friend, also a deaf mute. The second little girl woke up and watched as the first gestured with her hands. The words spelled out: "The President is shot."

As she had been sleep-walking, the first girl didn't remember next morning what had happened. At breakfast, however, with the other children and the superintendent gathered around the table, the second child related the story.

Two days later, on Friday, April 14, 1865, Abraham Lincoln was assassinated in Ford's Theater, Washington, D.C. Almost a hundred years later, also on a Friday, President Kennedy was shot to death in Dallas, Texas, also by a bullet in the head. Once more the twenty-year cycle was confirmed. And once more many Americans, children and adults, dreamed or had visions of their president being slain.

WILL HISTORY REPEAT ITSELF?

The Kennedy drama that unfolded in the 1960–63 period was astonishingly close in theme, plot, and characters to the Lincoln drama of 1860–65. But each president was the protagonist of a play within a play, for the entire decade of the 1860s parallels in many ways the decade of a hundred years later. Does history repeat itself? Compare the two periods:

In both decades America was "a house divided against itself" on the issues of war and civil rights.

The draft riots of the 1860s were matched by the draft resistance movement of the 1960s.

Three presidents were inaugurated in both decades, the first assassinated in each.

Lincoln was elected in 1860, Kennedy in 1960.

Lincoln's secretary was named Kennedy. Kennedy's secretary was named Lincoln.

On the assassination day Lincoln was sitting in Ford's Theater, and Kennedy was riding in a Lincoln.

Both were slain on a Friday, with their wives present.

Both were shot from behind, in the head.

Booth shot Lincoln in a theater and ran into a warehouse. Oswald shot Kennedy from a warehouse and ran into a theater.

Both assassins were killed before they could be brought to trial. Booth was born in 1839, Oswald in 1939. Both were Southerners.

Both vice presidents were named Johnson, and both were Southern Democrats who had been senators. Andrew Johnson was born in 1808. Lyndon Johnson in 1908.

The names Lee Harvey Oswald and John Wilkes Booth each contain fifteen letters.

The last names of Lincoln and Kennedy have the same number of letters—seven. The first and last names of the two Johnsons have the same number of letters—six and seven. The first, middle, and last names of Nixon and Grant, who were the third presidents in the two decades, have the same number of letters—seven, seven, and five. Here is how they match:

LINCOLN ANDREW JOHNSON ULYSSES SIMPSON GRANT
KENNEDY LYNDON JOHNSON RICHARD MILHOUS NIXON

What significance do these "coincidences" have for premonitions and prophecies? They may give hints of future events. There may be a hundred-year as well as a twenty-year cycle.

Perhaps in the year 2060, when another president is elected, the Lincoln-Kennedy drama will be played once more. He may be a tall man, as Lincoln and Kennedy were. He may lose a child by death in the White House, as the Lincolns and Kennedys did. He may be in office during a decade when once more there is agitation over the rights of minorities. And he may be assassinated by a bullet in the head, fired from behind.

"WHAT WILL BE MUST BE"

There are other parallels between the assassinations of Lincoln and Kennedy. One is that both sensed they would die suddenly. In her book *Office Hours: Day and Night,* Dr. Janet Travell, Kennedy's

White House physician, gives several examples of the president's preoccupation with death.

Shortly after his election in November, 1960, Kennedy went for a rest to his father's home in Palm Beach, Florida, accompanied by Dr. Travell. While they were sitting beside the swimming pool, the president-elect suddenly turned and said, "What do you think of the rule that for the last 100 years every President of the United States elected in a year divisible by 20 died in office?" Dr. Travell made light of this theory, but even as she spoke she saw the "shadow of death" in Kennedy's eyes.

On another occasion Kennedy had arranged to meet Dr. Travell near the Lincoln Memorial. His car intercepted hers and he invited her to join him in the White House limousine. On the way they passed a small boy, who suddenly pointed the lens of a movie camera at the president. Kennedy started nervously, then relaxed when he saw it was only a camera. He took a deep breath, then said quietly, "I will not live in fear. What will be must be."

One of John F. Kennedy's favorite poems was "I Have a Rendezvous With Death."

"I SHALL MEET A TERRIBLE END"

Just one hundred years before Dr. Travell first saw the "shadow of death" in President-elect Kennedy's eyes, Abraham Lincoln, returning to his home in Springfield after the 1860 election, also had a premonition of death. Lying down on the sofa to rest, he began to doze but woke up with a start. In the bureau mirror opposite the sofa he saw two images of himself.

He got up to take a closer look, but one of the images vanished. He lay down again and once more saw the double image, which he studied thoughtfully. The tip of the nose in one image was about three inches from the tip of the other nose. One of the faces was considerably paler than the other. To Lincoln it seemed death-like.

The president-elect told his wife Mary about the phenomenon. Her interpretation was that he would enjoy good health in his first term but would die in his second. From this time on Lincoln seemed to have the melancholy conviction that he would never return alive from Washington. On several occasions during his incumbency he confided his fears to friends. To Harriet Beecher Stowe, author of *Uncle Tom's*

Cabin, he said, "Whichever way the war ends, I have the impression that I shan't last much longer." Once he told Mrs. Lincoln, "I am sure I shall meet with some terrible end."

According to Mrs. Lincoln, she and the president had planned to visit Europe after the Civil War. About two weeks before the assassination, she told him that now they would have the opportunity to make the trip. Lincoln replied in a melancholy voice, "You can visit Europe, but I never shall." When she asked him why not, be answered that "something told him" he would never see Europe.

There is evidence that Lincoln was a deeply religious man, though not in a church-going sense, and that he was impressed with the dreams and visions of the biblical prophets. "If we believe the Bible," he was quoted as saying, "we must accept the fact that in the old days God and his angels came to men in their sleep and made themselves known in dreams." He believed that a Universal Intelligence sent messages in these subliminal states but that such messages were in code and needed to be deciphered.

Lincoln had many dreams and visions and took them all seriously. He saw running through them a thread that was leading to an inevitable personal disaster. According to his close friend Ward Hill Lamon, he believed that "the star under which he was born was at once brilliant and malignant; the horoscope was cast, fixed, irreversible and he had no more power to alter or defeat it in the minutest particular than he had to reverse the law of gravitation." Lincoln told Lamon that all his life, from boyhood on, his dreams had indicated that he would rise to a great height and then suddenly fall.

The famous death dream occurred shortly before the assassination, on a night, according to one version, when he had attended a performance of the opera *Faust.* Here are Lincoln's own words describing the dream:

> There seemed to be a deathlike stillness about me. Then I heard subdued sobs, as if a number of people were weeping. I thought I left my bed and wandered downstairs. There the silence was broken by the same pitiful sobbing, but the mourners were invisible. I went from room to room; no living person was in sight, but the same mournful sounds of distress met me as I passed along. It was light in all the rooms; every object was familiar to me; but where were all the people who were grieving as if their hearts would break? I was puzzled and alarmed. What could be the meaning of all this?

Determined to find the cause of a state of things so mysterious and so shocking, I kept on until I arrived at the East Room, which I entered. There I met with a sickening surprise. Before me was a catafalque, on which rested a corpse wrapped in funeral vestments. Around it were stationed soldiers who were acting as guards; and there was a throng of people, some gazing mournfully upon the corpse, whose face was covered, others weeping pitifully.

"Who is dead in the White House?" I demanded of one of the soldiers. "The President," was his answer. "He was killed by an assassin." Then came a loud burst of grief from the crowd, which awoke me from my dreams.

A few days later Lincoln told his wife about the dream and added, "Somehow the thing has got possession of me, and like Banquo's ghost, it will not down."

THE LAST DAY—LINCOLN AND KENNEDY

On Lincoln's last day of life, two more incidents occurred that could be classed as premonitions of death. Lincoln, who had awakened in a sombre mood, called a cabinet meeting late in the morning. Many distinguished Americans, including General Grant who was present as a guest, corroborated later what the president had said.

According to Secretary of War Stanton, Lincoln seemed more preoccupied and thoughtful than usual. He told no anecdotes and instead of slumping in his chair as was customary, he sat up straight and with an air of dignity. While the assembled group was waiting for news that General Johnston had surrendered the last of the Confederate forces, the President said slowly, "Gentlemen, something extraordinary is going to happen, and that soon."

His voice trailed off. "I had a dream, and I have now had the same dream three times." Lincoln paused, and his chin sank on his breast. "I am on a great, broad, rolling river, and I am in a boat . . . and I drift . . . and I drift. . . ."

Late that afternoon Lincoln was on his way to the war department to see if there was any news from General Sherman of Johnston's surrender. With him was his bodyguard, William Crook, who at one point had to remonstrate with two offensive drunkards. After they had walked awhile, Lincoln said, "Crook, do you know, I believe there are men who would want to take my life." Then he added, "And I have no doubt they will do it." They walked on in silence and

Lincoln said, almost to himself, "It would be impossible to prevent it."

Crook later recalled his feeling of uneasiness as the president left him. Instead of parting with his usual "Good night," he said, "Good-bye, Crook." Only a few hours later Lincoln sat in his box at Ford's Theater, while John Wilkes Booth waited with his pistol.

Almost a hundred years later, on the morning of November 22, 1963, President Kennedy remarked, "If anybody really wanted to shoot the President of the United States . . . all one had to do was get [into] a high building some day with a telescopic rifle, and there was nothing anybody could do to defend against such an attempt on the President's life."

Later that day Kennedy rode in a motorcade past a high building where an assassin waited with his rifle.

CHAPTER SEVEN

A Newspaper Predicts
An Assassination

Americans also respond psychically when there is a threat to other public figures whom they esteem. When, in addition, there are bonds of sympathy between those who have been or are about to be killed, the sense of impending disaster is felt even more strongly. The bond between President Kennedy and Robert Kennedy heightened the feeling of many psychics that Senator Kennedy would meet his brother's fate. And because the Senator and Martin Luther King, Jr., shared a feeling of sympathy for black people, their deaths were linked in many premonitions.

R. C. Anderson, an Alabama psychic, saw the killing of the Negro leader in a vision and told newsmen about it before the event. Anderson also said on television in 1968 that another "national figure" would be killed before the end of June. The psychic vibrations of the two assassinations were also felt across the sea. Malcolm Bessent, a young Englishman, was reading a book and saw the words "Luther King" flash across the page several times. Pendragon wrote, "I do not think Robert Kennedy will ever be President." The London Premonitions Bureau received several warnings that Robert Kennedy would be killed.

A PROMINENT AMERICAN WILL BE KILLED

Just as a misprint in a calendar foreshadowed the death of John F. Kennedy, a newspaper had a coded message of a murder soon to be committed. Such cues are picked up only by sensitives who know that predictions of the future may be received through any channel. Alan Vaughan read a newspaper that predicted an assassination, but it took an intuitive flash to find the meaning hidden in the newspaper's columns.

Vaughan began to have an uneasy feeling back on April 3, 1968, that a prominent American would be killed. In so many cases of this kind, the realization of tragedy builds up slowly. In the beginning the clues are obscure, as if an invisible playwright were tantalizing the psychic, arousing his interest and concern but not giving the show away too early. As time goes on and the event comes closer, the symbols often drop away or become clearer in meaning. Vaughan's first dream was about an unidentified public figure who would be killed. He had the pre-disaster feeling of apprehension but nothing specific to cling to.

Vaughan was in Germany at the time. After Martin Luther King's death, he had several more dreams indicating that the victim might be Robert Kennedy. In one of the dreams an American Indian appeared, whose swarthy complexion could have suggested Sirhan Sirhan. Also, in a sense the Indian was perhaps symbolic of someone who was in America but was alienated from the American scene, as was the case with Sirhan.

On April 19, 1968, Vaughan was reading the Paris edition of the *New York Herald-Tribune,* when something leaped out at him from the front page. The main story of that issue was about the FBI's hunt for Eric Starvo Galt, believed to be the murderer of Martin Luther King. In the next column Vaughan noticed another article about two victims of violence. The dominant theme of the news stories seemed to be violence and killing. As Vaughan's eyes travelled horizontally across the middle of the page, certain words stood out in each of the eight columns, and taken together, they spelled out a psychic message.

> Dr. King, killed by a single bullet/
> Both were hit ..../
> ...... Kennedy ..../
> believed dead ..../
> Two more Americans ...... and/
> .... the former president ...../
> from the north ..../
> ten weeks ..../

Taken consecutively, the words read: "Dr. King, killed by a single bullet. Both were hit. Kennedy believed dead. Two more Americans and the former president from the north. Ten weeks." Three assassinations are linked—that of the "former president from the north" (John F. Kennedy), Martin Luther King, and Robert F. Kennedy, whose murder would take place in about ten weeks—at the end of June or early in July. The actual date was June 5, 1968.

On May 25 Vaughan dreamed about Senator Kennedy in connection with a party. In the dream an assassin was concealed behind a grating. Taking Senator Kennedy's place in the dream, Vaughan walked through a central hall from a room with young people to another room at the end of the corridor. Here the "dirty deed" was done—that is, dirt falling as a symbol from the overhead grate where the assassin was concealed.

Vaughan debated, as most psychics do, whether to warn Kennedy. Such warnings are usually futile, as they were in the case of President Kennedy, but no one wants to carry around the knowledge that someone will be killed without making an attempt to prevent it. Accordingly, Vaughan sat down and wrote a letter, dated May 28, 1968, to Dr. Krippner at the Maimonides Medical Center, in which he voiced his fears:

This dream may presage the assassination of a third prominent American, one who has connections with John F. Kennedy and Luther King —someone young, married, who espouses equal rights for Negroes. Could that other martyr be Bobby Kennedy? His assassination would link synchronously. The initials of the three—KKK—would be symbolic of the divisive racialist fever in the U.S. . . .

If you can think of any way of drawing his (Kennedy's) attention to such a threat, I would be appreciative. If it happened, I think I should have it on my conscience; if it doesn't, then I need only feel a bit foolish.

This letter is now on file with the Central Premonitions Registry in New York City.

"TIRHAN, TIRHAN"

Joan of Arc had her voices that told her what was going to happen to France. Jeanne Gardner's Voice tells her what is going to happen in America. The tone of the Voice depends upon the nature of the psychic message. Good news is told in calm tones. If the prediction is tragic, the Voice cries. The Voice knew a year before it happened that Robert Kennedy would be assassinated, but it only doled out small clues to Jeanne.

As the year wore on the Voice filled in more and more details until Jeanne was certain that Robert Kennedy would be killed. She didn't tell anyone because she thought that Kennedy would not listen. It was more or less accidental that many persons in the publishing business did hear Mrs. Gardner's prophecy of the assassination—told a matter of hours before it happened.

On Sunday, June 2, 1968, Jeanne left her home in Elkins, West Virginia, and boarded a bus for Washington, D.C. The knowledge of Robert Kennedy's imminent death weighed heavily upon her, and she literally felt a weight on her head. She tried to push the thought aside. Her purpose in going to Washington was to see Mrs. Bea Moore, of Simon and Schuster, who was there for the annual bookseller's convention. She wanted to persuade Mrs. Moore to do a book about her life and prophecies.

Sunday evening Mrs. Gardner registered in a hotel. The following day, June 3, she was getting ready to go to the convention, when the Voice spoke and told her to write down the message. Kennedy would be assassinated in the early morning hours of June 5 and it would be in a "galley" (kitchen). The killer would be a short, swarthy man in his twenties. The Voice did not say where it would happen but mentioned the words "Tirhan Tirhan." But Jeanne did not associate the young, dark killer with "Tirhan Tirhan." She thought the words referred to a geographical location, perhaps Iran.

Now highly excited, she ran down to the Shoreham Hotel, where the bookseller's convention was in process, and begged the skeptical Mrs. Moore to come back and see what she had written in her journal.

Back at her hotel, she showed Mrs. Moore the entry. There would be a High Requiem Mass at St. Patrick's Cathedral in New York and another later at Hyannisport.

Troubled, Mrs. Moore suddenly flew back to New York on Tuesday, June 4. In the evening, just hours before the shooting, Jeanne walked into the Shoreham Hotel and headed for the Simon and Schuster hospitality suite. It had to come out now. Tearfully she told the booksellers and salespeople in the suite that Robert Kennedy would be killed in a kitchen in the early morning hours of Wednesday, June 5. Then she went back to her hotel and retired. She woke up at 3:00 A.M., turned on the radio, and heard the news she had been dreading.

It is seldom that the prediction of an assassination can be corroborated by so many witnesses. Bea Moore was overwhelmed and now she felt that the book about Jeanne Gardner had to be written. In September, 1969, Simon and Schuster published *A Grain of Mustard,* and the story of Mrs. Gardner's prediction is told there in graphic detail.

I asked Jeanne if the murder of Kennedy could have been prevented. She said that if the killing had been inevitable, the Voice would have left out one fact about it. Jeanne did not know where it would take place. "Tirhan Tirhan" kept ringing in her ears, but she only knew what the words meant when the news of the killing came in a radio broadcast.

"BRING THE KILLER TO ACCOUNT"

Martha Lynne Johnson is a young New York businesswoman who is being tested for psychic ability at the Maimonides Medical Center. She seems to have a talent for precognition and has had many dreams of accidents and deaths in her family that came true a short time later.

On the night of June 4–5, 1968, she had a frightening dream. In the dream the phone rang and she got out of bed to answer it. She heard the voice of her business partner: "We think you should know this—Mr. Keller was shot tonight." Keller was the accountant for her business. Miss Johnson woke up greatly disturbed and worried about Keller, then went back to sleep. In the morning she was awakened, as in her dream, by the ringing of the phone. It was her partner with the news that Robert Kennedy had been shot. Nothing had happened to Mr. Keller.

Miss Johnson knew immediately that her dream had been a veiled forecast of Kennedy's death. But why should she dream of Mr. Keller? She asked Dr. Karlis Osis, director of research at the American Society for Psychical Research, if he could explain the dream. He thought that "Keller" was a substitute for "Kennedy." Note the number of common letters in the name, the double "l" matched by the double "n."

When Miss Johnson told me later about her dream, these words flashed into my head: "Bring the killer to account." My interpretation was that subliminally Miss Johnson knew that Senator Kennedy would be killed. Not being able to stomach this, her dream-mind substituted Keller, who would not be harmed, a fact that Mrs. Johnson also knew subliminally. Mr. Keller was chosen to play his role because his name was similar not only to "Kennedy" but also to "Killer," and he was an accountant. In the dream she symbolically pre-viewed Kennedy's death and demanded that the "killer be brought to account."

FOUR PROPHECIES IN LONDON

Could the assassination of Robert Kennedy have been prevented? Jeanne Gardner thought not. Alan Vaughan sensed that he subconsciously wanted to join his brother in martyrdom. Jeane Dixon, who ascribes every event to "God's will," still thought that Kennedy should be warned and sent a friend to tell him about her premonition. Although Kennedy seems to have been disturbed by the warning, he didn't heed it, nor would he have listened to Alan Vaughan, Jeanne Gardner, and the many other psychics who envisioned his death.

The Premonitions Bureau in London and the Registry in New York were not in operation when President Kennedy was assassinated. Yet if 50,000 persons actually had premonitions of his death and had sent them to such a bureau, an early warning alert surely would have been sounded. Whether the president and his aides would have listened is another matter. The White House received many messages at the time but paid no attention to them.

Since the New York Registry was started in June, 1968, the month of Robert Kennedy's assassination, it was too new an organization to have any effect in averting the second Kennedy killing. The London Bureau, however, had been operating for a little over a year when messages about a future assassination began to come in. Of these, only four prophecies could be taken seriously, possibly because English psychics would not have as strong an emotional link to the Kennedys as do Americans. Two of the four who contacted the Bureau were American citizens, one of them Alan Vaughan.

On April 16, before Vaughan wrote to the Bureau, Mrs. Joan Hope sent this note from Canada: "Robert Kennedy to follow in his brother's footsteps. . . ." Another prophecy of the killing came in symbolic form from Miss C. E. Piddock of Kent, England. On June 5 she wrote in her diary, "Janitor will die today." She was puzzled by the reference but realized later that the word should be "Senator." Many predictions come in garbled form and must be interpreted.

The fourth prediction came from Lorna Middleton, who has both American and British citizenship. Her first intimation that Robert Kennedy would be assassinated came on March 15, 1968, and returned on March 21. At the beginning of April she told a reporter from a London newspaper: "The word assassination continues. I cannot disconnect it from Robert Kennedy. It may be that history will repeat itself." Later Miss Middleton wrote to Dr. Barker: "There may be another assassination. It may be in America shortly."

Once more the dark clouds began to form. On June 4, 1968, Miss Middleton was now positive that the killing would take place and wrote: "Another assassination and again in America." So emotionally overwrought was she that she telephoned the London Bureau three times and kept insisting that the killing was imminent.

Why only four valid predictions sent to the London Bureau? There are several reasons. One is that not enough persons yet know about the London Bureau and the New York Registry. Another problem is the difficulty of finding good psychics or training those who have an apparent talent for prediction.

If instead of four, there are forty, hopefully even four hundred letters or phone calls preceding another assassination attempt, the early warning alert may be sounded. After a few tragedies, when it has been demonstrated that there are human seismographs who accurately sense disaster, officials may then take heed and assassinations may be averted in the future.

LOOSE-TONGUED PROPHETS

Perhaps nothing could have prevented the assassinations of Lincoln, the two Kennedys, Martin Luther King, and others when the dark clouds gathered over them. But other important questions must be asked: Do self-appointed prophets put ideas into the heads of potential assassins when they make known their prophecies of death? And do they put an inordinate burden of fear upon public officials who are constantly in the limelight and are often easy targets for psychopathic killers? Are some public figures "scared to death" by the feeling that they are marked men?

No one knows for certain, yet it is possible that Jeane Dixon's prediction in the 1956 *Parade* magazine could have reached the impressionable Lee Harvey Oswald. Mrs. Dixon has a habit of blurting out her prophecies, both to reporters and to radio announcers. On one of Long John Nebel's all-night panel shows broadcast before November 22, 1963, she suddenly announced that President Kennedy would be assassinated, much to the discomfiture of Nebel and his associates. Later—still before the assassination—Oswald called Nebel long distance and asked to be on the program to discuss the subject of Cuba. Had Lee Harvey Oswald been listening when Mrs. Dixon made her prediction?

In September, 1967, an editor from the *Washington Daily News* was in a restaurant with Mrs. Dixon, when she told him that she had seen Robert Kennedy assassinated in a vision. How many persons in the restaurant heard her prediction? I don't believe that Sirhan Sirhan was there, but just to make public an ominous prophecy of this kind may be to set in motion harmful psychic forces.

Again, in her book Mrs. Dixon tells about attending a business convention and informing several executives that Robert Kennedy would never become president because he would be "assassinated in California this June. He will meet a fate similar to that of his brother Jack."

Prophets should be careful not to tempt the fate they so implicitly believe in. And the media also have a duty to keep out of print or off the air premonitions of death that name names. In the columns of current newspapers irresponsible reporters are blandly (and smugly) predicting the assassinations of persons in high office. In a syndicated article appearing in a Florida newspaper, Martin Gershen said that Daniel Logan had predicted the assassination of an important government official. Gershen gave the name of the official, but it won't be repeated here. At a time when violence is at its peak, this item could be an invitation to another killing.

One of the purposes of the London Premonitions Bureau and the Central Premonitions Registry is to prevent, if at all possible, an unfortunate tragedy that could result in part from public statements made by loose-tongued prophets and repeated by irresponsible reporters. If Mrs. Dixon or anyone else feels that an assassination is going to take place, details should be sent immediately to either of the two bureaus but told to no one else. Such messages are confidential, and action will be taken only if there are many such premonitions and the event seems close at hand.

Psychics are getting more and more publicity in an age when many sensational prophecies are coming true. They owe it to the rest of the world to use judgment and restraint, at least until the dreaded event is so near that some kind of preventive action seems necessary. It is understandable then that emotions will spill over and that there will be a sense of urgency about averting the tragedy.

At any time, however, the proper agency to contact is the Central Premonitions Registry.

CHAPTER EIGHT

Uneasy Lies the Head

Throughout history prophets have watched the dark clouds of death, natural and violent, gathering over kings, emperors, and others high in the ruling circles of many countries. In visions and dreams they have seen powerful governments crash into ruin and carry their leaders along. Eudemes the Cyprian had a vision in which he saw the imminent death of Alexander the Great. Julius Caesar was warned by a soothsayer to "beware the Ides of March." The Stoic philosopher Posidonius, who taught Cicero and Caesar, wrote about an inhabitant of the island of Rhodes who, on his death bed, named the order in which six officials would die.

Sometimes ill-fated ancients had premonitions of their own demise, as Lincoln and Kennedy did in modern times. Caesar saw himself going to heaven before he was killed. Nebuchadnezzar had a symbolic dream about his downfall. Alcibiades, a Greek rebel of the fourth century B.C., dreamed that his enemies had cut off his head and burned his body. A few days later his house was set on fire, and as he ran out he was mortally wounded by a swarm of arrows.

Many royal figures thought that the doctrine of divine right of kings conferred a kind of immunity upon them, and they ignored prophetic warnings. An Italian seer, Giuliano del Carmine, informed Alessandro de Medici, first Duke of Florence, that his throat would be cut by his own cousin, Lorenzaccio. The Duke, with a touching faith in the ties of blood, roared with laughter and told the prophet he was being ridiculous. But that night a soldier in the Duke's bodyguard also dreamed that de Medici's cousin would murder him. While he was telling the Duke about his dream the next morning, Lorenzaccio came by, and the soldier exclaimed, "That's the man!" De Medici rebuked the soldier, but later that day he was stabbed to death by his cousin.

Other rulers have been more responsive to warnings of death and disaster. To insure optimistic forecasts, many a prophet was put on the royal payroll, and if he valued his neck, he saw only good tidings for his king, particularly victory in war. When Ivan the Terrible of Russia pointedly asked his court prophet when he would die, the seer shrewdly answered that both of them would expire on the same day, thus guaranteeing his own safety during Ivan's lifetime.

Other prophets have been less tactful. An astrologer who predicted bad luck for the Roman emperor Domitian was immediately executed. King John of England was baited unmercifully by one Peter of Wakefield, who forecast an unhappy future for the monarch. Peter went around the country in the year 1211 proclaiming that by the coming Ascension Day, John would no longer be king. According to Grafton in his *Chronicles of England,* John sneered at the prophet: "Tush, sayeth he, it is but an idiot knave, and such a one as lacketh his right wits."

When Ascension Day came, John was still on his throne, but he had been put under sentence of excommunication by Pope Innocent III, and in the eyes of many Englishmen, he was as good as deposed. Meanwhile Peter "gate him abroad" to France and poured his prophecies into the willing ears of King Philip, who was anxious to invade England. John then had Peter thrown in jail and hanged, along with his son.

Medieval prophets seemed to enjoy naming not only names but also dates and circumstances of disaster that would overtake famous persons of their era. Tycho Brahe, an astronomer and astrologer, announced in 1572 the coming birth of a "valorous prince, whose arms would dazzle Europe but who himself would disappear in 1632." Gustavus Adolphus of Sweden was born in 1594, invaded

Germany many times, and finally "disappeared" in 1632 when he was killed in the battle of Lutzen.

Brahe tried to convert his brilliant pupil Johannes Kepler to a belief in prophecy through astrology, but for a time Kepler, who became a great astronomer, would have none of it. Later, however, he outdid his teacher in astrological predictions of death. Early in 1619 he prophesied that the emperor Mathias would die in March. Mathias, who might have been "scared to death" by this prophecy, obliged by dying on March 20.

"AYE, CAESAR, COME BUT NOT GONE"

In ancient times a group of Romans migrated to the colony of Capua. While they were digging into the earth to lay foundations for their homes, they stumbled on prehistoric graves, among them the tomb of Capys, founder of Capua. In this tomb was a bronze tablet with the following warning written in Greek: "When once the graves of Capua are brought to light, then a branch of the Julian House will be slain by the hand of one of his kindred; his death, however, will soon be avenged by terrible consequences in Italy."

The Capuan tablet was discovered in January, 44 B.C., during the reign of Julius Caesar. A Roman soothsayer named Vestricius Spurinna may have heard about the prophecy and decided that the "branch of the Julian House" referred to Caesar himself. Two months later Spurinna drew Caesar aside and solemnly warned him to "beware the Ides of March."

When Caesar retired for the night on March 14, he may have been worried by what appeared to be a double precognition—the inscription found in the tomb and the soothsayer's warning. Both he and his wife Calpurnia slept restlessly. Caesar dreamed that he had been carried up to the clouds, where he was welcomed by Jupiter. As he slept, the doors and windows of the room flew open, and a brilliant light came in. Caesar woke up and heard Calpurnia sobbing in her sleep. When he roused her, she said she had dreamed that he was stabbed and lay bleeding in her arms.

The next day Calpurnia begged her husband to stay away from the Roman Forum, at least until the Ides of March were safely past. But, as was true of so many kings and presidents in the centuries that followed, Caesar was a proud man and did not want his subjects to think he was afraid. While he hesitated, his friend Decimus Brutus, one of the conspirators, urged him to go, saying that a large crowd was waiting in the Senate to hear him. Reluctantly Caesar set out for the Forum, passing Spurinna on the way.

"Well, Spurinna," said Caesar bravely, "the Ides of March are come."

"Aye, Caesar, come but not gone."

An hour later Caesar was stabbed to death by Marcus Brutus. As the inscription had predicted, his death precipitated a stormy period in Roman history, the "terrible consequences" promised by the founder of Capua. Two bloody civil wars followed that kept Italy in turmoil for many years.

"TWO WOUNDS ONE, THEN DIE A CRUEL DEATH"

The physician looked at the King's three sons and thought to himself, "Two will die and one will rule." But he told the King, Henry II of France, that all three would occupy a throne. The Queen, Catherine de Medici, was delighted. She pictured two more European countries coming under the sway of the family.

The physician was not making a medical diagnosis but a prophecy. He was Nostradamus, the most famous seer of the sixteenth century and probably of all time. Henry had invited Nostradamus to his court in 1556 because of an earlier prophecy made in the psychic's strange quatrains. The prophecy had read:

> The young lion shall overcome the old
> In war-like field in a single fight
> In a golden cage he will pierce the eye
> Two wounds one, then die a cruel death.

The King wondered whether he himself was the "old lion." Some years earlier his court prophet, Luc Gauric, had warned him to avoid any one-to-one combat, such as jousting, after the age of forty. He would be in danger of receiving a wound in the head that might bring "blindness or death." Now Nostradamus had predicted that he would be blinded in a duel and would die shortly thereafter. A double precognition and therefore to be heeded.

Three years later, in 1559, a three-day tournament was held in Paris. Four days before the start of the tournament, a Captain de Montluc had a strange dream. He saw King Henry sitting in a chair, his face covered with blood. Doctors were examining the King's eye, while many persons stood watching. Some were saying, "The King is dead"; others, "No, he is not dead yet."

Henry may have wanted to tempt fate, but whatever his motive, he challenged the captain of his Scottish Guard, Comte Gabriel de Montgomery, to a joust. De Montgomery was reluctant but when the King insisted, they donned armor, each putting over his head a gilded visor that looked like a "golden cage." Twice they jousted without a decision. The third time Henry was wounded in the throat, then de Montgomery pierced the King's visor with his lance, and the point went into Henry's eye, blinding him.

Thus three premonitions came true—a triple precognition. The "young lion" overcame the old on a "war-like field." There were "two wounds," the King ruled briefly for ten more days, then died in agony—"a cruel death." The physician-seer's prophecy for Henry's sons was also fulfilled. The oldest son, Francis II, died soon after taking his father's place on the throne. The second son, Charles IX, also "occupied a throne" but died at the age of twenty-four. The third son was King Henry III, who ruled until 1589.

A SLAYING IN THE HOUSE OF COMMONS

The premonition of a leader's death often comes in a recurring dream, such as Lincoln's dream of a drifting boat. Lincoln's dream, however, kept returning at intervals over a period of years. John Williams' dream of an assassination in the British House of Commons came three times in one night, nine days before the actual shooting.

Unlike Nostradamus, Peter of Wakefield, or Vestricius Spurinna, John Williams was not a professional seer. He was a manager of mining properties in Cornwall, and the furthest thought from his conscious mind was that of murder and prophetic dreams—until the night of May 3, 1812.

That night he dreamed he was in the lobby of the House of Commons, a building completely unfamiliar to him. A man was standing there dressed in a "snuff-colored coat with metal buttons." Another man came into the lobby—"a small man, dressed in a blue coat and white waistcoat." The first man took a pistol from his coat and shot the man who had just entered. As the latter fell to the floor, mortally wounded, someone in the dream told Williams that the dead man was Spencer Perceval, Britain's Prime Minister.

Williams woke up and described the dream to his wife, but she was not impressed. He fell asleep again and had the same dream. Once more he woke up and told it to his wife. Now he went back to sleep and dreamed a third time about the murder, then awoke greatly excited and determined to go to London and warn Perceval. His friends dissuaded Williams, saying that Perceval would ignore him.

On the night of May 10 another man dreamed that Perceval would be murdered on the following day by a man wearing a "green coat with brass-colored buttons." The dream was identical to that of Williams, foretelling an assassination in the lobby of the House of Commons.

The second dreamer was Perceval himself. All week he had had a premonition that he would be killed and had told his wife it would happen very soon. He had even set his affairs in order, although he had no enemies and knew of no one who might plan such a bloody deed. On the night before he was to be killed, Perceval was the guest of the Earl of Harrowby. When he told the Earl the following morning about his dream, the latter urged him not to go to Parliament that day.

But just as Caesar went to the Forum in spite of his misgivings, just as President Kennedy went to Dallas in the face of many warnings, Perceval set out for the House of Commons. That afternoon, as he hurried through the lobby on his way to a meeting, he was shot by a man wearing a "green coat with brass-colored buttons."

Oddly enough, the killer, John Bellingham, had not gone to the House of Commons to kill Perceval. A convicted embezzler, he had brooded over his hatred for Lord Granville Leveson-Gower, a member of the House of Lords who had ruled against his petition for a review of the case. Perceval had rushed through the lobby in his haste to cast a vote on another measure before the House. Confused, Bellingham may have mistaken him for Lord Leveson-Gower and shot him.

This case has many strange facets. One is the recurring dream of John Williams. Another is the parallel dream and foreboding of Perceval himself. Both dreamers seemed to know that the victim would not be the intended one. The assassination of Perceval lends support to the theory that many events, although seemingly accidental, are predestined. All the logical signs pointed to Lord Granville Leveson-Gower as the man who would be killed. If he had been shot, a case could have been made for telepathy between the minds of the killer and the two dreamers. But if Williams and Perceval picked up the thought that was in Bellingham's mind, how did they know in advance that the bullet would kill the wrong man?

"MY WIFE AND I HAVE BEEN ASSASSINATED"

Closer to our own era, both professional seers and occasional psychics have envisioned the death of those in high places. The death of President Grant's widow was foreseen in a dream by Grant's sister. Madame de Thèbes, a remarkable French psychic, announced on January 1, 1899, that President Félix Faure of France would die that year. He succumbed on the sixteenth of February, perhaps "scared to death" by her prophecy.

Count Louis Hamon (Cheiro), the palm-reading psychic who warned W. T. Stead to stay away from water in 1912, was consulted by many kings who wanted to know about their future. In 1900 King Humbert of Italy, who had had a premonition that he would be killed, asked Hamon for a reading. The Count looked at him and sensed that he would be assassinated three months later. On July 29, 1900, the King was shot by Bresci, an anarchist.

Camille Flammarion, the astronomer, writes that a non-professional psychic also had a premonition of Humbert's death. The night before the King was killed, a man in Constantinople woke suddenly and said to his wife, "They have shot the King of Italy." An hour later he looked out the window and saw flags being lowered to half-mast.

One night in 1912 there was a gathering at the home of Archduchess Isabella of Austria. A medium was present who was known as Madame Sylvia. After going into a mild trance, Madame Sylvia suddenly turned to the Archduchess and said, "Your Royal Highness, I beseech you to soften your antipathy toward Archduke Franz Ferdinand and his wife. We must be kind to them; in two years they are fated to die from the same bullet."

Two years later, on June 28, 1914, Monseigneur Joseph de Lanyi, Bishop of Grosswarden, had a terrifying dream, in which he saw a letter bordered in black lying on his desk. The letter bore the arms of Archduke Franz Ferdinand, who had at one time been his pupil. In the dream the Bishop opened the letter and saw a strange drama being enacted. The Archduke was sitting in an auto with his wife, while a crowd milled around outside. A man stepped out of the crowd and fired two bullets into the car.

Superimposed on this scene were the words of the letter: "Your Eminence, dear Dr. Lanyi, my wife and I have been victims of a political crime at Sarajevo. We commend ourselves to your prayers. Sarajevo. June 28, 1914. 4 A.M."

The Bishop woke up trembling, looked at his clock and saw that it was 4:30 A.M. He got up immediately and wrote down the details of his dream, which he dispatched in a letter to his brother, Professor Edouard de Lanyi.

Later that morning, about ten hours after the Bishop's dream, Archduke Ferdinand and his wife were murdered at Sarajevo as they sat in an automobile. Two bullets were fired, one of them fatally wounding the royal couple.

Did Bishop de Lanyi get a psychic message from the Archduke, who subconsciously knew that he would be killed? Or was the dream a projection of the Bishop's own clairvoyant knowledge of what was to happen ten hours later? How did Madame Sylvia know two years earlier that the Archduke and his wife would be assassinated—and by the same bullet? Did the bullet "know" what its course would be?

The time sequence of this psychic melodrama staggers the mind. The Archduke wrote in the dream (if it was actually the mind of the Archduke that transmitted the psychic letter) that he had already been murdered, yet he meticulously recorded the time of the message as 4 A.M., ten hours before the actual killing. Do time and space exist as we know them or are they distortions of a reality we cannot clearly glimpse because of our physical and mental limitations?

"YOU WILL DIE IN THE ICY WATERS."

"NO, YOU ARE WRONG. I WILL NOT DIE."

The man with the cold, deep-set eyes looked penetratingly into the eyes of the prophet. It was a battle of wills—or rather a battle between a man of great will and hypnotic power and one who was quietly confident that his prophecies would be borne out.

The psychic repeated what he had said: "I foresee for you a violent end within the palace. You will be menaced by poison, by knife, and by bullet. Finally, I see the icy waters of the Neva closing above you."

The other man glared at the psychic.

"I shall laugh at the prediction," said the man in strong, measured tones. "I am called the Savior of Russia. I am the Maker of Destiny."

This scene took place in January, 1905. The psychic was Count Louis Hamon, and he was "reading" the future of Grigori Rasputin, the Mad Monk of Russia. There has been no more bizarre character in history than the Mad Monk. Winning the confidence of the Czarina, Alexandra, and later the Czar, Nicholas II, he fascinated almost everyone he met with the sheer force of his personality and mesmeric eyes. How could a mere palm-reader predict such an ignominious end for the great Rasputin?

The end almost came two years before the time predicted, when a peasant girl, Guseva, stabbed him in the stomach. "Menaced by knife," he recovered after being near death for several weeks. A year later, in 1915, Rasputin was the behind-the-scenes ruler of Russia, with the Czar and Czarina his willing subjects. But his list of enemies was growing, particularly among the nobility.

Prince Youssoupoff, who later wrote a book about the Mad Monk, plotted with one Pourkievitch and other nobles to kill him. Several attempts to trap Rasputin went awry, but finally a plan was worked out. Youssoupoff invited Rasputin to dinner at his palace, while the other conspirators waited on the floor above the dining room.

The food that was laid before the Mad Monk had been doctored with poison. On the table were decanters filled with red Crimean wine, and beside them were goblets containing powdered crystals of potassium cyanide. At first Rasputin refused to eat, and Prince Youssoupoff wondered uneasily if he was suspicious. Finally the Mad Monk picked up a chocolate cake and bit into it. The Prince sat back and waited.

Nothing happened. The Mad Monk seemed to enjoy the cake, and he ate another . . . then another. . . . Youssoupoff stared in dismay as Rasputin finished the last cake and smacked his lips in appreciation. They had had no visible effect on him.

Perhaps, asked the Prince in a trembling voice, he would like to try some of that excellent red wine? Rasputin nodded assent, and Youssoupoff poured the wine into a goblet. Rasputin downed it in one gulp, and the Prince filled up another glass . . . then another. . . . The Mad Monk's expression never changed. What manner of man was this who would be unaffected by enough poison to kill ten men?

Youssoupoff excused himself and went into another room, where he fetched a pistol. Coming back into the dining room, he aimed for Rasputin's heart and fired. The bullet was true to its mark. The evil genius fell to the floor, bleeding, and lay still. Surely he must now be dead.

Youssoupoff switched off the lights, locked the door, and went upstairs to join the other conspirators. For two hours they discussed what would be the best way to get rid of the body without drawing the attention of the police. A plan was finally worked out, and the Prince went back downstairs and turned on the light. Rasputin still lay where he had fallen.

As Youssoupoff bent down to look at the body, the "dead man" suddenly leaped up and grabbed him by the throat. The Prince struggled, but the strength of the Mad Monk was prodigious. Finally Youssoupoff broke away but not before Rasputin had torn loose an epaulet from the shoulder of his uniform. Clutching the epaulet in his right hand, Rasputin staggered up the stairs, but the other conspirators came down and fired four bullets into his body. He rolled down the stairs and lay still.

This time he must be dead. They wrapped the body in cloth, got into the Prince's car and drove to Petrovitch Island. Four men held him over their heads, then threw him into the river. His body hit a stone buttress, bounced into the air, smashed against a block of ice, and rolled into the river. The waters closed over Grigori Rasputin.

When Rasputin's body was examined later, there were signs that he had still been alive when thrown into the river. "Menaced by poison, by knife, and by bullet," only the "icy waters of the Neva" could finally kill him.

The story of Rasputin and the fulfillment of the prophecy comes from several biographies of the Mad Monk and from Count Hamon's autobiography, *Confessions of a Seer*. The Count, perhaps carried away by a sense of melodrama, added a girl to the conspirators, the dancer Karili, but she is not mentioned in Youssoupoff's account.

Was Cheiro's prophecy authentic? Doubt may arise when we have to take the word of the person who made the prophecy, without corroborating witnesses or other evidence. When is a prophecy or premonition genuine? Examples of thorough, scientific approaches to the study of premonitions are Dr. Barker's investigation of the Aberfan tragedy and Dr. Stevenson's careful evaluation of the *Titanic* cases. They both seek to determine the credibility of the prophet, along with details of the prophecy and written records and disclosures to witnesses.

The case is strengthened if there is more than one premonition of the same event—double or triple precognition. When there is only one witness, the prophet himself, the facts must be examined more closely. Was this Count Hamon's only prophetic utterance that came true? Hamon wrote several books filled with predictions of wars and other large-scale events—a risky business as Jeane Dixon and other contemporary prophets know. However, he did score amazing successes when he foretold the fate of individuals, one of them Mark Twain.

In 1895, when Twain was broke, Hamon predicted that he would be a rich man in 1903. In 1902 Twain was sixty-seven years old and bankrupt but in October he signed a contract with Harper Bros., guaranteeing him $25,000 a year from his books, regardless of sales. So popular were Twain's books that at the start of 1903, following a promotional campaign, he had earned $60,000 in royalties.

Hamon's warning to W. T. Stead is another example. Again, at a party Hamon attended in 1891, the future Edward VI of England asked him when he would die. Hamon said that Edward would live to the age of sixty-nine. King Edward was born in 1841 and died after ruling England for nine years—in 1910.

HITLER AND HIS COURT PROPHETS

It would have been fairly easy to predict the sudden death of anyone who got in the way of Adolf Hitler. To predict the time of death was a bit more difficult. On May 23, 1934, the Spanish psychic Tomas Menes foresaw that Chancellor Dolfuss of Austria would be murdered within three months. Two months and two days later a group of Nazis marched into the government office where Dolfuss was holding a cabinet meeting, and shot him.

Hitler himself was the subject of many death prophecies. In 1932 a hand-reading expert, Dr. Joseph Renald, studied Hitler's handprints and saw that his life would end violently. "I see that you will come into power," he told the future dictator. "It will bring woe to Germany and woe to Europe." Raging, Hitler stormed out of Dr. Renald's office and later did what many kings had done—he put in his own stable of prophets—all astrologers. Since Hitler's rise at that time was meteoric, his prophets were able to please him with glowing short-term forecasts.

One of his astrologers—Louis de Wohl—could see Hitler's violent end on the way, and he began to hedge his predictions or couch them in vague language. Foreseeing his own doom if he kept his professional integrity, de Wohl managed to escape from Germany in 1935 and resumed his forecasts in the more permissive atmosphere of London. Here he predicted success for the Allies.

Hitler's other astrologers were not so lucky. Karl Ernst Krafft first came to the dictator's attention in 1939, when he warned that Hitler would be threatened by violence during the November 7–10 period. An attempt was made on Hitler's life at that time in the Munich Bürgerbräu beer hall, but Der Führer escaped unhurt. As a court prophet, one of Krafft's jobs was to interpret the quatrains of Nostradamus—written four hundred years earlier—in favor of the Third Reich. These were used as propaganda during the war.

As Krafft's prophecies became less appetizing to Hitler, he fell from grace. In 1941 he was thrown into a concentration camp along with other German astrologers, occultists, and parapsychologists who were arrested after the Rudolf Hess flight. Among the parapsychologists was Gerda Walther, who later wrote about Krafft and the other Nazi astrologers in an article in *Tomorrow* magazine (Winter, 1956) entitled "Hitler's Black Magicians." In the article she mentioned another prophetess in Germany who courageously and openly predicted disaster for Hitler and Naziism. This was Elise Lehrer, a Bavarian.

Even when Hitler was winning his most impressive victories, Elise Lehrer insisted that a bad end awaited him. She spoke loud and often of Hitler's doom and never hesitated to show her contempt for him. She would often visit the studio of sculptor Ferdinand Liebermann, who made busts of the Nazi leaders. Once Elise stared at a bust of Hitler and said, "You needn't bother with that *Gitzkopf* (blockhead). You're wasting your time and might as well destroy the statues because they're going to be absolutely worthless." Elise was such a thorn in Der Führer's side that she was finally carted off to an insane asylum and later died in a concentration camp.

There were other prophetesses of Hitler's doom. One of the most remarkable lived in Hungary, and she was just as courageous as Elise Lehrer. Her name was Boriska Silbiger, and during the 1930s her predictions were published in newspapers throughout the world, including the United States. In 1934 she envisioned the killing of a king whose name began with an "A." King Alexander I of Yugoslavia was assassinated at Marseilles on October 9, 1934.

Also in 1934 Boriska predicted that a Nazi leader would be murdered by his friends. On June 30, 1934, Ernst Roehm was shot by order of Hitler. At the close of 1935 she announced that in January of the following year "the king of a great empire" would die suddenly. "He will be succeeded by his eldest son, but the reign of this successor will not last twelve months, whereafter he will renounce the throne." King George of England died on January 20, 1936, a few months after the prediction. The Prince of Wales ascended the throne as Edward VII, then abdicated on December 10, 1936.

Silbiger made several other accurate predictions during the 1930s, notably that in the early 1940s Naziism would collapse and Hitler would die. She made one mistake, however. She picked 1942 as the time of Hitler's death, three years too soon. Enraged, Hitler sent troops into Hungary to arrest her, and she too was thrown into a concentration camp.

Another German prophet made a remarkably accurate prediction of Hitler's death, saying that the dictator would die under mysterious circumstances before May 7, 1945. Wilhelm Wulff of Hamburg was able to escape Hitler's wrath because he was Heinrich Himmler's astrologer, and a forecast of death for Der Führer was pleasing to the power-hungry Himmler. As Hitler's last days approached, he was probably unaware of Wulff's prophecy. Hitler committed suicide on April 30, 1945.

Even the rulers of Soviet Russia, with its philosophy of materialism, have thought it might be possible to predict the future. Stalin himself used an astrologer, Yuri Yamakkin, who fell out of favor and was sent to a concentration camp. After Stalin died Yamakkin was brought back by Khrushchev and put into an official suite in the Kremlin. Another astrologer, Wolf Messing, was employed by Stalin's ministry of culture as an entertainer. Before a packed theater, he predicted in 1943 that World War II would end in May, 1945, probably in the first week, and that the Russian army would march triumphantly into Berlin.

Uneasy lies the head that wears the crown or directs the ship of state. Death and disaster are often waiting, psychically felt by the subjects or citizens of a country because of emotional links—whether of hatred or affection—to their leaders. Franklin D. Roosevelt could take calmly and philosophically the word of Jeane Dixon that he had six months to live. But King John was upset by his Peter of Wakefield, while Adolf Hitler screamed with rage when his downfall was predicted and sent his storm troopers to arrest the offending seer.

Prophets are often without honor in their own country, but so long as they have the "courage of their predictions," the future of honest and accurate prophecy is assured—with an assist from premonitions bureaus and scientific investigators such as Dr. Stevenson and the late J. C. Barker.

CHAPTER NINE

The Sound of Distant Drums

The strongest generator of premonitions is probably fear of death. In wartime, or in a prewar period, the person who has the psychic experience is often anxious about members of his family, his friends, or the fate of the community in which he lives. There are many striking cases of precognition in war activated by emotional ties, and these have been investigated by such parapsychologists as Hans Bender of the University of Freiburg in Germany, W. H. C. Tenhaeff of the University of Utrecht in Holland, and the French physiologist Charles Richet.

Unless prophecies of war are linked to someone *in* the war, however, they are not always reliable. The bond may be a deeply personal one with a city or nation that is threatened with destruction, as well as with individuals. Professional prophets who lack such ties often go wide of the mark in predicting the outbreak of war. Their predictions are like those of other large-scale events, such as violent natural upheavals, when there may be only a tenuous link to human beings in danger. Maurice Maeterlinck, the Belgian writer, studied eighty-three such predictions of World War I and found that it was "well-nigh inconceivable that this catastrophe, as it drew near bringing untold misery in its wake, did not more clearly cast its menacing shadow over us." Psychics such as Count Hamon, although quite successful in casting horoscopes for individuals, were somewhat less accurate in their prophecies of war.

Dr. Bender points out that "general, oracle-like prophecies of war," such as those investigated by Maeterlinck, rarely come true. "Only when it is related to one's personal destiny does the collective fate of mankind seem involuntarily now and then to light up in mysterious fragments." The more general prophecies lack what psychiatrist Joost Meerloo calls the "significant relation between the sender and receiver of the psi message. Often it is a cry for help or a last sign of life, or a signal of utter panic."

Dr. Bender compiled many cases of premonitions during World War II and wrote about them in *Tomorrow* magazine (Winter, 1956). In three of the cases described below, "cries for help" sent out before the event—in one case many years in advance—were answered by some of the most dramatic premonitions on record.

DISTRESS SIGNALS FROM THE FUTURE

February 8, 1945. The Soviets have captured a young German soldier, who has a bullet wound in his neck. He and his fellow prisoners are taken out to a field in the Ukraine and ordered to get down on their knees. Searchlight beams systematically criss-cross the field, exposing each of the men in turn. A shot rings out, and one of the prisoners slumps to the ground, dead. A beam lights up the face of another prisoner. He, too, is shot.

The young soldier starts to perspire as the searchlight beams come closer. The young man wants to live, not die so wretched a death. He thinks of his mother and the rest of his family back in Germany. Outwardly impassive, he is crying inside.

Now the two searchlight beams cross his face and body, revealing a shoulder strap loose and a large dark grey mark on his neck. The Russian soldier points a gun at him. His eyes grow large with terror and he cries for his mother. . . .

At the same moment his mother is praying for him. She has had a closeup vision of her son on his knees in a field, and she sees the torn shoulder strap and the dark grey bullet wound, and his terror-stricken eyes as he cries out to her. Her prayers are answered. A Russian officer intervenes and takes her son to headquarters for interrogation. The next morning he is placed in a tank turret, his life saved. All the other prisoners have been shot.

How did the soldier's mother know where he was on February 8? For years, long before the war began, she had had a recurring dream: She saw him with the wound in his neck, kneeling on a "fallow field," his eyes turned to her in mute appeal. On February 8 she felt that the "fateful day had come," and she prayed through the night for her son. The soldier returned from Russia in 1948 and verified every detail of his mother's vision.

Did an infant asleep in his crib send a "cry for help" to his mother to find his body in the sand twenty-seven years later?

This story started back in 1919, just after the close of World War I. Two weeks after her youngest son was born, a German mother had a frightening dream. She was walking along a beach completely unfamiliar to her, looking for her child. She knew he was buried there. She ran her fingers through the sand trying to find him.

The young woman woke up screaming and shouted at her husband, "You must help me look for our Hans! He is lying by the sea under the sand." He calmed her down, and she realized she had been in the grip of a nightmare. The child was sleeping peacefully in his crib.

As the boy grew up, the same dream kept coming back to her— Hans lying beneath the sand, while she frantically dug into it with her fingers as she looked for him. When World War II began, the boy was twenty years old, and he was drafted into the German army.

Seven years later, in the fall of 1946, the mother received word that Hans had died in a French prison camp. She tried to contact the other soldiers in his unit and finally located two who had been with him when he died. The sketch they sent to her was accompanied by this note: "Hans' grave lies in the dunes near Fort Mahon, 800 meters from the sea."

Another German mother dreamed that her daughter was trapped in a railroad train during an air raid. In her dream she saw the frightened girl start to leave the coach to lie on the ground at the edge of the railway embankment. The mother knew that certain death was waiting for her daughter there, and she cried out to the girl to go back.

When mother and daughter were reunited later, the girl recalled the incident. Dr. Bender writes: "On the night of January 30, 1945 she sought frantically to get out of a railway train under a dive-bombing attack. *All at once she felt herself drawn back into the coach* (italics mine). Another woman passenger, seeking refuge in the same spot on the embankment, was killed outright."

"As a result of deep emotional anxiety," says Dr. Bender, "a reciprocal telepathic condition seems to have come about, by which the mother's warning premonition was conveyed to the daughter and made the latter feel she was being drawn back into the train."

In another of Dr. Bender's cases, the collective fate of a community seemed to generate a premonition. In 1939 a resident of Freiburg had a waking vision of the destruction of his city. As he walked briskly down the street, the buildings appeared to melt away into a pile of ruins, with only the cathedral standing. Upset by his vision, he moved away from Freiburg that year. On November 27, 1944—five years later—the main section of Freiburg was destroyed by bombing, with only the cathedral untouched.

PREVISION OF A CASUALTY LIST

In World War I there were many examples of psychic links to those marked by death. One of the strangest of such experiences was that of the late Arthur Ford, who tells about it in his autobiography *Nothing So Strange*.

Ford was a young officer in training at Camp Grant, Illinois, when the worst plague of modern times broke out—the 1918 influenza epidemic. One morning he awakened from a dream and saw before his eyes the names of hospitalized soldiers who had died the night before. When the list of deaths was posted later, all the names were as he had seen them and in the same order. For several days thereafter, when Ford woke up he would immediately see the list of influenza victims.

One morning he visualized another list—those who had been killed in battle. In the afternoon newspaper the casualty list was made up of the same names and in the same order in which they had appeared to Ford. Every day after that he would write down the names he saw and check them with the afternoon newspaper. In every case they were the same and always in the same order. Sometimes the list he saw would not appear for several days.

What label should we put on Ford's vision—telepathy, clairvoyance, precognition? Some of the lists were of soldiers already killed when Ford saw the names. Others may have died after he pre-viewed the list. Or Ford may have had visualizations of the newspaper articles in which the casualty lists were printed.

WAR PROPHECIES OF TWO LADY PSYCHICS

We've met Madame de Thèbes and Madame de Ferrïem before. Since these two ladies were living in the period of World War I, it is natural that they should have had psychic experiences connected with it. During that time there were many "general, oracle-like" prophecies of World War I, most of them too vague or too far afield to be considered genuine premonitions. Madame de Thèbes, however, came closest to being an oracle of the war.

De Thèbes published annually her own *Almanac* in which she made forecasts. In 1905, nine years before the war started, she predicted: "The future of Belgium is extraordinarily sad . . . I repeat my earlier words: This land will set all Europe in flames."

In 1913 she wrote in her *Almanac:* "Germany threatens all of Europe in general and France in particular . . . After that [the war] neither Prussia nor the Hohenzollerns will keep their former dominating position. As I have repeatedly emphasized, the days of the Kaiser are numbered, and after him great changes will take place in Germany, I speak of his reign, not of the days of his life."

It took no great foresight to see in 1913 that Germany menaced Europe. The prophecy about the Kaiser and the Hohenzollerns, however, was quite remarkable and was realized a few years later. Although the Kaiser was deposed, he lived into the 1930s. Madame de Thèbes also hinted in her 1913 forecast that Archduke Ferdinand would never be King of Austria: "The Prince who awaits the Imperial Throne shall not reign; in his stead shall rule a young man who at present has no thought of succeeding to the throne."

In her 1914 *Almanac* Madame de Thèbes wrote: "The tragedy in the Imperial House of Austria, which was foretold a year ago, will come to pass. No-one is able to ward off destiny." On July 28, 1914,

Archduke Ferdinand, as foreseen by Madame de Thèbes, Madame Sylvia, and Bishop de Lanyi, was assassinated at Sarajevo, an incident that set off World War I.

Madame de Ferriëm, who scored amazing hits as the calamity seeress, is a classic example of a prophetess who lets her bias get in the way of her prediction, a failing common to many present-day seers. As a patriotic German, she saw the fate of her country through scenes of past Teutonic glories: "How bitterly it [the war] will be fought! Far more bitterly than in 1870 and 1871 . . . Somber years are before us, but we shall be the victors, we—not because we are German, no: the spirits of our ancestors will help us win!"

WHICH WAR WAS PROPHESIED?

Ask a prophet if war will break out in the near future, and he may give you details of the next two or three wars. Time and space are obliterated—what matters to the psychic self is the emotional linkage between events. Two predictions ostensibly about World War I were ignored at the time but made much more sense in later years.

Just before the outbreak of World War I, a member of the British Society for Psychical Research conducted an experiment with several mediums, which he later discussed in the Society's *Proceedings* for 1923. Each of the mediums put herself into another state of consciousness to facilitate automatic writing. (The hand of the medium writes involuntarily, as if another intelligence were directing it.)

One of the mediums, Dame Edith Lyttleton, had intimations of the war that was just over the horizon. Her hand wrote: "The terrible cry of the wounded . . . The hot breath of the war . . . The blending of many tears . . ." And à little later, "Now the trumpets blow, the bugles sound and all the world is at war." There was also a strange reference to the *Lusitania,* the American ship that was to be sunk later by a German submarine.

Another session, on May 24, 1915, produced some puzzling prophecies which members of the Society for Psychical Research tried, without success, to tie to World War I. "The hand stretched out to stay *Berchtesgaden* . . . the nemesis of Fate nearer and nearer, no respite now . . . the *Munich bond* remember that . . . You will see strange things."

In 1940 the reference to "Berchtesgaden" and "Munich bond" had meaning. But why was the automatic script of Dame Lyttleton concerned with the events of another war while the mediums were trying to get messages about World War I? A statesman has said that the Second World War was in many ways a continuation of World War I, interrupted by an armistice of twenty years. Perhaps the menace of the Nazis and Adolf Hitler was already present in the psychic world and was sensed by Dame Lyttleton.

Even stranger was a series of prophecies that began in 1908 and continued on and off for several years. A retired British army officer, John Alleyne, was also taking part in an automatic writing experiment, when a message came through in Old English, telling him where to find the hidden ruins of Glastonbury Abbey. During the experiments, Alleyne received predictions of war expressed in the enigmatic style of oracular forecasts. The following paragraph is made up of statements written at different times from 1908 to 1918:

> When the West falls, Britain shall endure . . . In May the advance carries the foe down the fair lands that lie to the west of him . . . slower, slower grows the advance . . . The pact is near its end in Europe . . . The East must of necessity extend the sphere of influence . . . the awakening of the soul of this great misguided German nation will be the termination of its warlike force . . .

The prophecy has only general application to World War I. More striking is its correspondence with World War II. The Nazis "advanced" in the month of May, 1940, and soon the "West," represented by France, had fallen. Britain withstood the terrific bombing by the Nazis, while in the summer of 1941 the "pact" between Russia and Germany came to an abrupt end when the German army invaded the Ukraine. The German advance was "slowed" in Russia.

"The East" may refer to Russia, which extended its "sphere of influence" after World War II. Although Germany became even more warlike after the First World War, there seems to have been a "termination of its warlike force" following the defeat of Hitler.

"THOU ART ON THE RHINE!"

In 1868 the Franco-Prussian War was still two years in the future. Dr. Tardieu, a young surgeon who had just graduated from medical school, was walking with his friend Sonrel one day when the latter suddenly stopped and seemed to go into a trance. Sonrel, a mathematician, looked at Tardieu as if he were part of a vision, and said, "How strange! I see you in uniform! Yes, you have a military cap and in it you are counting money, and you are on a railway!"

Sonrel also saw himself in uniform as an officer, but he was dying. "I shall die in three days, but you are there, you come in time to see me before I die, to watch over my children." Then Sonrel paused and watched time race ahead. He saw another war, one greater in scope than the war of 1870. "What bloodshed! God! What bloodshed! Oh, France! Oh, my country! Thou art saved! Thou art on the Rhine!"

In 1870 Dr. Tardieu was in charge of a military hospital. As in the vision, one day in August he had collected money for the wounded. On the way to the railroad station, he was counting the money in his cap when he remembered the prediction. A month later Sonrel, now an army engineer, contracted smallpox. Tardieu went to see him and found that Sonrel had been expecting him and had been repeating, "Tardieu will come. I see him coming." At this time Sonrel had been married a year. He had one child, and his wife was expecting another. Sonrel died shortly after Tardieu's arrival.

The second war previsioned by Sonrel came in 1914, when France, at first in great trouble, finally advanced to the Rhine and was "saved."

The story comes from Charles Richet's book *Thirty Years of Psychical Research*. Although Sonrel foresaw two wars, the events of 1870 were much more vivid and specific, those of the First World War greater in scope but vague in detail. The first part of the vision was generated by the close personal relationship between the two men. The second was more of an "oracle-like" prophecy.

"I WILL DIE AFTER CHICAMAUGA"

Sometimes the psychic link in wartime is to one's larger self, the company or regiment, the military community. Such was the case with John R. Davis, a soldier in the Civil War.

Davis was forty-four years old, past the usual age for military service. Although he had been born in South Wales, he enlisted in the Union Army in the early 1860s. Major E. C. Dawes of the 53rd Ohio Regiment had good cause to remember Davis, because the man seemed to know more about the Army's plans than either he or his superior officers.

In August, 1863, the 53rd Ohio was stationed at Messenger's Fort on the Black River, sixteen miles east of Vicksburg, Mississippi. Orders had come to Dawes from General Sherman to take the division to Natchez, Mississippi. While Dawes was riding into camp one day, he spotted Private Davis policing the grounds. The man did not look well, and Dawes told the sergeant to relieve him of duty. Then he invited Davis into his tent.

"Well, Davis," he said genially. "We are going to Natchez."

Davis shook his head.

"No, sir, the division is not going to Natchez. The regiment is not going."

"How do you know so much?" asked the astonished major. "When did you take command of the army?"

Davis repeated—respectfully but firmly—that the regiment was not going to Natchez. He had seen in a dream that the troops would be "marching off the transports at Memphis." Further, he could see Dawes "on the deck, pointing."

"And where will you be, Davis?"

"I am not there. I am going to die."

The order to go to Natchez was changed. One of Davis' predictions came true on September 5, after the battle of Chicamauga, when he died. Then the regiment was ordered to Chattanooga by way of Vicksburg and Memphis. Arriving at Memphis, the troops "marched off the transport," as Davis had seen in his dream. Dawes was about to leave the troop ship, when he saw the Lieutenant Colonel of the Regiment, who had been ill, standing on the wharf. Major Dawes leaned over the rail and called the attention of the guards to his superior officer, pointing at him. As he pointed, he recalled the third prediction of Davis.

In 1895 the *Proceedings* of the Society for Psychical Research published a letter from Major Dawes, in which he described the three predictions of John Davis that had come true.

ORACLES OF THE FRENCH REVOLUTION

There were perhaps more "oracle-like" predictions of the French Revolution than of other wars and uprisings. John Englebrecht, a

German of the seventeenth century, pre-viewed the storming of the Bastille, still 154 years in the future. Englebrecht was both clairvoyant (he could psychically "see" distant events and objects) and clair-audient (he could "hear" psychic messages). In 1625 he foresaw the events of the Revolution in a vision. Then a voice told him, as in the case of the modern prophet Jeanne Gardner, "Get up and write down what thou has seen."

Pierre d'Ailly, a philosopher and ecclesiastic born in 1350, predicted that one of the most fateful dates in human history would be 1789, the year the French Revolution was to begin. D'Ailly wrote, "Should the world remain in existence at that time, which God alone knows, then astounding upheavals and transformations will occur which will affect our laws and political structure."

Nostradamus, who probably comes closer than any other psychic to being an "oracle-like" prophet, named the Tuileries (the royal residence) as a point of attack for the revolutionaries. The Tuileries had not yet been built at the time of his prophecy. Nostradamus said also that King Louis XVI would be "crowned with a cockade" and mentioned the names of Narbonne and Sauce. Count Narbonne-Lara, born about two hundred years after the prophecy, was the first war minister for Louis XVI. Sauce, the mayor of Varennes, helped capture the fleeing king.

Nostradamus gives a graphic portrait of the future king and queen in this quatrain, written in the sixteenth century:

> Too good the times, too easy-going the King,
> He does and undoes, too negligent and sudden;
> He will follow the false ideas of his light but loyal wife,
> By his very good will he will be put to death.

"YOU WILL DIE ON THE SCAFFOLD,
YOU BY POISON, AND YOU . . ."

It is the year 1788, and a group of distinguished French citizens—men of letters, lawyers, philosophers—are having dinner at the French Academy. The Revolution is only a year away and these men do not have to be prophets to see it coming. But nearly all the cultured gentlemen and ladies sitting around the table look forward to the great change. When the oppressed classes rise up, the Age of Reason will be at hand. The life of the mind will replace the religious fanaticism and political excesses of the past.

One man does not share this glowing vision of the future. He is Jacques Cazotte, writer and philosopher, now in his seventieth year. He has a vision of the Revolution, too, and it is not a pretty one. He looks around at his friends with a feeling of sadness. He is fond of them and knows that there is terrible suffering and death in store for each one.

He watches in horror as his vision unfolds. The Marquis de Condorcet will be condemned to death, but he will take poison and die on the floor of a prison cell. Monsieur de Chamfort will sever his veins with a razor twenty-two times—but he will linger on for a few months before dying. Dr. Vicq-d'Azyr will also die, after he begs a friend to slash his wrists.

Cazotte tells each in turn what his fate will be. "You, Monsieur de Nicolai, will die on the scaffold, likewise you, Monsieur Bailly." So, too, Monsieur Roucher. The assembled guests whisper among themselves that Cazotte must be mad, but he assures them solemnly that all his prophecies will come to pass within six years. And the ladies present—they, too, will go to the scaffold, their hands tied behind their backs.

The last victim will be the King of France, Louis XVI.

The guests do not take Cazotte's prophecics seriously—they are too incredible. Besides, will not the Revolution usher in the Age of Sanity? No more violence, only intelligence and calm deliberation will prevail. Half-jokingly, Madame de Gramont asks what will happen to Cazotte himself.

Cazotte's head sinks to his chest and he tells the story of the siege of Jerusalem: how a man walked around the ramparts seven days in a row, crying, "Woe to Jerusalem! Woe to myself!" Then he was killed by a large stone that came from the Roman catapults.

This will be his fate—woe to France, woe to Cazotte!

In 1789 the Revolution broke out. One by one, in the following six years, all of Cazotte's predictions came true. Chamfort, about to be arrested, cut open his veins. De Condorcet died of self-administered poison while in jail in 1794. Bailly lost his head to the guillotine, along with Roucher. Madame de Gramont and the other ladies, including Marie Antoinette, were marched to the guillotine with their hands tied behind their backs.

And Cazotte himself? He was arrested in August, 1792, and sent to Abbaye prison. Now seventy-two, he was set free, but in a vision he saw his rearrest and death. He was taken into custody again on September 11 and guillotined on September 25.

"JEANNE! JEANNE! JEANNE!"

When she was a child, Jeanne d'Arc knew that there would be a war between the French and English. Her voices told her that she herself would lead the French armies. At the age of thirteen, when she was in her garden one day, the Voice called her three times—"Jeanne! Jeanne! Jeanne!"

Jeanne, who was clairvoyant as well as clairaudient, then saw a blaze of light, and she heard the Voice say, "Jeanne, go to France where there is a great pity." The Voice told her that she had only "a year and a little more" to accomplish her mission. Not only did Jeanne know in advance what the fate of France and her own fate would be. She knew also that she could convince the Dauphin that she had been sent by God to save France. She would do this by demonstrating her powers of telepathy and clairvoyance.

Four years later, at the age of seventeen, Jeanne d'Arc left her country town of Domremy and took charge of the French army. In "a year and a little more" she rallied France behind her in one of the miracles of history.

Jeanne d'Arc lived from 1411 to 1431. But the war between France and England and her part in it were prophesied long before by many psychics. Merlin, the Welsh prophet of the early Middle Ages, predicted that "a marvelous maid will come from a grove of oaks . . . for the healing of nations." A prophetess named Marie d'Avignon dreamed of arms and armor and a maid who "would restore France."

"DIVINE SALAMIS, YOU WILL BRING DEATH"

In ancient times the oracle at Delphi was often consulted about the many wars that threatened Greece and neighboring nations. Never were Athens and the other Greek city-states in greater danger than when Xerxes, the ruler of Persia, decided to invade Greece with his awesome army, the largest and most formidable in the world, in 480 B.C.

The war started as the result of a dream, in which Xerxes was told that he should invade Greece. As the Persian armies and fleet advanced west, the Greek leaders rushed in consternation to the Delphic oracle and asked what they should do. The oracle, too, was awed by the size of the Persian forces and in twelve lines of rambling verse, suggested that discretion was the better part of valor and retreat was the only sensible course.

But then the Pythia seemed to reverse herself and said, "Truly a day will come when you will meet him [the foe] face to face." The oracle added, enigmatically, that the Greeks would find their safety only in "houses of wood" and closed with this cryptic two-line prophecy:

> Divine Salamis, you will bring death to women's sons
> When the corn is scattered or the harvest gathered in.

According to the Greek historian Herodotus, "The professional interpreters understood these lines to mean that if they prepared to fight at sea, they would be beaten at Salamis [a seaport]." One of the Greek leaders, Themistocles, demurred. He thought that "houses of wood" referred to ships and that the Greeks would win the war at sea. He pointed out that if the Athenians were fated to lose, "hateful Salamis" would be more appropriate than "divine Salamis." If in later years the Greeks were to look back on Salamis as "divine," it meant that the oracle predicted a great sea victory there over the Persians.

The Greek leaders were won over by Themistocles' argument, and instead of a wholesale retreat, they readied their fleet for the battle at Salamis. Although the gigantic army of Xerxes swept over the combined armies of the Greek city-states, the smaller but more skillful Greek fleet overcame the Persian fleet at Salamis. This led to the defeat and withdrawal of the Persians from Greece.

The poetic and symbolic speech of the oracles often led simpleminded kings into trouble in ancient times, when they would base the wrong conclusion on the sometimes equivocal verse of the seers. This has been true throughout the centuries—the cloudy language of prophecy has frequently been misinterpreted. Even today, with dreams and visions clothed in symbolism, their message is often garbled.

The Greeks were grateful to Themistocles, not only for calling attention to the right interpretation of "houses of wood" and "divine Salamis," but also for the heroic part he played in the naval battle that resulted in victory for the Greeks. Still, if the oracle had prophesied "divine Salamis," she must also have known that Themistocles would correctly interpret the lines and that eventually the Greeks would fight and win at Salamis.

THE DRUM OF SIR FRANCIS

There is a tradition in England that the drum of Sir Francis Drake is sounded in the distance when the country is threatened with invasion. Perhaps it was this drum that the editor of *The Craftsman,* a weekly magazine, heard in April, 1776, when the British were being defeated by Washington's American army. The magazine predicted that by the year 1944, London would be in ruins and the world would be ruled by a "great North American empire."

For two thousand years and more the drums of war have been heard everywhere by individuals whose psychic centers were awakened by fear of death or of destruction to their country. In every war in history mothers have received telepathic messages from their sons. Friends have communicated mind-to-mind when danger threatened. Most of these psychic experiences were never recorded, but the investigations of Dr. Bender and others in modern times suggest that there were probably countless cases of this kind since the early tribal wars.

Prophets of today are still hearing the sound of distant drums. In the June, 1966 issue of *Fate* magazine, the English psychic Pendragon said, "I am not happy about the Near East and I am impressed that in 1967 . . . this area will become a war arena involving Egypt, Jordan, Syria . . ." In the summer of 1967 the Six Day War broke out between Israel and the Arab countries.

Early in 1968 a message came to the Central Premonitions Registry that Russia would soon invade Czechoslovakia. In August Soviet tanks rolled into Prague. A young woman dreamed on April 25, 1970 that there would be "exploding headlines" on May 2 in newspapers all over the world. She sent this prediction to the Central

Premonitions Registry. On May 2 the front page of the *New York Times* featured an eight-column headline about the U.S. entry into Cambodia. The *Times* uses such banner headlines only a few times a year, when the news is "explosive."

The Vietnam war has had its share of premonitions. In the spring of 1970, a young soldier from Pennsylvania heard a voice that he thought came from his dead uncle, predicting that on July 4 he would be wounded in his right side and would be home for Christmas. Both predictions came true.

CHAPTER TEN

Prophets of the Aquarian Age

As man emerged from his prehistoric past, he seems to have brought the prophetic sense with him. The ancient world swarmed with seers, soothsayers, diviners, necromancers, crystal-gazers, astrologers, dream-interpreters, augurs and oracles, many of them on the staff of kings and emperors. In his foreword to *Greek Oracles,* Robert Flacelière writes: "In antiquity divination was esteemed as an official institution. Everywhere, in Egypt and Mesopotamia, even in Israel and later in Rome, it was obligatory for political and military leaders to consult the oracles, to 'take the auspices,' before embarking upon any enterprise."

Today, two thousand years later, science and rationalism have become the dominant forces shaping the mind of Western man, and prophecy has retreated to the fringes of society, instead of being a vital part of it as in the time of Cicero, Socrates, and Jeremiah. With some exceptions mentioned later, governments no longer employ seers or consult oracles for portents of the future—although politicians and statesmen do make off-the-record visits to psychics.

Yet, paradoxically, a new era seems to be opening up for psychics. One sign is the birth of premonitions bureaus that in time may spread throughout the world. Another is the rise of a new crop of prophets, similar to the old in some respects, different in others. The seers of today's world use many of the same methods or variations of the methods of the ancients but with greater insight into the psyche and how it works.

Adrienne Coulter, a prophetess from Flushing, New York, is certain that in the generation of youths following this one—those who will be in their twenties and thirties in the year 2000—seers will be commonplace. She believes that the present Age of Aquarius—an age that occultists say will supplant a period of materialism with one of humanitarianism and spirituality—will see a universal acceptance of psychics and the reality of psychic phenomena.

While the hippie generation concentrates on rebelling against middle-class commercialism, another kind of revolution is in the making. By the twenty-first century, if the Rev. Coulter is correct, the children of the flower-children will be psychics.

THE "COOL" PROPHETS

Many of today's young prophets will be in their prime by the year 2000—mature prophets who are now setting the stage as the leaders of the next generation of psychics. This new breed is, for the most part, the product of a scientific age that is reexamining the values of religion and exploring new approaches to the unknown. They are cool and detached. They disdain artificial means of bringing on altered states of consciousness, unless in a laboratory setting. They do not purchase crystal balls or look up at the heavens for guidance. They take part in experiments and observe the workings of their own psyche.

One of them, Malcolm Bessent, studies the psychic process just as another student might study physics. Malcolm, now in his early twenties, is "in training" at the College of Psychic Science in London. To be chosen for study at the college, the candidate must first demonstrate that he has a psychic potential. Those accepted as students then do "readings" on a regular basis for the general public.

The method used is psychometry. The psychic trainee holds an object belonging to the visitor and makes predictions. In keeping with his cool approach, Malcolm is more successful with skeptics than with the more gullible visitors, a reversal of the usual situation.

His sense of detachment is appreciated by the skeptics, who get results guaranteed to make them lose their skepticism.

Before the young psychics go into action, an experienced older hand leads them in a period of meditation, the one practice almost universally followed by prophets of the Aquarian Age. If the new-age seers are in general less attached to old-style religions, their preparation for prophecy still has a spiritual base, borrowed from religious, mystical, and yoga disciplines. The purpose of the mind-calming silence is to put one's ego in the background and get in tune with others. The American Society for Psychical Research also begins its experiments in extrasensory perception with a period of group meditation.

Bessent was invited to give readings at the College of Psychic Science after he had studied for eighteen months with Douglas Johnson, the famous British medium who teaches at the college. A good psychic must have confidence in his ability to separate false impressions from genuine precognition. Johnson demonstrated his self-confidence many times for his young protégé. Once he told Malcolm that his father would die in the following week, a premonition that soon came true.

In June, 1969, Bessent visited America to be a subject of experiments in precognition at the Maimonides Medical Center. (These experiments are discussed in a later chapter.) Although the object was to have Malcolm dream of a target picture that would not be chosen until the next morning, he also had some dreams relating to his own present and future circumstances and, in one case, perhaps to mine.

As I was looking over the reports at the conclusion of the experiments, I discovered that my car, which had also had a "reading" from another psychic, had crept into Malcolm's dreams. When he was awakened after one series of dreams, he said: "I thought about an old black car . . . First of all, I thought about Canada and then I thought of this old car and then I was thinking I was going to be driving there. . . ." About the time of the dream I had just bought "an old black car" and I was thinking constantly of Canada and about "driving there." Malcolm knew of no one who owned a black car until he rode in mine one day, some time after his dream.

How do Bessent's prophecies come to him? They come "coolly"

in the form of mental statements. He no longer needs to hold an object to get his psychic mind on the move. Sometimes he has a prophetic dream, as he did under experimental conditions at Maimonides. Occasionally he hears a voice.

Once the "spirit-control" of the late Eileen Garrett, Uvani, spoke to him. Malcolm was visiting in Boston at the time, and he asked Uvani what Dr. Krippner was doing at that moment in New York City. Spirit-controls have personalities and moods of their own, and their responses are not always predictable. Uvani told him not to be facetious, then said that Krippner was with two persons and was standing on one leg in front of a fountain.

As it was not like the serious-minded Dr. Krippner to be so occupied, Bessent thought it was Uvani's turn to be facetious, and he was inclined to discount this experience. But it turned out later that Krippner had indeed been standing with two friends at a soda fountain at the time mentioned. One foot had been resting on a rail.

THE WATER LEVEL WILL BE RISING

Alan Vaughan, now in his early thirties, should be a mature prophet in the year 2000. He joins Malcolm Bessent in predicting that the water level will be rising in a few years and that New York City will become uninhabitable. This will be gradual, however, and there will be enough time for people to leave the city.

Vaughan and Bessent gave me this prediction at the same time. It was impressive to see two cool young seers quietly confident of the same prophecy. But could one have influenced the other through telepathy? During his stay in America, Malcolm was the guest of Vaughan and his wife, and there could have been an unconscious mind-to-mind communication which resulted in similar prophecies.

Vaughan, who has worked closely with experimental parapsychologists, believes in the scientific approach to ESP and admits the possibility of mutual influence. Now associate editor of *Psychic* magazine, he was formerly a science editor and brings this orientation to his research in psychic phenomena.

A graduate in classical studies at the University of Akron, Vaughan finds parallels among the personages and events of ancient times with those of the twentieth century. He believes that what the Swiss psychiatrist Carl Jung called "synchronicity" (the way in which people and events seemingly unrelated are linked by strange coincidences) operates in human affairs, and that predictions of the future can be based on studies of the past. He gives as an example the correspondence between the Kennedys and the Gracchi family of Rome. Two of the sons in the Gracchi family dedicated themselves to political and social reform, and their pattern of early deaths may have foreshadowed the fate of the Kennedy brothers.

The cool young prophets offer themselves as subjects of experiments. Vaughan has participated in projects at the Maimonides Medical Center. He has also been a subject at the Masters-Houston Foundation for Mind Research in New York City, where he was put in the "Witch's Cradle," a device for inducing altered states of consciousness. His predictions made in the Witch's Cradle are described in a later chapter.

Vaughan does best as a prophet in areas that intrigue him, such as the space program. Unlike some subjective prophets who become emotionally involved with their dreams and visions, he must be a bit detached although interested for his predictive powers to function.

Although Vaughan and Bessent agree on the "water calamity" facing New York City, their predictions in the political area are at variance. Vaughan believes that Nixon will be reelected but that there will be trouble and possibly scandal in his second term. Among his other short-term forecasts:

The year 1970 would be bad for the stock market. The low point would come in September, and there would be a recession for several months. This prediction was made in 1969. Actually, the low point in the market came in May, 1970, but the *New York Times* of October 29, 1970, stated that the Government's index of leading indicators of general business activity reached its lowest level in September.

Eventually, the U.S. and Russia will cooperate peacefully on the space program. In the '70's a new form of propulsion will increase the speed of spaceships 10 to 100 times. It will take only a month to reach Mars.

Some of Vaughan's predictions that came true: He foresaw the blizzard of 1967 that followed the New York subway strike. One day, while walking along the street he heard the strains of "Thanks for the Memory" sung very sadly. Believing that there would be a tragedy connected with Bob Hope, who had made the song famous, Vaughan sent his prediction to the Central Premonitions Registry. Five days later, Hope's brother died.

Vaughan also uses meditation as a way to develop extrasensory powers, and conducts his own meditation group. One night in 1966, while he was concentrating on predictions of world events, a voice told him that he would marry in 1967. Shortly thereafter, he met his future wife, Iris. Both worked for companies with the initials ABC, which Vaughan believes to be an example of synchronicity.

A RELIGIOUS PROPHET OF THE '70S

There are still seers with a religious orientation. One of them is the Rev. Adrienne Coulter. She also hears a voice giving predictions from time to time, but works mainly as a trance-medium. Her "control" is a mischievous spirit-sprite called Sunbeam, who is rather unconventional in her prophecies.

When a group once gathered in the Rev. Coulter's home during a seance, Sunbeam suddenly announced that there would be an accident in about fifteen minutes: a minister present would split his britches. Fifteen minutes later the minister stood up, and as he did so there was the sound of ripping cloth. He hurried off in embarrassment.

Was this a self-fulfilling prophecy? Only Sunbeam would know and she wasn't telling.

Less amusing, to me at least, was the prediction Sunbeam made about my "old black car" that had appeared in Malcolm Bessent's dream. She mentioned the color and described it correctly as having a "funny" rear. Sunbeam announced that the car was a "lemon," specifically that the carburetor was no good and the gas line was blocked. I had ambivalent feelings about her prophecy; if she were correct, it would make good copy but would also cause me trouble I didn't need.

The next day the car wouldn't start. Was it the carburetor, I asked the mechanic? No, he replied with emphasis, the carburetor was fine. New distributor points were installed, along with new spark plugs and a rebuilt starter. For a week or so the car was all right. Then, mysteriously, it began to balk again and refused to start after a cold night.

Once again the car was towed to the garage. The next day I went to see what the trouble was.

"I've got bad news for you," said the mechanic. "Your carburetor's no good."

"That's what Sunbeam said," I murmured. He gave me a puzzled look, but I didn't explain. A new carburetor was installed. Two weeks later the car resumed its early-morning policy of not starting.

"Do you suppose," I asked the mechanic timidly, "it could be the gas line?"

"Absolutely not," said the mechanic. "It's not the gas line. I think you need another carburetor."

"But Sunbeam said . . ."

Another carburetor was put in. As I write this, the third carburetor has gone bad and has to be replaced. At the moment, I can't make up my mind whether Sunbeam is a prophet or a witch.

In her ordinary readings, the Rev. Coulter makes predictions without the aid of her spirit-control. Before a big snowstorm in February, 1969, she had a vision of a wavy bridge and people leaving stranded cars. Later she saw the identical scene on television. She also forecast the Alaskan earthquake of 1964 and a tidal wave in Hawaii.

Unlike the cool prophets who have a tendency to analyze their psychic impressions, Adrienne says that her spirit-teachers tell her not to try to understand her powers but to be merely the channel through which these powers work. At various times each of her senses has been involved in her psychic experiences—she sees clairvoyantly, hears clairaudiently, even feels invisible objects touching her. She is also a healer and has relieved persons of injuries or illnesses by placing her hands on the affected part.

A FOOTNOTE TO THE ABOVE

I just went over to see my car mechanic.

"Well, we found the trouble," he said. "It was in the gas line."

Verdict: Sunbeam is not a witch but an authentic prophet.

THE WEST VIRGINIA SEERESS

Another prophetess with a religious orientation is Jeanne Gardner, who should be one of our most famous seers when the twenty-first century rolls around. Jeanne is passionately committed to the building of her Cathedral of Prayer for all religions in Elkins, West Virginia. Whatever she makes from her books and her career as a psychic will go to this project.

Jeanne confesses that she is a simple soul, totally wrapped up in her spiritual life, and not given to the self-analysis of the cool prophets. She is an attractive woman in her late thirties, and her stories about her Voice pour out in a constant, enthusiastic stream. The psychic gift runs in her family. Her mother and grandmother used to hear the same Voice with its predictions. Now, together with an aunt and uncle, Jeanne has a three-way communication with the Voice. Even when they are widely separated, the Voice will give each of them different clues that spell out a prophecy when put together.

Surprisingly, considering the gloomy forecasts of other seers, Jeanne's Voice tells her that there will be a good outcome of our relations with China. The problem, says the Voice, will be solved through "Chilean Negroes." When Jeanne first heard this, she was puzzled, but the Voice said, rather snippily, "Use your head—look it up." Jeanne opened her encyclopedia and found that "Negro" is a port in the Philippines. There is a Chile off the coast of China, and in some manner, according to the Voice, the Philippine port and the Asian Chile will be instrumental in bringing America and China together.

The prophecies often come in rhymes. The Voice has explained that it exists in a timeless dimension and therefore is aware of what will take place in the future. "Your time," says the Voice, "is not my time."

EVERYBODY'S PROPHETESS

Jeane Dixon, in the limelight following her prediction of President Kennedy's assassination, is probably America's most popular living psychic. Her books are best-sellers, and she has a syndicated newspaper column. Crowds line up to hear her lectures.

Mrs. Dixon takes her role as a religious prophet quite seriously. At times she gives the impression that she is a modern Jeremiah or Elijah and that the Lord has chosen her to express His divine will and to warn nations and individuals of their fate if they ignore her advice.

Her prophecies come in many forms. One is an apocalyptic vision sent by the Lord, of a future event that cannot be changed. Her vision of "dark clouds over the White House" was such a revelation—nothing could have prevented the assassination of President Kennedy. On the other hand, the murders of Robert Kennedy and Martin Luther King were not fated and could have been averted.

Mrs. Dixon is a "scryer"—she often uses a crystal ball in which to view the future. Her forecasts cover a wide range. For one, she is a "gossip-prophet," closely following the fortunes of Jackie and Aristotle Onassis, Tricia Nixon, and others in high society. She is also a political prophet and in this area combines seership with the moral exhortations of the biblical prophets.

In her book *My Life and Prophecies,* she chides the late Martin Luther King for allegedly associating with the Communists, and believes this led to his assassination. Correctly predicting that there would be racial riots in the late '60s, she has gone one step further by putting the blame squarely on Russian intrigue. Kosygin and Breshnev invariably show up in her crystal ball, revealing their plans for her benefit. She frequently adopts a preaching tone on her television broadcasts—the President should do this, America should do that. She predicted disastrous consequences if we signed the test-ban treaty.

Along with spontaneous impressions and the use of her crystal ball, Mrs. Dixon also brings on the psychic state through meditation. Her prophecies often come in dreams and in the twilight period between sleep and waking. Another psychic channel for Mrs. Dixon are her fingers; she receives vibrations from people when she touches them.

Mrs. Dixon is an authentic psychic, but her religious and political bias may interfere with the accuracy of her predictions. As is the case with most psychics, her prophecies seem to be more reliable when they are stimulated by emotional links with persons than when she is envisioning broad-scale political and social events.

A CREATIVE-ARTIST PROPHET

At the other extreme from the cool prophets of the new-age Aquarians is Lorna Middleton, whose wealth of predictions in every area may stem from her creativity. Miss Middleton is a dance and piano instructor and has been associated with the theater all her life. Inheriting her psychic sense from her mother, her prophetic range is unlimited, covering everything from falling bridges (she predicted the collapse of the Silver Bridge at Point Pleasant, West Virginia, on December 8, 1967) to upheavals in nature.

Miss Middleton's subliminal consciousness may see the world as a stage, for many of her predictions come in dramatic form (and in this she is not alone—prophetic dreams often appear as drama). On February 5, 1970 she hurried off a note to the Central Premonitions Registry with this warning: "Someone is going to be shot. Someone is going to be shot." Three days later three persons were shot in the ancestral home of Earl Fortesque in Gloucester. A prediction that someone will be fired upon in America is not statistically significant, but murder in England is far more rare.

On January 23, 1970 Miss Middleton was upset by a ghastly vision: "A holiday camp . . . the worst train crash I have ever known . . . hundreds of people killed . . . blood gushing in the air like fountains . . ." the *New York Times* of February 2 carried this news item from Buenos Aires, Argentina: "A passenger express train smashed into the rear of a parked commuter train filled with people returning from a weekend holiday last night, crushing two of the five commuter cars and knocking the others off the track. Casualties estimated at 500. . . ." The total number of dead was over 150.

On July 29, 1969 Miss Middleton sent a sketch to the Central Premonitions Registry showing an airplane half-submerged in a lake: "It will be an unusual plane crash. I see woods, a lake, evening." A few days later, on August 3, a plane overshot the runway at the Marseilles airport in France and fell into a nearby lake. All forty-five passengers were saved, and the picture of the half-submerged plane appeared in a London newspaper.

A SHOWBIZ PROPHET

Many seers of the '70s perform for the public via radio and television. One of them is Daniel Logan, a former actor who is at home before the camera.

Although he has made many predictions of public events, he

admits he feels more confident working with individuals. He has not hesitated, however, to prophesy broad-scale events on order. Logan has predicted a depression for the early '70s, a formal alliance between Russia and the United States by 1975, and strange deaths in space. He claims also that our Mars probes have revealed life on the red planet, but that this information is being suppressed.

Logan is also a gossip-prophet and has joined the parade of seers who probe the future of Jackie and Aristotle Onassis. His prediction: they will be divorced. He sees the war in Vietnam going on for several years—"well into the '70s."

Logan says that he rarely hears voices and that psychic impressions come to him as thoughts. "The only effort involved is that of clearing the mind and tuning in." In common with other prophets of the Aquarian Age, he believes that the best way to develop psychic power is by meditation.

Still in his thirties, Logan should continue to divert television audiences in the year 2000 with his prophecies and Fu Manchu mustache. Although not particularly a scientific prophet, he could be classed with the "cool" ones.

INSTANT PROPHECY

An even stagier performer than Daniel Logan is Maurice Woodruff, the Instant Prophet. Since television time is too expensive to permit looking into crystal balls, meditation, or other kinds of preparation for prophecy, Woodruff has to make snap predictions in a way that will satisfy both the person he is "reading" and the vast television audience. When Woodruff looks at a guest who stands before him, he gets or at least gives the impression of getting an immediate glimpse into the future.

Sometimes his predictions are accurate, and his audience is reminded of it at a later date. The predictions that do not come true are not mentioned, of course. One that comes to mind is Woodruff's prediction that Sam Yorty would be reelected mayor of Los Angeles but would not serve. At the present writing, he is still in office and gives no sign of stepping down.

Woodruff has done some remarkable forecasting, however, some of it during private readings in his apartment, when he can dawdle for a moment or two before making his predictions. In a book written before Judy Garland's death, he prophesied that in the ensuing year a world-famous actress who had been in show business since childhood would die. He also wrote that her initial was J or G.

As a showbiz prophet, Woodruff is consulted by many theater personalities, including Peter Sellers, Britt Ekland, and Arlene Dahl. With an eye to his nation-wide following, his prophecies include many gossip-items. Perhaps to make America happy, he predicted that Frank Sinatra and Mia Farrow would have a baby and that George Hamilton would marry Lynda Bird Johnson, forecasts that were somewhat wide of the mark. He also made the startling prediction that Princess Grace of Monaco would have no more babies, but to soften this blow he said she would again star in a successful film.

Woodruff makes prophecy a fun thing. Always genial, even his pessimistic forecasts are couched in such cheerful terms that he sends his television and private clients away smiling. If he is still alive in the year 2000, he will continue to make prophecy an exciting and theatrical pastime.

MORE GOSSIP-PROPHECIES

As a footnote to the above, an item in the *New York Post* of December 26, 1969, gives a few forecasts by French gossip-prophets for the year 1970. The prognosis was both good and bad. Marcellus Toeguor foresaw a divorce for the Onassises but first a bouncing baby girl for Jackie. At the end of the year Mrs. Onassis' pregnancy still had not been announced. A psychic named Frederika saw the parting of the ways for Elizabeth Taylor and Richard Burton. More sensational were the predictions that Brigitte Bardot would be kidnapped and Queen Elizabeth would abdicate.

So far, in 1971, the ladies and gentlemen mentioned in the prophecies show no inclination to make them come true.

THE OLD PROS AMONG THE PROPHETS

The new prophets in the Age of Aquarius will build on the work of the old, and no discussion of prophets young and old should omit mention of the "two deans" of modern psychics who died in the past year—Eileen Garrett and Arthur Ford. Mrs. Garrett, although she was known as a warm individual personally, shared some of the detachment of the cool prophets in being curious about her gift and cooperating with scientists in experiments to test it.

Mrs. Garrett, a trance-medium, had psychic experiences since early childhood, and her talent was developed during a five-year training period at the College of Psychic Science in London. One way in which she first saw scenes of the future was on a "tiny screen, containing images, places, and events" that were not familiar to her. Then later she would meet the persons she had seen on her "screen."

Mrs. Garrett worked with J. B. Rhine at Duke University, psychologist Ira Progoff, and many other professionals who were interested in the nature of her psychic gift and wanted to learn where it came from. She was not successful in the purely clairvoyant experiments at Duke, in which the cards were viewed psychically as objects. In the telepathic experiments, when she would "see" the cards in someone else's mind, her scores were much higher, probably because another mind was involved.

The prophetic experiences of Mrs. Garrett spanned more than sixty years and two world wars. One of her best-known premonitions was of the crash of the British dirigible R-101 near Beauvais, France, on October 5, 1930. The first intimation of disaster came to her four years earlier, in 1926, when she "saw" an airship over Hyde Park in England that seemed to be in trouble. Two years later she had a similar vision of a dirigible that was buffeted by the wind and dipped toward earth. The most frightening vision came in 1929, when the dirigible "appeared" overhead, sent out puffs of smoke, then exploded into a "dense cloud."

More spectacular perhaps, although not precognitive, was a later spirit-communication while Mrs. Garrett was in trance, from the dead commander of the R-101, who described how the accident happened. The technical details given by the alleged spirit could not have been known to anyone else, certainly not to Mrs. Garrett.

Mrs. Garrett founded one of the most important organizations devoted to paranormal research—the Parapsychology Foundation in New York City. The Foundation gives grants for research in psychic phenomena, maintains a library for the use of students and researchers, and has published several journals, including *Tomorrow,* the

International Journal of Parapsychology, and a newsletter, the *Parapsychology Review,* that describes the latest work being done in the field.

Arthur Ford became aware of his prophetic gift during World War I, when he "saw" the casualty lists in the newspapers before they were in fact printed. Also a trance-medium, it was through him that the late Bishop Pike allegedly communicated with the spirit of his dead son. Another famous case involving Ford was the controversial spirit communication from the late Robert Houdini. Houdini, a magician who exposed mediums during his lifetime, had arranged with his wife that if he lived in the spirit after death, he would send a code message to her through a medium. After a session with Ford, Mrs. Houdini signed a statement that her husband's message had come through.

Ford was an ordained minister and a lecturer on the relationship between religion and psychic phenomena. He tried to overcome the resistance of the church to a belief in the psychic, pointing out that the greatest sensitive of all was Jesus, and that the miracles described in the Bible were simply examples of psychic phenomena. Ford was one of the founders of the Spiritual Frontiers Fellowship, a church-affiliated group that studies all aspects of the paranormal.

There are, of course, many other prophets in the Age of Aquarius, some advanced in years, others young enough to be seers in the twenty-first century. Peter Hurkos and Shirley Harrison have helped police apprehend criminals by the use of their psychic powers. Gerard Croiset, the remarkable Dutch psychic, has an extraordinary talent for finding lost children. He admits that he has a strong bond with children, and this sharpens his psychic sense when they are in danger.

The prophetic gift is not confined to known psychics. There are numerous cases on record of persons in public and private life—actors, poets, musicians, politicians, and ordinary citizens—who have had premonitions of coming events. Unlike many professional psychics of today or the oracles of two thousand years ago, they do not look into crystal balls or make other preparation for stirring up their minds. Their visions and hunches come without warning—often in dreams—with the uneasy knowledge that "something terrible" will happen.

The Central Premonitions Registry and the British Premonitions Bureau are staking their futures on the emergence of more such human seismographs during the Age of Aquarius. The home- and office-based psychics will increasingly dream or have visions of newsworthy events—the sound of distant drums, natural catastrophes, plane accidents, traffic deaths, and murders. But these amateur seers will also foretell with greater accuracy events in their own lives or the lives of those with whom they have emotional ties. The dream-and-vision prophecies of ordinary persons, along with some extraordinary ones, will be discussed in the next few chapters.

CHAPTER ELEVEN

The Death-Portents of Ordinary People

There is a widely held theory that everyone has a psychic sense but may not know it. According to this belief, people are bombarded day and night with thoughts coming from other minds and with images and impressions of events far removed from present time and space. Many of these impressions are of something that will happen in the next minute or next hour, perhaps the following day or not for many years. The average person, going about the practical business of living, must screen out these thoughts before they become conscious. Otherwise, he could not function in the present and would likely go mad.

If this is true, then unconsciously everyone knows what is going to happen but hides such knowledge from himself. Occasionally, however, awareness of the future breaks through when he is off guard, frequently in dreams and visions, sometimes in a sudden flash when he is occupied with other thoughts. Generally, the intimation is of an unpleasant experience—loss of money, an accident, possibly death that will come to him or to members of his family or his friends. A young lady told me that she had dreamed her father appeared to her, holding his severed head in his hand. A few days later he was decapitated in a plane crash.

Ordinary persons get premonitions in the same way that psychics do—through unusually vivid dreams, uneasy feelings, graphic visions, mysterious voices, even pictures seen in mirror-like objects. One young lady was startled when she saw in the reflected surface of a metal cabinet a death-scene that would take place in ten months. In 1903 a Mrs. Leeds woke up and went into the kitchen for a glass of water. As she started to drink, she saw in the water an image of a train accident. Her husband, who was a railroad man, came home later and told her that the brakeman had been hurt in an accident. The details were the same as in Mrs. Leeds' vision.

Ordinary people react in different ways to their death-prophecies. When a person has a foreboding of his own death, he may meet it reluctantly or, in many cases, with calmness and courage. He can have nothing but anxiety, however, if the premonition is about members of his family. Most poignant are those stories of men and women who sense that their children will die.

"SHE'LL NEVER NEED IT"

Mrs. Davidson's premonition of tragedy began with a vision of the crib burning with the baby in it. Horrified, she thrust the thought out of mind.

In early July she began to have the feeling that an unusual "burden" would fall upon her family. What it would be she didn't know, but the feeling kept coming back to her, all through July and August. She mentioned it to her husband, and talked it over with her sister who lived in the neighboring state of Connecticut. Her sister didn't believe in premonitions and told her to forget about it. But Mrs. Davidson couldn't, and she prayed constantly to be relieved of this weight on her mind. The thought of disaster would not go away. Instead it grew stronger and stronger.

Many times between August and the fatal day in December, Mrs. Davidson thought fondly of her little girl Lettie, almost two years old. One day it occurred to her that the child would have her own bedroom when she was older, and Mrs. Davidson wondered how to furnish it. A voice said, "She'll never need it." Mrs. Davidson looked around the room, but no one else was there.

After she had her vision of the burning cradle, Mrs. Davidson worried about matches lying around. Once she thought she smelled smoke and went down to the cellar, but nothing was on fire. She decided to destroy all the loose matches around the house and in the baby's room, but she put off doing so.

Mrs. Davidson kept a diary for Lettie, in which she recorded what happened to the child each day. When Lettie grew up, it would be fun for her to read about her baby days. One evening late in November, her mother was writing in the book, when the voice said, "She'll never need it."

Two weeks later, on the morning of December 2, Lettie was running around the house in her old shoes. "Your feet must be cold," said Mrs. Davidson. "We'll have to get you a new pair of shoes."

The voice said, "She'll never need it."

It was time for the baby's morning nap. Again the thought came to Mrs. Davidson that she should get rid of the matches. But as she picked up the box on the table, she decided she needed them to light the gas stove. She would dispose of the matches when her older boy came home.

As she was putting Lettie into the crib, the voice spoke again, saying, "Turn the mattress." Mrs. Davidson was in a hurry to get back to work. She could turn the mattress after the baby's nap. She went downstairs.

About half an hour later she heard Lettie crying and she rushed upstairs. The room was full of smoke and the cradle was on fire. The child must have found the match in the crib, perhaps under the mattress, and set fire to her bedclothes. She was so badly burned, she died in three hours.

A week before the tragedy Mrs. Davidson's sister, who had scoffed at the idea of premonitions, had a strong feeling that there would be a calamity in the family. She prayed for each of her relatives, but when she came to Lettie, she choked up and the words would not come out.

The story of Mrs. Davidson (a fictitious name) and the voice that said, "She'll never need it" was reported in the 1898 *Proceedings* of the Society for Psychical Research by Dr. James Hyslop, a professor of logic at Columbia University.

THE BLUE COFFIN

Another case of a mother's premonition of her child's death was investigated by the Society for Psychical Research. It came in a dream and portended death for two other children as well.

Annette Jones, the wife of a London tobacconist, had her dream while her little boy Peter was ill. In the dream a cart drove up to her house and the driver removed a black cloth from three coffins. Two of the coffins were white and one was blue. They were of three sizes, the blue coffin the largest. The driver left the larger white coffin with Mrs. Jones and drove off with the other two.

A few days later a friend of Annette's, Mrs. Devonshire, gave birth to a baby boy, Eric. Eric was healthy at first but his lungs collapsed and he died two weeks later, on a Friday. On Monday Peter, who was sixteen months old, also died. The Joneses, knowing that Eric would be buried on Wednesday, arranged to have Peter buried on the same day. The parish priest told Mr. and Mrs. Jones that another child who had just died would be buried at the same time.

The third child was the son of Mr. and Mrs. Jupp, whom the Joneses did not know. There were three coffins in the church. The larger of the white coffins held the body of Peter Jones, the smaller that of the infant Eric. The Jupp boy, who had died at the age of six, was buried in a blue coffin, the largest of the three.

"THOU WILT LOSE A SON"

The Quaker lady, who lived in Philadelphia, often heard a still, small voice whenever a sad event was about to take place. She kept a diary in which she recorded what the voice said. One day she wrote, "The Lord showed me that I should lose a son. It was often told me, though without sound of words. It said: 'Thou wilt lose a son; and he is a pleasant child.'"

The "pleasant child," her son James, often went swimming in the Delaware River near Philadelphia. Once, soon after his mother had written down her premonition, he was in the river with a friend. The friend was in danger of drowning, and James tried to rescue him but was also drowned.

A messenger was sent to tell his mother, who lived eight miles from the scene of death. When he arrived, he was struck dumb and unable to recite the bad news. The Quaker lady heard a voice say, "James is drowned." She said calmly to the messenger, "Thou has come to tell me that James is drowned."

The story is related in *The Life of Isaac T. Hopper,* by Ludia Marie Child. The Quaker lady lived in the early part of the eighteenth century.

SNOW ON THE GROUND

Premonitions of death in the family may come within a relatively short time of the event or even just before the tragedy. But sometimes the event may be foreseen years in advance, and the moment of recognition comes as a strange and eerie experience to the person who had the premonition.

In *Hidden Channels of the Mind,* Louisa Rhine tells about a man in New York City who dreamed he was driving a car down the street where his mother and father lived. It was a cold winter night, and there was snow on the ground. In the dream he got out of his car and walked into the house. His father was sitting by the window, and there were several people in the living room, no one familiar to him. His father motioned him into his mother's bedroom. He went inside and saw her lying on the bed, dead.

At the time of the dream the man did not own a car, nor was there snow on the ground. It was not until ten years later that he received word his mother had died suddenly. He got into a car which he now owned and drove down the street leading to his parents' house. The ground was covered with snow, as in the dream. As he was getting out of the car, he saw his father sitting at the window. In the house were several people, relatives and friends whom he knew. His father motioned him into the bedroom. There he saw his mother lying dead as in the dream.

The real event matched the dream in every detail, except that the man knew the visitors in his father's home. Because so much that is emotionally motivated gets into the precognitive dream, there was probably a reason that would be apparent to a psychiatrist why the man didn't recognize his friends or relatives in the dream.

Sometimes psychic news of death comes in the form of printed matter seen in visions or dreams. Arthur Osborn describes a case of this kind: A woman dreamed that the front doorbell rang and she went down to answer it. The mailman gave her a letter from a woman who was a distant acquaintance living in her home town. In the dream she was surprised to hear from this woman, whom she knew only slightly.

The dream-letter was so vivid that when the woman awoke, she could still see the heading, signature, and handwriting. She immediately wrote down the contents of the letter and showed it to other people living in the house. In the dream no one else had been home.

About a month later she was at home alone when the doorbell rang. The mailman handed her a letter with the return address of the woman in the dream. The heading, signature, and handwriting were exactly as they had been in the dream. She was requested to return immediately to her home town. When she arrived, the clergyman told her that her brother had been killed. The clergyman had asked a local woman to write the letter.

Her brother had died on the night she dreamed of receiving the letter. The news of his death probably came telepathically, although she had no conscious awareness of it, and in the dream she previewed the contents of the letter.

A MAN WILL DROWN ON THIS SPOT

If there are no ties of blood or friendship to the person who will die, the setting itself may forge an emotional link with the one having the psychic experience. A case in the *Proceedings* of the Society for Psychical Research tells about a woman in Castleblaney, Ireland, who saw a man committing suicide a week before it happened.

The woman sat down upon a rock at the edge of the water and was lost in the stillness and beauty of the scene. A slight fatigue and the quiet ripple of the water served to take her out of present time and into a slight trance. Suddenly she felt a cold chill and her limbs grew stiff. She was frightened, yet held to the spot by a kind of paralysis. She found herself staring into the water and waiting. A black cloud slowly rose above the water, and in it appeared a tall man in a tweed suit. The man leaped into the water and disappeared.

The dark cloud lifted and once again the woman felt the warmth and sunshine. She went home and told her sister and brother about her vision. They laughed at her.

A week later a bank clerk resembling the man in the vision committed suicide by leaping into the water where the woman had been sitting. She was not acquainted with him.

A DATE ON A GRAVESTONE

Beneath the layers of conscious awareness, each person may know the time he is to die. Occasionally the knowledge breaks through, usually a short time before the end. Aniela Jaffé tells about two schoolboys standing at a well. One of them suddenly looked puzzled and said, "How can I be lying down there when I am standing here?" He was later drowned in the well. Knowledge of his future death had momentarily penetrated his consciousness.

Most often such knowledge comes in a dream. Charles Richet writes about a man who dreamed he was at an inn, where he met several dead friends. He promised to visit them again in six weeks. Exactly six weeks later he was killed in an auto accident.

Sometimes, although rarely, the time of death is far in the future. Richet also tells of a Mr. Banister, who saw the date of his own death seventy years in advance. When he was a schoolboy in 1813, he dreamed of a gravestone with his name on it. The date was "Jun(e) 9, 1883" with the "e" in the month missing. On June 9, 1835, his oldest son died. Mr. Banister died Jan. 9, 1883. The dream had combined the dates of his own and his son's death, striking the "e" from June and changing the "a" of January into a "u."

"MY END WILL BE TERRIBLE"

Knowledge of one's death may come, like other kinds of premonitions, in any one of the altered states of consciousness. One young lady predicted her own death while she was hypnotized, a case reported in Flammarion's *Death and its Mystery*.

When Mademoiselle Irene Muza attended a seance on January 30, 1906, she was a young actress at the dawn of her career. While she was in a trance, she was asked if she could visualize her future. She wrote:

My career will be short. I dare not say what my end will be. It will be terrible.

The others present were alarmed by what Mlle. Muza had written, and they quickly erased it before she awoke. Had she known about her premonition, it could have become self-fulfilling.

On February 22, 1909, about three years after the seance, Mlle. Muza was at her hairdresser's. The latter accidentally dropped some antiseptic lotion containing mineral oils on a lighted stove. The flames wrapped around the actress, her hair and clothing were set afire, and she died in a hospital a few hours later.

THE ACCEPTANCE OF DEATH

The actress, the boy who looked down the well, the dreamer who died in six weeks' time—all had little or no consciousness of impending death. In other cases, the premonition is so vivid that the person facing death quietly accepts the fact and makes preparation.

Richet writes about a Russian who in 1895 dreamed he was on a ship that collided with another ship at sea. In the dream he fell into the water with another passenger and was drowned. When he awoke he was convinced he would die and began to put his affairs in order. A few months later he received instructions to sail for a port in the Black Sea. He told his wife: "You will see me no more; when you hear of my death, put on mourning. . . ."

Two weeks later his ship, the *Vladimir,* collided with another vessel and he was drowned. Another passenger who survived said that he and the drowned man had been clinging to the same lifeboat for a short time.

Dr. Gustave Geley in *Clairvoyance and Materialization* writes about an elderly man in good health who predicted his own death six months in advance. He would die, he said, sometime before winter and every day thereafter he repeated his prediction. Eight days before his death, he announced that he would die on All Saints' Day. Five days later he was examined by Dr. Geley, who found "no organic lesion" and his heart in perfect condition.

The next day he said, "I shall die on All Saints' Day at midnight precisely. I shall have no pain nor death-pangs. I shall seem to fall asleep, but it will not be sleep; it will be death." On All Saints' Day, two days later, he woke up with a pain in his left side. He went back to bed, saying he would never get up again. At 11:30 P.M. he asked his wife what time it was, and when she told him it was 2 A.M., he replied that he knew it was not yet midnight.

At midnight he turned over and seemed to be sleeping. Then he raised his hand and pointed to the clock, which struck twelve. His arm fell back, and he died.

"IN THREE DAYS YOU WILL BE DEAD"

She was a young grandmother, only forty-nine. During Ascension Week in 1900, she dreamed one night that someone had appeared very early in the morning and knocked on the kitchen window. When she opened the window in the dream, the mailman handed her a letter and said she must read her newspaper very carefully that day. There was an announcement in the dream newspaper addressed to her: "Magdalene S—, get ready, in three days you will be dead."

When she woke up, it was with the conviction that she had only three days to live. She went into the garden and filled a basket with beans, added a piece of smoked ham, put on her Sunday dress and her white "death stockings" and went to see her daughter in town. When her daughter asked her why she had come so early, she told her about the dream. She was very cheerful about it. She gave the food to her daughter to be eaten on Ascension Day, the following Thursday, and helped the young woman clean up the house. When Ascension Day came, she did not feel well when she woke up. She lay back and died of a heart attack.

This is one of many cases collected by Aniela Jaffé, a Jungian analyst, for her book *Apparitions and Precognition* from personal experiences sent in by residents of Switzerland. The young grandmother lived in Berne.

DREAM OF A SEVERED HEAD

Many premonitions of the death of friends and relatives are sent to the Central Premonitions Registry, but as these are personal and not public events, they are of no use to the Registry. Sometimes, however, a death-prophecy may be associated with a newsworthy item, although the person who dies may be unknown to the public. A classic case of this kind was the "hands" dream of psychical researcher Walter Franklin Prince. Prince did what everyone who has a premonition should do and what the two premonitions registries recommend—he made a careful record of his dream before it came true and told two other persons about it who could corroborate his account.

During the night of November 27–28, 1917, Prince dreamed that in his hands was an order printed in red ink for the execution of a woman. Prince was not sure why she was condemned but he had a feeling that the French Revolution was somehow involved. The woman herself had brought the order for her own execution and said she was perfectly willing to die, if only Prince would hold her hand.

Dr. Prince saw the woman clearly in his dream: she was "slender of the willowy type, had blonde hair, small girlish features, and was rather pretty." She was about thirty-five. She sat down and waited for death without fear, as if well prepared to die.

Suddenly, in the dream, the light went out. Prince sensed that the woman was being put to death, and when her hand grasped his hand in the dark, he knew the execution was taking place. He wrote later: "Then I felt one *hand* (of mine) on the hair of the head, which was loose and severed from the body, and felt the moisture of blood."

Dr. Prince felt the fingers of his other hand "caught in her teeth, and the mouth opened and shut several times as the teeth refastened on my *hand*, and I was filled with the horror of the thought of a severed but living head. Here the dream faded out."

As soon as Dr. Prince woke up, he recorded the details of the dream. Then he visited the offices of the American Society for Psychical Research and related the dream to Gertrude O. Tubby, an officer of the society. The following morning, the twenty-ninth of November, 1917, Prince set out for church with his wife and narrated the dream to her.

So far nothing had happened to indicate that the dream was a prophetic one. Dr. Prince was an experienced psychical researcher, however, and believed he could distinguish a premonitory dream from an ordinary one. Another person would have felt foolish in making a careful record or even repeating the dream. But Dr. Prince was so shaken by the gory details that he was sure the dream was precognitive.

Returning from church, Prince saw this headline in the afternoon newspaper:

HEAD SEVERED BY TRAIN AS WOMAN ENDS HER LIFE

A woman by the name of Hand had placed her head on a track of the Long Island Railroad, directly in front of a train coming out of the station. She was decapitated. She had left a note in her handbag stating that her head would continue to live after it had been severed from her body.

The accident happened at 11:15 P.M. on Wednesday night, less than twenty-four hours after Prince's dream. Mrs. Hand was thirty-one years old, was slender and pretty and had golden brown hair. The dream corresponded in other ways with the real event: the dramatization of the "hand" (the woman's name); the fact that she "ordered" her own death; death by decapitation; death occurring "in the dark"; the belief of Mrs. Hand that her head would continue to live, as it did in the dream.

Two other significant details are that the suicide took place a short distance (six miles) from Dr. Prince's home and within twenty-four hours of the dream. The time element in particular is an important factor that would be considered in the evaluation of the dream by premonitions bureaus.

The dream of the severed head was Dr. Prince's second premonitory dream in which a train was involved. Just as Morgan Robertson and W. T. Stead were drawn in their thoughts to ships and water, it is possible that trains held a certain fascination for Prince. In any event, the severed head dream is one of the most remarkable death-portent dreams on record, especially because of the careful steps taken to make the dream known before the event.

Had the Central Premonitions Registry been in existence in 1917, this would have been one of its most celebrated cases. Unfortunately, such meticulous recording is rare, but the Registry and the Premonitions Bureau hope the day will come when this kind of documentation is commonplace.

"A YOUNG, BLONDE-HEADED GIRL"

It was a simple matter for the Central Premonitions Registry to verify the details of a dream about the Yablonski murders. On January 8, 1970, Mrs. Mildred Barton dreamed that three men and a girl were present during the killing of the United Mine Workers official, his wife, and daughter. "Two killers and the director of it," she wrote to the Registry, "and a young blonde-headed girl involved. . . ."

Two weeks later three men were arrested and on February 5 a blonde housewife was also indicted for murder. Robert Nelson, head of the Central Premonitions Registry, pointed out that at the time of the dream the authorities had no information about the murders.

Mrs. Barton, a Cincinnati housewife, would be considered not an established psychic but an "ordinary person" who dreamed of death and murder. A few more "hits" such as her dream of the alleged Yablonski killers may help to bring her into the class of Aquarian prophets and swell the ranks of psychics developed by the Central Premonitions Registry and the British Premonitions Bureau.

CHAPTER TWELVE

Appointments in Samarra

A merchant in Bagdad sent his servant to the marketplace to buy food. While the servant was examining some produce, he felt a touch on his arm and looking up, saw a white-faced woman. It was Death. She gestured at the man. Trembling, the servant ran back home and told his master that Death had threatened him. He begged his master to loan him a horse so that he could leave the city and go to the town of Samarra, thus avoiding Death. The servant was given his horse and he rode quickly out of town and away from his fate.

The merchant then went down to the marketplace and saw Death standing there. He asked her why she had made a threatening gesture at his servant. No, replied Death, that was not a threatening gesture, only a start of surprise. Death couldn't understand what the servant was doing in Bagdad, when she had an appointment with him in Samarra.

The above story comes from W. Somerset Maugham's play *Sheppey* and suggested the title for John O'Hara's first novel, *Appointment in Samarra*. Few of us know about our "appointments in Samarra," but knowledge of one's imminent death has often come to people in dreams and visions. In some cases, like that of the young grandmother who saw the announcement in the dream-newspaper that she would die in three days, death is accepted calmly and with no attempt to escape. In other cases, the frightened dreamer will move heaven and earth to cancel his "appointment."

As in the Samarra legend, a man who dreams of death—his own or that of someone close to him—often tries to arrange each detail of his life so that he can elude his fate. If the dream, vision, hunch, or voice says he will die in a certain country, he will go to another country. If he has seen himself dying in a plane, he will vow never to fly again. But—like W. T. Stead who was warned to stay away from water but eventually found himself on the *Titanic*—circumstances somehow arrange for him to be in the "wrong" place at the "wrong" time, and he keeps his appointment with Death.

The fascination of many of the "Samarra" stories in this chapter lies in the desperate attempts of the protagonist to move all the pieces on the chessboard—only to see them rearrange themselves in the end in exactly the pattern he tried to avoid. In another story, that of the Marston family, several persons fated to die could only watch helplessly and fearfully as each one was picked off in the order predicted.

The final Samarra story illustrates how a person may be impelled to act in an irrational and unaccustomed way to keep his appointment—as if an unconscious force were driving him, possibly against his conscious will, to the very spot where Death is waiting.

"YOU WILL DIE AT TWENTY-SIX"

"You will lose your father in a year to this very day. You will soon be a soldier but not for long. You will marry young, have two children, and die at twenty-six."

Only seven years to live! The young Frenchman, nineteen years old, looked at the psychic anxiously, but the face of Mme. Lenormand, Necromancer, was impassive. She knew the future like a book. The present date was December 26, 1879. He would live until 1886 and no longer.

The young man's father died on December 27, 1880. As the psychic had predicted, the boy enlisted in the army but was out in seven months. Still very young, he met a girl and was married. When his twenty-sixth birthday was approaching—February 4, 1886—he was the father of two children. Was there no way to avert his own death?

The young man consulted a well-known psychologist, Dr. Lié-beault, on January 7, 1886. Was it true, he asked the doctor, that he had only one month to live? What could he do to change his fate? The doctor laughed. This was pure superstition. The lad was young, vigorous, healthy. He had a long life ahead. He must push this fear out of his mind.

The doctor hypnotized the young man and gave him the suggestion that he would live not for a few more days but for forty-seven years. The suggestion seemed to work. His birthday, February 4, came and went, and he was still alive. The psychic had been wrong. He would live for at least forty-seven years longer. The doctor had said so.

But on September 30, 1886, the young man, still twenty-six years old, died suddenly of peritonitis. In spite of every precaution, he was called to his appointment in Samarra.

"I WILL BILK THE GHOST"

The young man who died at twenty-six might quite literally have "scared himself to death." In spite of the countersuggestion instilled in him by the psychologist, deep down he may have been afraid he would die, anyway. The fear of death may sometimes be stronger than the will to live.

The case of Lord Lyttleton seemed to be different. Lyttleton, a member of the House of Lords in England during the eighteenth century, had a premonition of death in a dream, but made light of it. In the dream a bird flew into the room, then changed into a woman dressed in white. She told him to prepare for death.

"I hope not soon," he said in the dream. "Not in two months."

"Yes, in three days."

Two days later he told a lady friend about the dream. She looked worried, but he laughed about it, saying, "I have lived two days, and, God willing, I will live out the third."

When he woke up the following morning, he felt fine and he told his friends he would "bilk the ghost." All day he acted unusually cheerful and, before retiring, told his servant to be sure to provide tasty rolls for breakfast. Lord Lyttleton had every intention of living through the fourth day and many days and years thereafter.

At a quarter after twelve, Lord Lyttleton looked at his watch, smiled triumphantly, and said to his servant, "This mysterious lady is not a true prophetess, I find."

The servant then stepped into the dressing room to prepare a tonic, went back in and found his master on the bed, dead.

Walter Franklin Prince comments in his *Noted Witnesses for Psychic Occurrences:* "The question comes up whether Lord Lyttleton died from autosuggestion, but it does not appear likely from the account that his apprehension was anything of the degree which would make such a theory plausible."

Despite Lord Lyttleton's promise to "bilk the ghost," in three days' time he kept his appointment with the white-faced lady.

"THE BODY I SEE IS MINE"

Sometimes the appointment in Samarra is death by accident. In such cases the person threatened may do everything possible to avoid the circumstances in which he will accidentally die. A Scottish gentleman dreamed he saw a crowd standing around a lake. Presently a body was fished out, and on close inspection he saw that it was his own corpse. He woke up trembling, for it had been one of those vivid here-and-now dreams, and he made up his mind to avoid the lake at all costs.

But later that day his business made it necessary for him to travel down the lake with his associates in a rowboat and meet another group on the other side of the water. The day was calm, and an accident seemed unlikely. He decided, however, to take this precaution: he would be rowed directly to the opposite shore and would then walk the remaining distance on land, while his partners went by boat the rest of the way.

He was rowed safely to the other side, and he sighed with relief as he got out of the boat, for the danger was apparently past. After walking for awhile, he came to the place of meeting. No one else had arrived. He stood on a promontory while he watched the approach of the boat with his friends. Suddenly the promontory, loosened by water underneath, gave way. The man fell into the water and was drowned before help could reach him.

In many Samarra cases, the threatened person may think that the fatal moment has passed. But it is just when he relaxes that death may be near.

THE SALUTE THAT KILLED

Nothing could be clearer than the dream of Robert Morris, Sr., that he would be killed during the firing of a salute by a foreign vessel. Yet he thought he could outwit the white-faced lady by taking every precaution at the scene of the salute.

The incident is described in the biography of his son, Robert Morris, Jr., an American financier in the eighteenth century and one of the framers of the Constitution. Robert Sr., an agent for a Liverpool shipping firm, was expecting the arrival of the ship *Liverpool* at Oxford, Maryland. The night before, he had dreamed he received a mortal wound from a salvo fired in his honor.

Morris was uneasy about the dream and decided it would be best not to join the party. Captain Mathews of the *Liverpool* thought Morris was being foolish and superstitious. Morris replied, "Call it superstition if you like, but our family is reputed to have the gift, or curse, of receiving premonitions of impending disaster."

The captain finally reassured Morris that no salute would be fired, and Morris reluctantly consented to join the party. But later the captain told him that the crew was upset at not being able to fire a salute. Morris replied, "Very well, but do not fire the salute until I or someone else gives the signal."

Captain Mathews said that he would go ashore with Morris when the time came and give the signal himself when they were a good distance away. Then the captain told the gunner not to fire until he raised his hand.

Before their boat had rowed clear of the guns, a fly lighted on the captain's nose. When the captain raised his hand to brush the fly away, the gunner, thinking this was the signal, fired the salute. The wadding from one of the guns struck Morris' arm above the elbow, breaking the bone and imbedding itself in the flesh. Infection set in, and Morris died a few days later.

Whatever unfeeling entity puts the dream into the head of the ill-fated man often is careful to leave out details that might help to prevent the tragedy. Had Morris dreamed of the total sequence of events, including the appearance of the fly, he might have been on the alert. As it was, he saw only the crucial act, the firing of the salute that wounded and eventually killed him.

Incidentally, how did the fly know that Morris was supposed to die and pick the strategic moment to alight on the captain's nose?

A BLOW FROM AN IRON WEAPON

Sometimes the appointment in Samarra is for a beloved relative. The premonition comes to a sister or brother, father or mother, who then does everything possible to keep the white-faced lady at bay. Maurice Maeterlinck writes about a young mechanic who dreamed that he had come home at 5:30 in the afternoon and seen his little niece run over by a street-car in front of their house. He told his family about the dream, every precaution was taken, and the child carefully watched at all times. But a few days later, at exactly 5:30 P.M. the child was killed as in the dream.

King Croesus of ancient Lydia dreamed about the death of his son and woke up vowing to prevent it. Herodotus writes that Croesus, who had already paid for the crime of an ancestor who killed an earlier king of Lydia, was punished by his son's death "presumably because God was angry with him for supposing himself the happiest of men."

Croesus dreamed that his son Atys would be killed by a blow from an iron weapon. The king, who was very fond of Atys, immediately put his vast resources to work to prevent the tragedy. First he got his son a wife, thinking that time spent with her would take him away from dangerous situations. Then he relieved Atys of his command of the Lydian soldiers, for in war it was quite likely that one could be struck by an "iron weapon."

The cautious Croesus had all the weapons in the palace collected and piled up in the women's quarters, as he was afraid that a javelin or a spear hanging on the wall might accidentally fall on Atys' head and kill him. He was not worried about this happening to the women, but of course the Samarra dream had been about his son.

Atys was no sooner married and presumably safe in his wife's arms than he decided he wanted to hunt a wild boar that was roaming around Mount Olympus. This outsize animal had been eating the crops and was so fearsome that expeditions against him always came away in terror. According to Herodotus, "The unfortunate hunters received more damage than they were able to inflict."

The Mysians, in whose territory the animal was loose, asked

Croesus to help them by sending his son with other young men and some dogs. Croesus wouldn't fall into this trap. He explained that the boy was too busy being married, but he said he would send an expedition of other young men to rout the boar.

Atys, being a vigorous and lusty lad, insisted that he go along. When Croesus refused, the boy pointed out that he would lose the esteem of their Lydian subjects, not to mention that of his adoring wife. Croesus told about his dream of the iron weapon, but Atys replied that since a boar had no hands, the animal couldn't inflict such a wound.

Croesus reluctantly agreed to let him go, but he took a further precaution. One Adrastus, a Phrygian, had at this time escaped from his country after killing his brother in an accident, and asked to be admitted to Lydia. The gracious Croesus welcomed him and also saw a chance to use his services. He asked Adrastus to go along with Atys and protect him from cutthroats and other lawless characters they might encounter who could harm Atys.

Croesus' own act sealed his son's doom. When the party of young men spotted the wild boar, they let their spears fly. The Phrygian's spear, unfortunately, went wide of its mark and killed Atys.

Again, the dream only showed an "iron weapon" but omitted the other details. Why wasn't Croesus allowed to see that Adrastus would be the agent of his son's death? It may be that Atys was fated to die and that Croesus not only could do nothing to prevent it, but every act of his seemed calculated to hasten the dreaded end.

Croesus might also have stopped to reflect whether a man who killed his own brother through carelessness would be a fit guardian for his son. In any case, the white-faced lady was not to be denied her prey.

DANGER—MURDER AHEAD

An appointment with death, although seemingly impossible to avoid, may still be a painless and relatively peaceful experience. An appointment with murder, seen in dreams and visions, holds the terror of a Greek tragedy. Many persons, famous and ordinary, have dreamed of being set upon and killed and have tried desperately to prevent the inevitable.

One such case was reported by Robert Dale Owen in his *Footprints on the Boundary of Another World*. It concerned a locksmith's apprentice, Claude Soller, who lived in Germany about the middle of the last century. One night Soller dreamed he was attacked by a brigand while travelling between Hamburg and Bergedorf, and slain.

The young man had no intention of going to Bergedorf, but the dream bothered him and he told his master about it. That proved to be a mistake, for the latter not only laughed at the premonition but determined to put it to the test. He had some money to send to his brother in Bergedorf and decided that the apprentice should be the messenger. The young man protested, but in vain.

From Hamburg to the village of Billwaerder, the apprentice walked in fear and trembling, casting nervous glances over his shoulder. Arriving safely in the village, he called upon the magistrate and told about his dream, asking for a companion to go with him through a wooded area on the way to Bergedorf. The magistrate designated a workman to accompany the young man and see that he came to no harm.

The apprentice never reached Bergedorf. He was found in the woods the next day, his throat cut. The workman who had been with him was located and charged with the crime, to which he confessed. The young man had confided to him that he was carrying the money and so gave the workman the idea of killing him.

The moral of the story, if there is one, is to keep your premonitions of personal disaster to yourself. If the apprentice hadn't told his dream to his master in the first place, he wouldn't have been asked to make the trip. Then revealing his fears to the magistrate and the workman led directly to his Samarra.

Whoever or whatever fashioned the apprentice's dream of murder evidently knew that he would put the noose around his own neck, but the dream didn't reveal this. Again, as in the case of Croesus, the very person who was asked to be the protector turned out to be the villain.

DEATH IN THE FIFTH HOUR

When a king or statesman dreams he is to be murdered, he has good cause for alarm. Men in public life are often targets of conspiracies or psychopathic killers, and the dream may well presage the event in real life.

After the assassination of Julius Caesar, there was murder in the air, and other Roman statesmen were nervous about their safety. Cinna, a good friend of Caesar's, had no cause for worry, however, as the public temper was inflamed against the killers. Yet Cinna had a disquieting dream, in which Caesar invited him to dinner, but he declined. Caesar kept insisting and finally took him by the hand and led him into a "very deep and dark place against his will." Cinna slept very restlessly that night.

In the morning news came that Caesar's body was to be interred. Still disturbed by his dream, Cinna tried to put off going to the ceremony. Then he reflected that he was Caesar's friend and it would not be fitting for him to stay away from the services. Reluctantly, as Caesar himself was when he went to the Senate on the fatal day, Cinna dressed himself and joined the throng listening to the oration of Marc Antony. Whereupon the angry crowd fell upon Cinna and murdered him.

It was a case of mistaken identity. Another Cinna had in a previous speech spoken harshly of Caesar, and the crowd thought he was the man. Although he had no reason to believe the crowd would turn against him, Cinna should have paid closer attention to his dream. Yet, because he was already condemned to his appointment in Samarra, he had, however reluctantly, to join the crowd at Caesar's funeral and be killed.

The emperor Domitian had much better cause than Cinna to believe he would be murdered. Domitian, leader of Rome in the latter part of the first century A.D., was a tyrant who made many enemies and was constantly in fear for his life. So mean was this emperor that he amused himself by catching flies and sticking pins in them.

When he was a young man astrologers had warned Domitian that he would die violently—even naming the date and the hour. He kept his equilibrium, however, until a soothsayer told him that in the fifth hour of September 18, 96 A.D. he would be murdered.

As the fateful day approached, Domitian grew more and more anxious. To discourage any attempt on his life, he had his secretary, Epaphroditus, put to death and followed his execution with that of the emperor's cousin, Flavius. Then he ordered the gallery where he exercised lined with highly polished moonstone, so that he could see in the reflecting surfaces the approach of any would-be killer.

On the night preceding September 18, Domitian dreamed that the goddess Minerva told him she could no longer protect him and walked out of the chapel he had consecrated to her. So terrified was Domitian that in the middle of the night he leaped out of bed with a cry.

In the morning the emperor woke up in a cold sweat and refused to leave his closely-guarded bedchamber. He sat all morning on his bolster and thought about the sword underneath that he could pull out quickly in an emergency. As he sat, he counted the minutes to the fifth hour.

Finally word came that the fifth hour had come and gone, and the prophecy would not be fulfilled. Relieved, Domitian left the bolster and went into the next room to bathe. He was stopped by Parthenius, his chamberlain, who persuaded him to stay in his room on the pretext that a visitor had news of a plot against his life. No longer fearful, Domitian agreed. Stephanus, a freedman, then entered the chamber and stabbed the emperor to death.

Was the prophecy fulfilled? Actually, it was still the fifth and not the sixth hour when Domitian rose from his bolster, for the conspirators had lied to him. The soothsayer's prediction was accurate. He saw only the murder at the appointed time and knew nothing of the conspirators' plans.

An interesting sidelight is that the seer Apollonius of Tyana was making a speech at Ephesus, several hundred miles from Rome, at the time of the slaying. He stopped short, glanced at the ground, and said, "Strike the tyrant, strike!" In his vision he saw Domitian killed. Then he said, "Take heart, gentlemen; the tyrant has been slain this day. This day? Why, by Athena, it was but now, just now, at the very moment of uttering the words at which I stopped."

"YOU WILL GO FIRST, CISSY, THEN NELLY, AND THEN . . ."

Dr. Westland Marston was an accomplished man—a happy man. A poet and playwright, he had a charming wife, two talented daughters, and a son who was a sensitive and gifted poet. The family's mansion in London was a literary salon, frequented by such distinguished guests as Robert Browning, William Thackeray, and other literary lights of the mid-nineteenth century. The house in Regent's Park was a place of continual excitement and activity.

Yet Dr. Marston was fated to end his days alone in the house— every other member of his family dead. He had heard of the prophecy in 1871 and he tried to forget it, but through the years it haunted him as each one of the family left for his appointment in Samarra.

The first to die was Mrs. Marston, the gracious hostess who had supervised so many literary gatherings in the home. Then in 1871 Cicely Marston was visited one night by the spirit of her mother, who said, "You will go first, Cissy, then Nelly (Eleanor), and then Philip, and last of all your father."

Cicely was anxious about the future of her poetry-writing younger brother, Philip Bourke Marston. Philip had been blind since he was a small boy and had been the special concern of his mother. Since her death Cicely, an excellent poetess in her own right, had sacrificed her career to watch over Philip. But the prophecy had said both she and Eleanor would die before Philip. Who would care for him then?

With all his sorrow, a bit of happiness came into Philip's life. He was engaged to a beautiful young lady, Mary Nesbit, and had written fifty-seven love sonnets for her. A year after their engagement, Mary died suddenly. Philip needed Cicely more than ever.

It didn't seem reasonable to Dr. Marston that the father of a family should be the last to die, and he tried not to worry about the prophecy. But Cicely died suddenly in 1878, still a young woman. She was followed by Eleanor seven months later. Only Philip and his father were now left. Philip carried on by himself and in 1883 published a volume of poems, *Wind Voices,* that received critical acclaim. The book sold so well that it was out of print three months after publication.

Philip was only thirty-three years old at the time. His father was overjoyed but still fearful of the prophecy. Then, early in 1886, Philip had an attack of brain fever, followed by a slight stroke. He died early in 1887. The prophecy was fulfilled. Dr. Marston was now alone in his spacious house. He lived for three more years, then died in 1890.

Louise Chandler Moulton, who published the story in the November, 1891 issue of *Cosmopolitan,* prefaces her account with a quotation from a Matthew Arnold poem:

> But who is this, by the half-opened door,
> Whose figure casts a shadow on the floor?

The figure was that of the white-faced lady who had set up a schedule of appointments in Samarra for the Marston family and left the oldest member, Dr. Marston, until the very last.

A similar story is told by a physician, W. E. Anthony, in a letter to the Society for Psychical Research. He had been the doctor for the family of Hiram Maxfield, a New England hotel keeper. One day, after attending a slight illness of Mrs. Maxfield, he was standing at the bay, waiting for the return boat, when the Maxfield's oldest daughter, a girl of twenty, came out on the porch to talk to him. Worried, she told him that a voice had said to her: "You will die first, then Harry, then father." She was alone in the house at the time and had no idea where the voice came from. The voice had added: "And Dr. Anthony will be present in each case."

All members of the family were in good health at the time. The girl married, and two years later Dr. Anthony was called to her bedside. She had had a stroke and died a few minutes after his arrival. Six months later the son, Harry, was dead of consumption. Dr. Anthony also arrived at his bedside just before he died. A year later Mr. Maxfield caught cold on a fishing trip and died soon after he returned home, with Dr. Anthony present.

"YOUR HUSBAND OR DAUGHTER MUST DIE—CHOOSE!"

Flammarion in his *Death and its Mystery* writes about a Parisian woman who woke up one morning in 1914 during a terrifying nightmare. A ghost was clutching her arm and saying, "Either your husband or your daughter must die. Choose!" She would not choose. Her husband and her daughter of seventeen were in perfect health. There was no reason why either should die.

But the nightmare and the specter's ultimatum haunted the woman. Mentally she debated—if she had to make a choice, whom would she condemn to death? She didn't want to think about her conflict, but it kept pounding on her mind. Finally she told herself that if she had to choose between husband and daughter, perhaps maternal love should be the stronger. Then she forgot about her dream.

Five days later her husband, who had never been ill, suddenly died after a brief illness. There had been no symptom of any disease—his heart had just stopped beating. It was not a case of being "scared to death" because he did not know of his wife's vision.

Flammarion does not say what the woman's reaction was to her husband's death. Did she believe that in some way she had condemned him to die because she was forced to choose between him and her daughter? Chances are that he already had his appointment in Samarra and that the vision dramatized not only his coming death but also some psychological problem that beset the woman. It is possible also that subliminal knowledge that he and not her daughter would die made her mentally choose him as the victim of the white-faced lady.

APPOINTMENT ON A STREET-CORNER

Danny Davis had no conscious awareness of his premonition, yet his strange behavior indicated that he was being controlled by an irresistible force from the future. Everything he did was a mystery to his friends and seemed to lead him to a foreordained death.

Davis was a television comedy writer and performer living in New York City. In February, 1970, he made arrangements with a producer, Peter George, to do a pilot series for a new situation comedy show. The setting was to be a store.

While discussing the show with George, Davis came up with a strange idea: He wanted a plate glass window put up in front of the store. The actor who played the role of proprietor would drive through the window in an automobile at the start of each program in the series. George and others involved in planning the show argued with Davis, pointing out that the device was not only costly but unnecessary. Davis was adamant about it, a fact that surprised the executives of the show. He had always been reasonable and easy to get along with.

Davis lived on Manhattan's East Side, on 65th Street near the East River. As a rule he never left his apartment in the morning, generally going out about 3:00 P.M. In the middle of February, two weeks after the discussion about the plate glass window, he made an appointment with a fellow comedian to meet in his (Davis') apartment at 11:30 A.M.

Davis was known to be very prompt in his appointments and regular in his habits. Yet for some mysterious reason he left his apartment about 11:15 that morning and started to walk west toward Third Avenue, about three long blocks away. Then he turned south toward 59th Street. When his guest arrived for the appointment, Davis was not there.

At 11:30 A.M. an auto driving north on Third Avenue went out of control as it approached 59th Street. The car knocked over a lamppost on the south side of the street, careened across the intersection, hit a woman, then hurtled over the curb and headed for a store window on the north side of the street.

Standing in front of the store was Danny Davis. The car carried him through the plate glass window and came to a stop inside the store, with Davis pinned under the wheels. He died twenty minutes later.

Why did Davis insist that his show open each week with an auto driving through the window of a store? What compulsion made him leave his apartment on the morning of an appointment, walk about a mile south and west, then station himself in front of a store window at the exact moment when a car leaped the curb and drove him through the plate glass window?

Somehow, unconsciously, he must have known about his appointment in Samarra.

CHAPTER THIRTEEN

Is Your Fate Irreversible?

Is every man's future fixed, without possibility of change? When you dream of death or other ill-fortune, is there any power that can save you or must you resign yourself to the inevitable?

If one's fate is irreversible, the Central Premonitions Registry and the Premonitions Bureau might just as well dismantle their offices and forget about early warning alerts. A thousand premonitions would not have prevented the Aberfan tragedy. The *Titanic* would somehow have sailed and sunk even if the British Government had threatened the White Star Line with heavy penalties. And every master or servant who encounters the white-faced lady, Death, has no recourse but to pack up and leave for Samarra, because he will not be able to escape her.

There is, however, a large body of evidence to the contrary. Many premonitions of disaster have come as warnings, and by taking heed the person threatened was able to avert tragedy. Often it is no more than a feeling of impending disaster but one that is so strong that immediate action is taken. A locomotive engineer in the caboose of a train once had a feeling of uneasiness that mounted to panic as the train tore down the tracks. Impulsively he stopped his train and found that someone had separated the rails on a section of track just ahead.

In other cases, the circumstances of the dreaded event have been so graphically dramatized in dreams and visions that the dreamer could change his fate by closely following the dream-scenario in his waking life and intervening at the strategic moment. This kind of premonition gives specific details, whereas the Samarra type omits important facts.

If Jeanne Gardner's Voice had told her the meaning of "Tirhan Tirhan," perhaps the assassination of Robert Kennedy could have been averted. If the young mother whose child died in the burning cradle had turned the mattress over when told to do so, she might have found the match at the bottom that set the child's bedclothes on fire. But the Voice neglected to add that the match was underneath.

Even in cases where, in retrospect, the future event seems to have been fated, there were often warnings, vague or specific, which for some reason were not heeded. The young mother, for example, who had previously seen the cradle burning in a vision, resolved to get rid of the matches but had neglected to do so. Perhaps, however, the death of the child was inevitable and the mother subconsciously felt it—along with the veiled warnings, the Voice had mournfully said of the child: "She'll never need it."

Similarly in the case of the Scotsman who dreamed of drowning in the lake: had the dream been more specific, picturing the exact details of the death scene, he could have cancelled his appointment with death.

HEAVY HANGS OVER THE BABY'S HEAD

The emotional bond between a mother and child is so strong that mothers often have dreams and hunches warning of death or injury to the child and they take prompt action. Louisa Rhine writes of a young mother who dreamed one night that a large chandelier hanging in the nursery had come down upon her sleeping baby and crushed the child to death. In the dream the hands of the clock on the dresser pointed to 4:35.

Terrified, she awoke and told her husband of the dream, but he thought she was unduly anxious and suggested going back to sleep. Unable to do so, she went into the other room and took the baby out of his crib and back into her room. Although in the dream the weather had been stormy with a strong wind blowing, in reality it was a calm night, and she wondered if her husband was right. But she was unwilling to take a chance.

Two hours later there was a resounding crash in the next room. The young mother and her husband leaped out of bed and ran into the baby's room. The chandelier had fallen and crushed the crib. The hands of the clock pointed to 4:35. Outside a storm had come up, and the rain pelted the window while the wind howled.

In an article written for the *Journal* of the American Society for Psychical Research, Ian Stevenson tells about another mother's warning premonition. She dreamed one night that she had walked into her little girl's room and had seen her sitting on the sill of the bay window, one leg hanging over the edge. As the child lost her balance and began to fall out, her mother woke up in terror and ran into the baby's room. The little girl was sleeping soundly.

In the days that followed, still worried about the dream, the mother never failed to look anxiously into Vivien's room when the child was there. She reassured herself that the girl was too small to climb up on the windowsill. One afternoon, however, she went into the yard to get some clothes hanging on the line, thinking that Vivien would follow her as she usually did. But when she turned around, the child was not there. She rushed upstairs and found Vivien perched precariously on the window ledge, in the same position as in the dream. As the baby started to fall, her mother caught her.

Somehow Vivien had managed to climb from her bed onto the windowsill. She was wearing the same clothes as in the dream—a playsuit and white sandals. Another corroborating detail was that the sun came into the west window of the baby's room at the exact angle as in the dream. It was the first time the child had ever climbed on the window.

The "voice" premonition of a mother is described by Maeterlinck in *The Unknown Guest*. A child who loved to watch the trains go by had left her house to walk to the nearby seashore. She had to cross through a "railway garden," a strip of ground between the sea-wall and the railway embankment, and just beyond the wall she would sit near the tracks and wait for the trains.

A few moments after the girl left, her mother heard a voice coming from nowhere: "Send for her back, or something dreadful will happen to her." In a fright, the mother told the servant to fetch the girl. A few moments after the maid took the girl away, a train ran off the track and crashed through the wall onto the very stones where the child had been sitting.

Another case involving a baby, a mother, and a nurse was described by Dame Edith Lyttleton, at one time president of the Society for Psychical Research. It was the nurse's custom each day to put the perambulator in the garden so that the child could have a couple of hours of fresh air. One morning the mother had a sudden feeling of apprehension, with an inner voice saying, "Don't put the baby near the shrubbery." Every few minutes the voice kept repeating the warning. The mother finally told the nurse to wheel the perambulator onto the lawn.

A short time later a bull escaped from a zoo, got into the garden of the next house, jumped over the hedge and charged into the shrubbery—through the exact spot where the perambulator had been standing a few moments before.

Mothers worry about big children, too—in this case a distinguished churchman. Since Cardinal Bembo couldn't be snatched away from danger by the maid, however, he got into trouble after his mother warned him to avoid a gentleman named Giusto. She had dreamed that Giusto wounded him in the right hand with a sword.

Cardinal Bembo was in Venice in the early part of the sixteenth century, where he was starting a lawsuit against one Simon Goro. Goro was sending his nephew Giusto to plead his case in court. Bembo's mother beseeched him to avoid any argument with Giusto that day, merely to give the judge the papers and leave the courtroom. Bembo promised his mother he would stay away from Giusto, but when he met the other man in court, and showed him the legal papers, Giusto snatched the papers from Bembo's hand and ran off.

Bembo, a man of peace, was not sure what to do. A short while later, however, he met Giusto on the Rialto and was incensed by the arrogance of the man. In a few moments they were quarrelling and each drew his sword. Giusto wounded Bembo in the second finger of his right hand, almost cutting it off.

Cardinal Bembo fortunately lived to tell the story of his mother's dream, and it is a safe bet that he paid heed to her warning premonitions in the future.

"STAY AWAY FROM THE THEATER"

A story in the *Journal* of the American Society for Psychical Research tells about a man who saved his two children and his sister by heeding a voice warning him that fire would destroy a theater. There was nothing ambiguous about this warning, no detail left out that would have been essential to averting this tragedy.

The year was 1877 and the man was a soldier on leave of absence. He promised to take his two boys to see a play and made reservations for the following evening, also arranging to meet his sister there. When he bought the tickets, something impelled him to examine the interior of the theater, including the stage and a rear exit. The following day a voice kept saying, "Do not go to the theater; take the boys back to school."

The soldier tried to ignore the voice, but as the day wore on, it grew stronger, more insistent. He described it later as "someone talking inside me." The Voice kept repeating, "Take the boys home, take the boys home." An hour before the performance, the man cancelled his reservations. His sister, however, attended the performance.

That evening the theater, filled with people, caught fire and more than three hundred persons died. The soldier reasoned that if he had been there with his sons, he would have taken them over the stage to escape by the rear exit he had examined. But they would have perished because the passage to the exit was blocked. The man's sister was also saved—she left before the performance was over and was home when the fire started.

The soldier must have sensed that something would happen, even before he heard the voice. It is rather unusual for a playgoer to inspect the interior of a theater with the object of escaping if a fire should break out. As it turned out, the soldier's premonition saved three members of his family from death.

The fear of drowning may be almost as great as that of death by fire. A New Jersey woman dreamed that her son had drowned. The next week her husband and boy were thrown into the middle of a lake when their canoe tipped over. The boy was saved—because his mother had insisted that he wear a life-preserver.

There are emotional links, of course, between members of a family other than the bond between parents and children, and these often bring on premonitions when there is danger of death in the water. In 1833 a boy named Adrian dreamed that he was captain of a ship and that his family on another ship were in danger of losing their lives. He told his dream to his brother Thomas.

Many years later, in 1880, Adrian was captain of the *British India* on its voyage from Sydney, Australia, to Rangoon, Burma. One night Adrian dreamed that another ship was in danger of sinking. At the end of the dream the word FAMILY appeared in bright letters. The next night he dreamed again of a ship in distress and got the impression that the other ship was due north of his own vessel. Although his officers objected, he altered course and two days later caught up with a ship that had just started to sink. Among those rescued was his brother Thomas. The name of the sinking ship was *The Family*.

Adrian was able to save his brother and the other passengers on *The Family* because he knew the direction in which to take the ship. Had that one fact been omitted from the dream, his premonition would have been to no avail.

THE WRONG SIDE OF THE ROAD

There are many premonitions of death in an automobile or other moving vehicle. Sometimes the warning is clear but is ignored. Louisa Rhine tells about a girl named Rosemary who felt strangely depressed on what should have been a festive occasion, the wedding anniversary of her parents. She refused an invitation to attend a dance. As her younger sister was leaving to go to the dance, she suddenly cried out, "Don't ride in that car, Frances. Ride in this one!"

Frances took her sister's advice at first and rode in the other car, a new model that had to be driven slowly. It was too slow for her, however, and she switched to the first car. Late at night she was killed in an accident. Could the warning have saved her life if she had heeded it, or was she fated to be killed in the second car?

Another man was saved from death in an auto because he saw in a vision the one detail that enabled him to avoid a collision. The incident is related by Arthur W. Osborn in his book *The Future Is Now*. The man, a music teacher, was looking over some Bach piano music, when the notes faded away and he saw the road on which he would drive to London later in the day. The vision showed a very sharp bend in the road and a car coming around the curve from the opposite direction, going very fast on the wrong side of the road.

Driving up to London in the afternoon, the music teacher approached the sharp curve he had seen in the vision. He pulled over to the other side of the road a split second before the car of his vision came hurtling at great speed around the curve but on the side the music teacher had just left. If the vision had revealed the accident without the detail of the sharp bend, he would probably have been killed.

Another possibly fatal accident was averted by the intervention of a warning voice. Jean Dupré, the French sculptor, was in a carriage with his wife, driving on a narrow mountain road along a steep cliff. A voice that seemed to come out of the mountain cried, "Stop!" Dupré and his wife both heard the voice, and they stopped the carriage and looked around. There was no one in sight. They resumed their journey and several times the voice called out, "Stop!"

Finally Dupré, sensing that something was wrong, got out of the carriage and saw that one left wheel, perilously close to the edge of the cliff, had lost its linchpin and was about to separate from the axle. In a few moments the carriage would have gone over the cliff.

THE LADY AND THE COACHMAN

An English gentlewoman in the early part of this century was very fond of her coachman, an old and trusted servant. She was quite disturbed, therefore, when she dreamed one night that he had fallen on his head in the road. She was planning in the morning to take her child to a relative in a town near London, and the coachman was going to drive the brougham. In the dream she saw the carriage turn into a street in Picadilly. Then, in a flash, the coachman had fallen out and landed on his head, his hat smashed in.

The next morning the woman, Lady Varden, told the coachman that she would go by train, but he insisted that he was all right and would take her. They left in the carriage and there was no mishap on the way to Woolwich, their destination. As they entered Picadilly on the return journey, she saw through the glass front of the brougham that the driver was leaning back in his seat, holding the reins tightly as if losing control of the horse. They turned into a street north of Picadilly, Down Street, as in the dream, and the dream sequence flashed into her mind.

As the coachman began to sway in his seat, she yelled for him to stop, then grabbed the child and jumped out. She called to a nearby policeman who rushed over and caught the man just as he toppled out of the coach. If he had hit the ground, he would have landed on his head.

The coachman had been ill but kept this knowledge from his employer. Thus the future was changed because of the graphic warning in the dream.

"RUN TO THE WINDOW, QUICK!"

The frequent warnings sent through voices and dead persons in dreams bring up the possibility that another entity may be intervening to prevent tragedy. When apparitions appear in dreams or visions, one wonders whether the subconscious mind is dramatizing the future or an actual spirit is present. The same holds true for a voice that suddenly comes out of nowhere. Is it an auditory hallucination, a projection of one's subconsious knowledge that danger threatens, or the voice of a concerned though disembodied entity?

In a case reported by the Society for Psychical Research, a man was sleeping on board his anchored yacht. Suddenly a voice spoke to him, warning that another ship was headed his way and would crash into his boat. The man went up on deck and looked out over the sea, but there was no other vessel in sight. He went back to his cabin and lay down once more, and as he dozed off the voice spoke again, this time more urgently. He jumped up and went back on deck. A fog had come up and through it he could see a ship headed directly at the yacht. He yelled at the captain of the other boat, who steered clear just in time to avoid an accident.

One of the strangest cases of a warning voice involved a dentist back in 1894. He was working on a set of teeth at his workbench, which was partitioned off from the rest of his office and at the farthest point from the windows. Suddenly a voice said, "Run to the window, quick!" Twice the voice gave the same command.

Finally, the dentist walked over to the window and looked out into the street, but nothing unusual was taking place. At that moment there was a deafening sound back in the laboratory. The copper vessel in which he vulcanized the rubber setting for false teeth had exploded and blown up into the ceiling. Although it weighed ten pounds, the explosive force was so great that it was embedded there. A safety valve supposed to open automatically at a certain degree of pressure was defective. The workbench was broken in two by the concussion.

"BEWARE OF THE TRIANGULAR DAGGER"

There are many weapons that can cause injury or death—knives, guns, explosives, etc.—and they generate fears both for ourselves and for others. Sometimes warning premonitions come in dreams that counsel us to use caution. A woman once had a strange dream in which she saw a hand grasping a pearl-handled revolver. The revolver fired and killed her daughter who on this night was sleeping on the living-room couch. The worried mother woke up and took her daughter to her room. In the morning she found a bullet in the pillow on the couch.

Sometimes the dream warns of one kind of accident but comes in the form of another. If the dreamer understands the symbolism, he may save himself and others from injury or death. Arthur Conan Doyle, in *The Edge of the Unknown,* writes about a young man just out of Cambridge who had a prophetic dream. On vacation in Switzerland, he dreamed one night that he was in the tropics, a country of sand and "shimmering heat and intensely blue sky." In the dream a huge man loomed in front of him holding a triangular dagger, and menaced him with it. The man then disappeared.

On the day following the dream, the young man went exploring an old abandoned tunnel. Here he found magnificent icicles hanging from the roof. One just above his head was very large, in the shape of a triangle that came to a very sharp point. The dream of the triangular dagger came to him, and he backed away quickly. The next moment the icicle crashed into the ground in front of him. He said later that it must have weighed about 200 pounds and would certainly have killed him if he had not remembered the warning dream in time.

THREE DREAMS PREDICT A MURDER

When two or more persons have the same dream of future tragedy on the same night, the diagnosis of a premonition seems reasonable. Yet, in psychic cases as in legal ones, the evidence may be circumstantial but misleading. Take Henry Armitt Brown's dream of a horrible street murder.

Brown was a law student living in New York City in 1865. One cold winter night he lay down at twelve midnight (the witching hour for dreams of future death), dozed off, and suddenly—in his sleep—heard loud noises and felt a strong hand clutching his throat. In his dream he was lying on cobblestones on a narrow New York street, a bearded, unkempt man with long hair on top of him. One powerful hand tightened over his throat while the other held a hatchet. Friends of Brown's were rushing to his rescue but before they could reach him, the hatchet struck his forehead and he felt his body relax as blood flowed over his face. He heard his friends weeping, but the sound died away.

Brown woke up, glad to be alive but still shaken by his dream. Later that day he met a classmate who told him that he, too, had fallen asleep at exactly midnight. He dreamed he was passing through a narrow street and heard murderous cries. He saw Brown on his back fighting the burly man, and rushed forward to save him. But it was too late—the hatchet came down on Brown's head and killed him instantly. Brown's other friends were there, too, and they wept bitterly. Then he awoke and his cheeks were wet with tears.

A week later Brown went to Burlington, New Jersey, to visit another friend. "My husband," the wife told him, "had such a horrible dream about you the other night. He dreamed a man killed you in a street fight. He ran to help you, but before he reached the spot, your enemy had killed you with a great club."

At this the husband interrupted, "Oh no, he killed you with a hatchet."

Fortunately, the dream-scene never did take place and Brown was spared the horror of being slain by the blow of a hatchet while his friends watched helplessly. The dreams are striking enough as examples of telepathic communication involving several minds. One could conjecture as to why Brown had such a dream in the first place. Perhaps, as a law student his thoughts were taken up with murder cases, which would also have been true of his classmate. What the associations of the third man were that led to the same dream are not known.

Not every vivid dream presages the future. When one has a dream of this kind in which death or other gloomy events seem to be indicated, the attitude should be one not of panic but of watchful waiting, with the option to intervene in some way if the dream seems about to come true. Fortunately, as in Brown's case, even the most realistic dreams of future sorrows may never materialize.

THE PROTECTIVE WALLS OF PRISON

If a dream warns that a friend or relative is bent on following a self-destructive course of action, one way to prevent it is to get the man confined in jail.

Nicholas Wotton, Dean of Canterbury, dreamed in the year 1553 that his nephew Thomas Wotton was going to be involved in a scheme that would ruin the Wotton family and cost the young man his life. The Dean was at first inclined to dismiss the dream, but it was one of the recurrent kind. He had the same dream the following night. Being a thoughtful man, he decided that this phenomenon should not be ignored.

Any other man would have taken direct action, that is, he would have pleaded with his nephew to abandon his plans. But nephews, like most other people, are headstrong and if his particular future was to be one of disgrace and death, something would have made him continue regardless of his uncle's entreaties. Nicholas Wotton realized this and decided on an ingenious trick that would change Thomas' future in spite of himself.

He wrote to Queen Mary of England and suggested that she "cause his nephew, Thomas Wotton, to be sent for out of Kent; and that the Lords of her Council might interrogate him in some such feigned questions, as might give a colour for his commitment into a favorable prison; declaring that he would acquaint her Majesty with the true reason of his request, when he should next become so happy as to see and speak to her Majesty."

Today uncles and other adults are not held in the same high regard as they were four hundred years ago, and it is not easy to arrange for a nephew's confinement in jail. Nicholas Wotton, however, was also ambassador to France and was respected by the Queen. Accordingly, Thomas Wotton, for his own good, was hustled off to prison.

The Queen soon learned of a plot to prevent her forthcoming marriage to King Philip of Spain. Among those opposing the marriage was Thomas Wotton, but during the plotting he was in jail. The conspirators, including their leader Sir Thomas Wyatt of Boxley Abbey, were apprehended, taken into custody, and executed.

Thomas Wotton, chafing in jail, was therefore saved from the gallows by the Dean of Canterbury's ingenuity. He realized that he too would have died if his uncle had not "so happily dreamed him into prison."

CHAPTER FOURTEEN

Oracles on the
Psychiatrist's Couch

High up in the Swiss Alps, on a mountain spur overlooking a pano-
ramic valley, three scholars dressed as priests are watching the re-
enactment of a scene from the days of classical Greece. Instead of
statuary and vases, there are books piled high around them. The air
is filled with the fragrance of incense. A modern oracle, who has just
put herself in a trance, sits on a tripod and stares with glazed eyes at
a crystal ball resting on a slab in front of her.

The oracle Jeane, dressed in flowing white robes, sees strange and
frightening events unfolding in the magic ball: mountains exploding
in torrents of fiery ash and billowing smoke, lands sinking from sight
as rivers rush over their banks, highways collapsing and carrying
autos into the depths of the earth, torrential rains with hailstones the
size of baseballs pouring down from darkened skies . . .

The oracle closes her eyes and sways as the odor of incense wafts
into her nostrils. She mumbles something. The three scholar-priests
—Freud, Jung, and Adler—lean forward and listen intently to a
stream of free-association words that tumble from her lips. They write
quickly in their notebooks, then begin to chant in unison:

> Mountains shall tremble, the frightened shall flee
> Parts of the country shall sink in the sea

> Forty days and nights will it rain
> Men in high places shall die or be slain.

Freud pauses and clears his throat. The other two scholar-priests wait.

"It is quite clear to me," says Freud, "that the oracle longs to return to the womb. The symbolism of raging waters, the terrifying world outside the mother's womb suggest the birth trauma. Since what you call premonitions, Jung, are obviously nonsense, the psychiatric, I may say more specifically the Freudian, interpretation is the correct one."

"Not so, my dear Freud," interrupts the scholar-priest Adler. "I agree with you that it is impossible to see the future except as a result of rational inference, and that such resort to magical thinking is a form of compensation for not reaching one's life-goals. However, it is not necessary to go back to the birth-experience. Let us instead consider the unrealistic demands of the patient. . . ."

The priest Jung, who has been puffing thoughtfully on his pipe, now speaks up.

"I agree with you reverend gentlemen that the prophet-patient may be suffering from a form of hysteria in which she projects her fantasies upon the outside world. However, the projection may stem from a physical cause within herself. The scene in the crystal ball may mirror some adverse condition in the lady's organism, some illness that has not yet manifested itself.

"There is yet another possibility that would partially corroborate both interpretations you gentlemen have made. We know that the dreamer is a resourceful dramatist who is able to create many plots and subplots symbolic of her psychic state, and weave them into a surrealistic whole. The young lady who sits here with her eyes closed, her body swaying to the rhythm of her subliminal consciousness, may have integrated the drama of her birth trauma and of her striving for compensatory goals with a projection of her physical condition—in a sense what you would call her organ inferiority, Adler.

"So we have three interpretations. There is possibly a fourth. The collective unconscious may indeed have brought forth memories of primordial cataclysms which have merged with her present psychophysical state to produce this stirring melodrama in the crystal ball.

And perhaps—who knows?—there are future catastrophes portrayed here which the young oracle has somehow divined. So you see, reverend gentlemen, that we are all correct. I believe, however . . ."

The scholar-priest Freud feels his blood pressure rising. "What you are saying, Jung, is mystical nonsense. The explanation is perfectly simple. The principle of wish-fulfillment in dreams and fantasies . . ."

Adler speaks up again.

"Reverend gentlemen, let us not quarrel. The phenomena known as premonitions, which both Freud and I disbelieve but which Jung seems to credit, may be a dramatization solely of the needs of the psyche. You reverend gentlemen would agree that before the public is made hysterical and possibly traumatized by the extravagant prophecies of popular seers, it would be well for medical scholars of our standing to examine the individual in question and make some kind of psychiatric determination."

Freud stares coldly at Adler, who annoys him no less than does Jung. He changes the subject: "Now as to the last line in the prophecy—'Men in high places shall be slain.' Obviously the young oracle, who has been disappointed by the real father, longs to kill the father figure. . . ."

The above scene never took place, of course. Most sensitives do not care to bring their predictions to the psychiatric couch. Yet, astonishing as is the overall record of foretelling the future, the prophetic sense might be sharpened immeasurably if our leading seers would allow psychologists and psychiatrists open to the idea of psychic phenomena to study their prophecies against the background of their emotional makeup. It might then be possible to separate what appears to be a valid forecast from one that reflects a political or religious bias, or a personal problem that can often stir up the prophetic sense but may also distort it or produce only fantasies.

An outstanding example of prophecy gone wrong is the panic created by the belief that California would break away from the mainland in April, 1969, and sink into the Pacific Ocean. The psychics were overstimulated by Edgar Cayce's trance-prediction many years before that this would be California's fate. And in one case, that of Mrs. Elizabeth Steen and her seven frightening visions of the catastrophe, the Jungian interpretation of physical disease would probably have been correct. Mrs. Steen died suddenly at the young age of twenty-nine, and chances are that her visions had been symbolic of a pathological condition that would lead to her untimely death.

General, oracle-like prophecies of a large-scale event are often unreliable, and even a layman can frequently spot the bias behind the prediction. Madame de Ferriëm's attachment to her native Germany colored her prediction of the outcome of World War I. Jeane Dixon's political and religious orientation obviously interferes with her predictions. And for many other authentic prophets their attachment to one of the two major political parties somehow dims the psychic aura surrounding the other one. So, too, in the religious sphere. Jeanne Gardner, a devout religionist, believes that America will be saved only when we return to prayers in public schools.

Without going too deeply into the emotional background of each psychic, a psychologist should be able to determine when a bias is the motivating force behind a prophecy. The cool prophets solve this problem to a large extent through self-analysis. Malcolm Bessent's work at the College of Psychic Science is an example. Eileen Garrett subjected her psychic gift to examination by detached professionals such as Ira Progoff, and she was constantly trying to understand and evaluate her talents.

But, as someone like Jung would be the first to point out, too much rationality and self-analysis can water down the prophetic sense, which seems to function best in a non-rational dimension. The passionate convictions of Jeane Dixon and Jeanne Gardner may help to generate their premonitions. But with more self-understanding, they could separate true prophetic impressions from those colored by opinions and needs.

This is an important consideration for those of you who will send predictions to the Central Premonitions Registry. Do you feel confident that your hunches are accurate or do they merely reflect your fears and desires? Does the scene portrayed in your dream seem to come from the future or is it merely a dramatization of a personal

problem? Surprisingly, it could be both, as Dr. Jule Eisenbud and
other psychiatrists have discovered in observation of their patients.
More of this later.

HOW PSYCHIATRISTS LOOK AT PREMONITIONS

What do psychiatrists in general feel about extrasensory perception, especially precognition? They, too, are not free of bias but
many have made an earnest attempt to understand psychic phenomena. Freud believed in telepathy and clairvoyance, although he did
not dwell much on the subject in his writings. After mulling over the
idea of precognition, he finally decided that it was not possible to see
the future, although he had some evidence for it in his practice.
Stekel believed strongly in the existence of telepathy but also tended
to ignore precognition. Adler seems to have discounted the whole
area of extrasensory perception.

Carl Jung, on the other hand, thought there were no limits to the
scope of the mind, and he cited many cases of precognition in his
experience. In 1910 there was a startling confrontation between
Freud and Jung that must have given the former food for thought.
While Freud was explaining why he believed precognition was impossible, Jung had a peculiar feeling. "It was as if my diaphragm
were made of iron," he wrote later, "and were becoming red-hot—
a glowing vault."

The next moment there was an explosive sound in the bookcase.
Jung, seizing advantage of the situation, said, "There, that is an example of a so-called catalytic exteriorization phenomenon."

"Oh come," said Freud, "that is sheer bosh."

"It is not," Jung replied. "You are mistaken, Herr Professor. And
to prove my point, I now predict that in a moment there will be
another such loud report."

Immediately there was another explosion in the bookcase.

Jung noticed many cases of precognition in his practice, which
dovetailed with his principle of synchronicity. A woman patient,
whose determinedly rationalistic approach to her problems kept her
from getting well, told him about a dream she had had in which
someone gave her a golden scarab. As she lay on the couch describing it, there was a gentle tap on the window. A large insect was trying

to get into the office. Jung opened the window and caught the insect as it flew in. It was a scaraboeid beetle, with a green gold color very close in appearance to that of a golden scarab.

Jung handed the beetle to the young woman, saying, "Here is your scarab." He wrote later: "This experience punctured the desired hole in her rationalism and broke the ice of her intellectual resistance. The treatment could be continued with satisfactory results." The woman's dream-precognition of the appearance of the scarab was thus combined with her own need for a breakthrough in the analysis. In her dream-drama, the "someone" who handed her the scarab was Jung himself, who in doing so presented the "gift" of improvement in the analysis.

In Jung's explanation the appearance of the beetle goes even deeper and indicates that the symbols of the ancients, including magical properties assigned to animals, were far more than mere superstition. The scaraboeid beetle was a rebirth symbol, so that the patient's dream also pictured the "rebirth" of her healthy personality in the analysis. An old Egyptian fable tells how a dead sun god changed himself into Khepri, the scarab, and was thus reborn.

But this does not account for the sudden appearance of the scarab-beetle itself at exactly the right moment. Did it, in its own wisdom, understand that it was a rebirth symbol and respond telepathically to the young lady's need? Why, as Jung asks, would it go against its normal habits and demand admittance to a darkened room?

Another of Jung's cases suggests that the ancient augurs and diviners who studied the behavior of birds for signs of the future may have been acting out of an unconscious wisdom. One of his patients, who had been well before, collapsed on the street on his way home and later died of heart failure. When he was brought home dying, his wife was already in a state of anxiety because a flock of birds had settled on her house. When her grandmother had died and later her mother, "a number of birds had gathered outside the windows of the death-chamber."

The man's wife evidently had a premonition that her husband would die, and the birds appeared as an objective symbol of what was to happen. Jung writes that in ancient Egypt the *ba* or soul was akin to a bird and that "some archetypal symbolism was at work" in the premonition. Again, did the birds know that they were symbols of approaching death and obligingly gather at the house in response to the coming event precognized by the man's wife?

In sophisticated societies today the behavior of birds is no longer taken as an augury of approaching death. Certainly the cool prophets would disdain this type of prophecy. Yet naive persons, perhaps closer to their unconscious and to the symbolism of the ancients, still regard bird behavior as prophetic. As recently as 1912, when the *Titanic* was sailing out of port, a passenger from Cornwall in England was highly disturbed by the crowing of a cock, suggesting to her that the ship would sink.

Since the patient usually looks upon the doctor as a mother or father figure, the emotional link between the two will often give rise to telepathic and precognitive dreams connected with the analysis. Sometimes the patient dreams of circumstances in the psychiatrist's life that would not be known to him, often of future situations that the doctor will face. Hollos, Servadio, and other psychiatrists have noticed that this is generally something the doctor is trying to suppress at the time.

Sometimes, as Dr. Joost Meerloo has pointed out, the analyst senses the future actions of his patients. Meerloo believes also that telepathy and precognition are often the patient's substitute for the usual flow of words. When oral communication seems to be getting nowhere, the patient attempts to reach his doctor through telepathic and precognitive dreams.

Dr. Ehrenwald and other psychiatrists have noticed that what is repressed in the patient's unconscious, such as hostile feelings, sometimes takes the form of extrasensory images. Death-portents are often tied to unconscious hostility, so that someone who dreams of a death that later does occur may feel that his wish was responsible. He probably has unconscious knowledge that death will come to the person in the dream, and when it happens he suffers feelings of guilt. He has been able to perceive the future death through the emotional link of his hostility.

Many psychiatrists are making an active study of ESP in their practice. Dr. Berthold E. Schwarz of New Jersey estimates that from 1955 to 1965 he consulted with 2,013 patients who were responsible for 1,443 telepathic events. Other psychiatrists are cooperating with the Central Premonitions Registry by watching for premonitions voiced by their patients that can later be verified.

Psychiatrists such as Schwarz, Riesenman, Greenbank, and others mentioned in this book are discovering that their patients are often becoming minor oracles as they try to work out their inner conflicts on the analytical couch.

SUBLIMINAL DRAMA IN THE DOCTOR'S OFFICE

In recent years perhaps the most interesting and meaningful studies of premonitions on the psychiatric couch have been those reported by Dr. Jule Eisenbud, a Denver psychiatrist who has also investigated and written about psychic photography in *The World of Ted Serios*. For Dr. Eisenbud the premonition is the starting point of an exciting subliminal drama that ties the future to the present and past and involves many characters.

Dr. Eisenbud's cases read like detective stories. The analyst himself is the sleuth who traces the premonition to its roots in the patient's psyche. But the psychiatrist is also one of the two chief characters in the mind-drama. The patient's premonition is intended to call to the attention of the doctor something in the dynamics of their relationship. And the doctor's needs, sensed by the patient, are a sub-theme that accompanies the main thread of the psycho-story.

Nothing in the premonitory dream is irrelevant, for the psyche is a skilled dramatist who leaves no loose ends. Sometimes there are gaps that puzzle the doctor-detective. He has uncovered all the secondary characters in the play—the mother, father, sister, or others who are important in the life of the patient. But something is missing. And into the breech steps another of the doctor's patients who has intruded into the drama with his own needs that happen to dovetail with those of the doctor and the first patient. Finally the doctor fits all the pieces of the puzzle together, and the mystery of the dream-premonition is solved.

What of the future event itself? How did the patient come to dream of it or visualize it? How does it happen to fit so neatly into the psychiatric picture? Dr. Eisenbud points out that many psychiatrists, when they have satisfactorily analyzed a patient's premonitory dream, tend to ignore the fact that the dream does come true, since they are interested only in the patient's thoughts and their significance. He mentions Wilhelm Stekel's patient who kept dreaming of the winning number in lotteries. Dr. Stekel discovered *why,* from the analytic point of view, the woman had these dreams but he slighted the fact that the dreams did come true.

"It is as if," writes Dr. Eisenbud, "Stekel had seen one of his patients flying unaided over the rooftops, only to pass the occurrence off as completely understandable in the light of the deep unconscious significance to the patient of this highly symbolic act."

So the event that has been foreseen becomes important in its own right as an example of the uncanny power of the subliminal mind. And when tied to the drama of the psyche, it takes on an even greater significance. There was the case, for instance, of Eisenbud's patient who dreamed he was in bathing trunks in a hotel lobby, where he had gone for a swim.

The dreaming mind finds nothing unusual about swimming in the lobby of a hotel. In the first dream-scene, the patient had an argument with his mother-in-law, who tried to talk him out of going swimming. In the next scene he was wearing swimming trunks in the lobby of a New York hotel, either the old Pennsylvania or the Wellington. He took the elevator to the top floor and was let off in a service corridor, where he was afraid of being stranded.

The morning after the patient's dream, a crew of workmen was cleaning the interior of the elevator in the Pennsylvania Hotel, when a drum of cleaning fluid blew up on the top floor. The water main burst on one of the lower floors and flooded the lobby with five inches of water. At the time of the incident, the Cornell University swimming team was staying in the hotel.

The elements of the later hotel scene were present in the patient's dream: his anxiety at being stranded on the top floor of the hotel, where the explosion did in fact occur; his wearing swimming trunks in the lobby which later did resemble a swimming pool; and the presence in the hotel of the college swimming team, a link to his dream.

Why, asked Dr. Eisenbud, did the patient pick this specific event to dream about? The day before the patient had been very disturbed during the psychiatric session. He had outlined a grandiose scheme for a new kind of X-ray machine, but Dr. Eisenbud had not responded to the idea, and the patient interpreted this as indifference. Thus in the dream-drama the analyst becomes the antagonist.

"The top floor [of the hotel]," writes Eisenbud, "represents the patient's head or mind and . . . his anxiety refers to his feelings at being left stranded on the morning before the dream, when I had declined comment on the ideas with which he was bursting." The hero of the drama, the patient, protests: "You cannot leave me stranded, bursting with this stuff on my 'top floor.' I'll explode."

The "explosion" does of course occur in reality, and this leads to the entrance of another character—the patient's brother-in-law. Years before this man had gone into a career that his mother (the patient's mother-in-law) had disapproved of, and had made an outstanding success. But the brother-in-law had at the height of his career died suddenly from a brain tumor, developing, in Eisenbud's words, "a fatal explosion on the 'top floor.' " He had also been in analysis at the time, so the dreamer's situation was even more perilous.

The mother-in-law's role is now linked to that of the doctor. She had disapproved of her son's career; the doctor seems to disapprove of the patient's scheme for an X-ray machine. The dreamer is saying that, like his brother-in-law, he will be a success anyway, despite the doctor. But the brother-in-law died from the "explosion" and the patient is in jeopardy.

The patient turns to the psychiatrist to save him from disaster. Eisenbud, a Freudian, now brings another concept into the dream related to a childhood conflict. The "explosion" takes on another meaning. "If you abandon me," Eisenbud's dreamer is saying in effect, "leave me stranded and about to burst on the 'top floor,' I'll not be able to contain myself. I cannot endure this tension any more than I could endure the tension in my bladder as a child. I must let go, 'burst a main.' "

Thus several psychic plots emerge in the dream, all related to the dreamer's present problem. The hero-dreamer is hanging on the edge of a cliff, as it were, at the mercy of the antagonist-doctor. But he still has an ace up his sleeve, and now the spotlight shifts to the analyst's problem, which the patient has telepathically divined and has cunningly brought into the dream. On the night of the dream, Eisenbud had been conducting an experiment with another patient, who tried to pre-view the headlines of *The New York Times* two days in advance. The experiment had been a failure.

The dreamer has, says Eisenbud, "hijacked" the task given to the other patient, and in doing so has drawn even in his battle with the doctor-antagonist. Eisenbud writes that he, too, was excited by "revolutionary visions" of piercing the wall of the future, as the dreamer had been excited by his idea of an X-ray machine. But Eisenbud's experiment had failed, and he, too, was "left stranded on the 'top floor.'"

The dreamer is telling the analyst that he will make a deal with him. If Eisenbud wants the future headlines of a newspaper, the patient will give it to him. In return the doctor must approve of the patient's idea for an X-ray machine, also a "revolutionary way of seeing." Thus the anxiety-allaying feature of the dream is that "the patient may expect from this bargain the encouragement he needs and perhaps a reprieve from the punishment unconsciously feared."

Now we know why the patient picked the hotel incident: it dramatizes his problem of the moment for which he seeks a solution that may be provided by the analyst. Thus the dream ties his present problem to a future event and brings in conflicts from the past that have not yet been resolved. Altogether an extremely well constructed dream-drama, with the striking symbolism of the "explosion," "swimming," "burst water main," and other elements.

Each character has his or her significant place on the dream-stage to work out the chief character's conflicts: the doctor-antagonist, the mother-in-law, the brother-in-law, the shadowy influence of the patient's own mother and father, and the "extras" in the hotel. The analyst-detective painstakingly uncovers clues to the dreamer's problem, then finds the main link in the doctor-patient conflict.

Perhaps every precognitive or premonitory dream, if so carefully unveiled, would also reveal *why* the psychic chose a particular event in the future to dream about. It would probably have a dynamic relationship to a personal problem at the time, with emotional links to individuals close to the dreamer as well as those involved in the later event.

In another of Eisenbud's cases, a young lady dreamed that a plane leaving Philadelphia had crashed, killing her roommate who was on the way to join her fiance in the Midwest. The next day a plane did crash as it left the Philadelphia airport, but it was a later plane, not the one on which her roommate was a passenger. The woman's dream precognized the accident and—in her unconscious—placed her roommate on the doomed plane.

The death-dream of Eisenbud's patient seemed to be motivated by feelings of ambivalence toward the other girl and her fiance. On the one hand, she was angry because she had been "abandoned" by the roommate, who was leaving her for a man who would now be the central interest in her life. On the other, there was the "deeply galling fact that Nora [the roommate] had got the man whom [the] patient had earlier had fantasies of winning." The easiest way to get back at both antagonists was by "killing" the girl on the plane.

In a sense, however, the dream-drama was like a waking fantasy in which the girl might imagine horrible things happening to someone who has betrayed her. She knows she doesn't really "mean it" but it helps to discharge her hostile feelings. In the dream, too, the girl may have known subliminally that her roommate would be safe because it was another plane that would crash. She would not have to feel guilty later. Thus it was safe for her to pick out the events of the next day and manipulate them according to her desires.

The case of Eisenbud's bird-watcher again shows the intimate connection between the present problem and the future event. A man woke up one morning feeling certain that if he went to the park he would catch sight of a rare bird called the worm-eating warbler. This species generally appeared in the park no more than one day a year. After ten minutes of searching, the man caught sight of the bird. A year earlier this same man had awakened with a feeling that he would see another rare bird—a kingfisher—and did so as he was driving on Long Island, New York.

This case is interesting enough as an example of precognition. But the psychiatrist, as detective-reporter, must go further and ask certain questions. Why precognition about a bird? "Conjuring up" the bird was an attempt, in Eisenbud's words, to "conjure up" his mother. The patient had felt abandoned because his wife was out of town for several days and he was left alone in his apartment. Then, just before the incident of the worm-eating warbler, the maid had failed to show up to make his breakfast. To complete the abandonment of mother-figures, his secretary had to leave town because of a family emergency. "Small wonder," writes Eisenbud, "that he had to fall back on the infantile illusion that one could conjure up the mother by sheer force of inner need, the last desperate device of the forlorn child."

By making use of his unconscious knowledge that the bird would appear, the patient reverted to the "omnipotence" of the child and believed he could cause the bird to appear, thus "creating" the future. The bird obliged by being in the right place at the right time, defying all the odds, just as Jung's scaraboeid beetle and death-omen birds came in response to the unconscious needs of the women involved.

But why, specifically, a bird? Again we go back to the symbolism of the ancients. In addition to representing death and the soul in Egyptian mythology, Eisenbud points out that archaeological and historical evidence shows that in early cultures the bird was "equated at once with the nursing mother and the hope of immortality." Thus the premonition that a particular bird would appear was tied to the patient's emotional need at the time.

Although Eisenbud stressed the Freudian interpretation of what he calls "psi-conditioned" cases in analysis, other interpretations are possible—Jungian, Adlerian, or what have you. A dream can be analyzed on many levels, and the dreamer always cooperates by providing elements acceptable to any school of psychotherapy. The essential fact, at least for this book, is that precognition does take place. The psychiatric dimension proves that premonitions can be traced to motivations in the unconscious and that emotional links are forged to the future event. Further, the choice of event is no accident but is selected from an infinity of future happenings known to the subliminal mind.

Apart from the psychiatric scene, one experiment conducted by Eisenbud was of particular interest—the attempt to "see" headlines that would appear later in a newspaper. There are many times when a psychic envisions not the actual future event but an account of it that will appear in the press, which he then dramatizes. Although Eisenbud's experiment failed, it did succeed in effect when his other patient "hijacked" the test and dreamed of swimming in the lobby of the Pennsylvania Hotel.

CHAPTER FIFTEEN

Seeing Tomorrow's Headlines—
Yesterday

One day early in November, 1952, shortly before the presidential election, I went with a friend to visit Frances, a sensitive who lived in a cabin in the Malibu mountains of Southern California. In the evening the three of us sat near the fire while Frances described the impressions that were coming to her.

An atmosphere of this kind often brings out the psychic in a person without paranormal abilities, such as myself. The stillness of the night, the cool fresh air, the softly crackling logs in the fireplace all played a part. I heard strange sounds and got telepathic messages from both Frances and my friend Lloyd.

Suddenly a headline passed in front of my mind's eye: EISEN-HOWER WINS. Although I had planned to vote for Adlai Stevenson in the election, I knew at that moment that General Eisenhower would be the next president.

There was nothing remarkable about picking Eisenhower to win at this time; he was the overwhelming favorite. As a Stevenson follower, however, I was looking for a minor miracle that would put my candidate in office. Seeing the headline that would be out a few days later dashed my hopes. I knew with the certainty that comes of psychic glimpses that the election would go to the hero of World War II.

More noteworthy are the many cases, some of which have already been described, of persons who "see" verbatim newspaper articles that have not yet been written or photos that will not appear in the press for days or weeks, sometimes months or years. Occasionally a scene from a later television program flashes into the mind of a psychic, as with Mrs. Milden's vision of the little boy with the long fringe of hair who was seen on the television screen two days after the Aberfan coal slide. Often a psychic who is clairaudient tunes into a "pre-hearing" of a radio announcement that has not yet been prepared and will not be broadcast for a day or more.

Included in this category of psychic experiences are "reading" passages in books that have not yet been opened, viewing scenes from moving pictures or plays that have not been attended or perhaps not even written, and—in at least two cases—anticipating in dreams a future part in a stage or film production. The psychic is drawn to this experience of the future by the same kinds of links forged in other premonitions or previsions.

The sense involved may depend on which—seeing, hearing, touching, even smelling—is the most acute in ordinary circumstances. An artist is likely to visualize snapshots, press photos, or reproductions of paintings. One artist, for example, painted in her dream a picture of a landscape that was described in a book she read later.

One of the strangest cases involving possible precognition of a future newspaper article was that of Barney and Betty Hill, a couple whose alleged encounter with a flying saucer was described by John G. Fuller in *The Interrupted Journey*. Returning by car from a vacation in Canada one evening, the couple noticed a peculiar-looking craft hovering overhead and got out to take a closer look. After that they appeared to have blacked out for two hours and later had nightmares about being taken aboard a spaceship and interrogated by visitors from another planet.

A psychiatrist hypnotized them separately and they gave identical descriptions of their dream-experience. It was never decided whether the dreams were replays of a real event or subliminal fantasies telepathically shared. One item, however, could possibly be explained as precognition. Mrs. Hill said that a physician aboard the spaceship had shown her a map of the heavens and the area the craft had come from. She sketched the map for the psychiatrist. A year later, in April,

1965, a similar map appeared in the *New York Times,* designating the origin of mysterious radio signals from outer space.

In her altered state of consciousness, either in dreams or under hypnosis, Mrs. Hill may have had a psychic look at a newspaper map that would not be printed for another year.

PRE-VIEWS OF DISASTERS IN THE NEWS

A friend of writer J. B. Priestley claimed that he often had previsions of "jet-age" disasters, with the name of the victim, a well-known personality, superimposed as a headline over the scene. Three weeks before the Duke of Kent died in an air crash during World War I, this man "saw" the plane hitting the ground and over it the words "Duke of Kent." Two days before a film star died in an auto crash, a vision of the accident appeared to the psychic in the form of a moving picture. Over the scene was a headline with the name of the star, "Bonar Colleano."

Priestley's friend may have had a psychic sensitivity to death by accident and with it an understandable emotional link to the fate of famous persons. His experiences would have made notable copy for the London Premonitions Bureau if it had been in existence at the time.

In another Priestley case, described in his book *Man and Time,* a woman dreamed about a train accident that was later mentioned in a radio broadcast. In the dream the woman and her husband were riding in what seemed to be a "motor-coach train"—they could see the engine and driver through a window as though they were in a bus. The train suddenly stopped and the driver got out and looked under the wheels, whereupon the train started up again and went off without the engineer, finally coming to a "bumpy halt."

The woman woke up and told the dream to her family. Everyone laughed because it was obvious that trains do not behave so erratically. But that evening during a radio program, the announcer told about a "very curious thing" that had occurred in the south of France. The events of the dream had actually taken place, and an engineerless train had gone off by itself. The woman had taken the facts of the radio broadcast and dramatized them. The combination "motor-coach" and "train" may have been related to something personal in the woman's life that was symbolized in the dream.

News articles, headlines, and photos of other jet-age disasters involving ships, planes, and dirigibles have been seen weeks in advance by psychics. In *Some Cases of Prediction,* Dame Edith Lyttleton tells about a woman who had a vision of one ship colliding broadside with another. At the same moment a voice said that the picture would appear in the London *Daily Mail* in just two weeks. Two weeks later the woman opened her newspaper and there was the photo exactly as she had seen it in her dream.

The crash of the dirigible R-101, which had been previsioned by Eileen Garrett years in advance, also figured in two more of Dame Lyttleton's cases. Several weeks before the accident, a lady had a dream in which she saw the dirigible dive to earth, burst into flames, and then explode. She had the same dream a week later. On October 5, 1930, the R-101 crashed at Beauvais on its way to India. Just as the scene had been pictured in the dream, a newspaper photo showed the ship hitting west of a hill with its nose slightly down.

On October 3, two days before the accident, another woman dreamed of a dirigible crashing into a hill and bursting into flames. In the dream was an officer on horseback with a small company of soldiers. The day after the crash a photo of the disaster scene appeared in the London *Times,* showing a mounted officer in the foreground.

DEATH IN SPACE—OR A DRAMATIC RETURN?

Fortunately, the accident to *Apollo XIII* does not have to be included with fatal jet-age disasters that have been sensed in advance. Yet who would have predicted during the perilous return journey that the astronauts would be back on earth a few days later, alive and well and the toast of the world?

On April 14, 1970, the day after the oxygen tank burst as the craft was nearing the moon, Alan Vaughan sat in his bedroom and meditated. What did the immediate future hold for the three men trapped two hundred thousand miles from home? A vision came to him, and he recorded it in a letter of April 15 to the Central Premonitions Registry:

> Yesterday, when I heard that the Apollo 13 astronauts were in very serious trouble, I meditated on whether or not they would return safely.
> They will return safely and get a tremendous heroes' welcome. I had an image of them being showered by confetti and, oddly, the

astronauts were holding flags or banners. It may be that a photo in the press will depict them like that.

On May 2 there was a picture in the *New York Times* showing the men being greeted by enthusiastic crowds in Chicago. As in the vision, they were covered with confetti. But there were no flags in their hands.

Vaughan turned to the next page and there, directly behind the first picture was another photo of three men holding flags. In his vision he had combined the two pictures and put the flags in the hands of the astronauts. This "telescoping effect" was also evident in Vaughan's prediction of trouble for *Apollo XII* that actually developed during the flight of *Apollo XIII*.

"HEARING" THE FUTURE

If a psychic is absorbed in public affairs, it may be natural that he or she will "see" newspaper articles and photos well in advance of their publication dates, and also "hear" future radio newscasts. Lady Rhys-Williams of London was a professional woman with a keen interest in government and social welfare. She held several important posts and was an economist.

On January 17, 1964, Lady Rhys-Williams turned on her radio at 4 A.M. and heard a Voice of America broadcast. The news was disturbing. There had been riots in Atlanta, Georgia, with fighting between members of the Ku Klux Klan and a crowd of blacks. According to the account, the police arrived and charged into the crowd. There were many injuries and several arrests were made.

Later in the morning she told her daughter about the broadcast, but there was no mention of the riots in the newspapers that day, nor on the following day, January 18. More than a week later, on January 26, Lady Rhys-Williams heard a BBC announcement at 8 P.M. that riots had broken out in Atlanta. The next day several newspapers featured articles about the rioting. Puzzled, Lady Rhys-Williams wrote to the Voice of America and received a copy of the *New York Times* of January 19, describing the scene in Atlanta as she had heard it on January 17.

The riots had occurred on the evening of January 18, about forty-eight hours after Lady Rhys-Williams had "heard" the Voice of America broadcast. There had indeed been a broadcast about the riots, but at a much later time. With her concern about social problems, it is possible that Lady Rhys-Williams sensed that the riots would break out, then pre-heard the Voice of America account.

Sometimes her psychic experience involved two media—radio and the press. On February 24, 1964, Lady Rhys-Williams thought she heard an early morning announcement that Archbishop Makrios had asked General de Gaulle to mediate a dispute in Cyprus. She later told this news to her daughter and the chauffeur. But neither the newspapers nor the radio said anything that day about such a request. Two days later, however, on the twenty-seventh, a political correspondent wrote that in an interview with a Paris newspaper on the twenty-sixth, the Archbishop said he would like de Gaulle to mediate.

Lady Rhys-Williams "heard" the news twenty-four hours in advance of the interview with Archbishop Makrios and dramatized a meeting between the Archbishop and General de Gaulle. Although no mention is made of a radio broadcast, it is probable that the early morning French news bulletin, which Lady Rhys-Williams thought she had heard, did feature it later.

As an economist Lady Rhys-Williams had a penchant for seeing nonexistent articles and photos relating to her specialty. She would act on the information, only to discover that the article she thought she had "read" was not there. This would often cause her embarrassment, but invariably the article would appear, the next day or a few days later.

In 1957 she "saw" a paragraph in the London *Times* about a heavy drop in the earnings of small farmers. She immediately sat down and wrote a letter about it to the Prime Minister, but when she opened the newspaper to clip out the article, she couldn't find it. Mystified, she sent the letter without it. The following day the article appeared in the *Times,* and a puzzled Prime Minister may have wondered how she was privy to news that had not yet been announced.

A year later she "saw" another paragraph in the *Times,* accompanied by a photograph of a three-bedroom house that could be built for a thousand pounds. At the time she was chairman of a town council and was concerned about the high cost of homes. She asked her secretary to clip out the article and picture and show them to the chief architect. The secretary combed the newspaper but found no such items. The next day the news story appeared along with the picture of a home with a sloping roof on one side—just as Lady Rhys-Williams had seen it in the imaginary photo.

THE BROWN BEAR IN THE BASKET CHAIR

Ann Jensen's crystal ball often acts as a therapeutic aid, mirroring the problems of people who come to her and projecting symbolic pictures that may give answers. One day a mother brought her fourteen-year-old boy to Mrs. Jensen's home in Dallas, Texas, for some crystal-ball therapy. The boy had been having problems in school. Perhaps the crystal ball, in its mysterious way, would come up with a suggestion.

While the boy's mother waited in the next room, Mrs. Jensen and her charge sat in front of the crystal ball and waited. The surface of the ball clouded over, the mist then dissipated, and there—sprawled in a basket chair—was a large brown bear. What did this bear have to do with the young boy? Had he been reading a story about a brown bear? The lad shook his head no. Had he been to a zoo recently? No. Then why the bear? Mrs. Jensen and the boy stared hard into the ball, but the bear just sat there and stared back.

Mrs. Jensen called the boy's mother, and she came into the room and looked at the bear. Thus another person besides Mrs. Jensen could see the bear in the crystal ball, and neither one understood what the picture meant.

Mrs. Jensen took her guests to their car, then walked back to her porch slowly, puzzling over the mystery. She picked up her morning newspaper and read on the front page about a bear that had been found in a back yard by a boy. According to the story, the boy kept insisting the bear was in the yard, but his mother paid no attention to him. Finally she went outside, saw the bear and screamed.

In the photo over the article, a brown bear was sitting in a basket chair, in the identical sprawl of the bear in the crystal-ball scene. In some way the boy who came to Mrs. Jensen for help had identified with the other boy, and the picture of the sprawling brown bear was in his subconscious mind. With this mind-to-mind linkage Mrs. Jensen was able to conjure up the scene in the crystal ball.

What psychological significance there was for the lad who had trouble in school was not apparent. It is rare, however, that two persons will see in a crystal ball the image of a photo on the front page of a newspaper.

The story of the snapshot, although a newspaper was not involved, was in some respects similar to that of the brown bear. Again a mother and her fourteen-year-old son, Pete, were the chief characters. Friends of Mrs. Jensen, they asked her to look into the crystal ball and read their future.

Mrs. Jensen studied the ball for awhile and then saw scenes that appeared to be in Mexico, perhaps Acapulco. Pete was standing on a hill near a body of water, alongside a burro decorated with flowers. Mrs. Jensen thought it meant that they would be taking a trip to a southern country. The other woman also saw the crystal ball scene.

Some time later the woman's married daughter wrote that she was planning a trip to the Virgin Islands and asked if her mother would take care of her baby while she was gone. If so, she could take Pete along on the trip. Pete spent a week in the Virgin Islands. When he returned, he brought pictures that had been taken during his stay.

In one of the photos Pete was standing by a burro which was decorated with beautiful flowers around its ears, reins, and saddle. The photo was almost identical with the one that had appeared in the crystal ball.

THE ENGAGEMENT PICTURE

Sometimes there is a pre-view of a personal item that will appear in a future issue of a newspaper, such as the announcement of an engagement or wedding. The psychic's link to the article may only be the fact that she is happy about the news. This is particularly true of women, who take delight in the marriage plans of other women. A lady bank teller once "saw" a newspaper photograph of an engagement picture, yet at the time she didn't even know the young lady who was engaged.

The girl's father was in a cheerful mood when he came into the bank. His daughter Barbara had just been engaged and he was looking forward to the announcement and to the wedding itself. As he passed his bankbook to the lady teller behind the window, the latter smiled and congratulated him on the forthcoming marriage.

"You know," she said, beaming, "that was a beautiful picture of Barbara in last Sunday's newspaper."

The man was puzzled. What picture? The announcement would not appear until May 23, and it was only the thirteenth. But the teller insisted that she had seen the picture along with the announcement in the May 9 issue. What was even more puzzling was that she had not even known that the man had a daughter. Yet she knew the girl's name and described her appearance, including the unusual hair style in the picture.

She said also that the photo had appeared in the second column of pictures, "just off center." There had been one photo in the second column of the May 9 issue, but it was not of Barbara. The engagement picture had been taken on May 11, two days before Barbara's father came into the bank.

Barbara's engagement picture finally appeared in the May 23 issue of a Florida newspaper—in the second column of pictures, just as the teller had "seen" it. It was an exact replica of the psychic photo, including the unusual hair style. As for its position on the page, the society editors had made a random choice of where to put it.

"SMELLING" THE FUTURE

Sometimes a psychic will experience well in advance the events of a play or motion picture, even the contents of a book. In *Psi and Psychoanalysis,* Dr. Eisenbud tells about a patient who dramatized a personal problem in a dream that was later duplicated in a movie. In the dream a "burly thug" came into the man's bedroom and had sexual relations with his wife. The dreamer grabbed a hammer and attacked the intruder with it, but his blows lacked force and he felt "like a baby, weak and uncoordinated." The dream-villain just laughed at him and began to approach him menacingly.

That evening the patient decided to see a movie and after some deliberation went to a performance of *Major Barbara.* Along with the feature film there was a comedy from the silent screen era, in which a baby picks up a hammer and hits the head of a large villain who is sleeping beside him. The sleeper pays no attention to the baby's weak blows. Dr. Eisenbud analyzes the psychological conflicts behind the dream, but of interest to us is the subliminal process that led the dreamer to the very theater where the events of his dream were being reenacted.

In another case the sense of smell was tied to a later scene in a film. A woman was watching a newsreel when she smelled the odor of a substance that had been used in the biology laboratory when she was an undergraduate years before. The odor stayed with her for fifteen minutes, well into the next film, a short feature showing a study of fish in the ocean. One of the actresses opened a bottle containing a specimen and made a wry face as she held it to her nose. At this point the psychic smell went away.

The same woman, who was an artist, had earlier dreamed of looking at the show window of an art store, a scene that was exactly duplicated in another film she saw later. Artists think visually and may be subliminally aware of the background of a later movie sequence, painting a picture of it in their dreams.

Another woman artist "pre-viewed" a passage of a book she had not yet read. In her dream she was in a summer cottage, painting a landscape of a familiar scene nearby but somehow "much more sweeping and magnificent" in the dream than in reality. While she worked, she felt compelled to use "blacks" and "yellows" to reproduce the sky, and tried to "paint the effect of dark clouds with sunshine or sulphurous yellows bathing the scene." The effect was of a storm brewing, with a deep, odd yellow light of approaching sunset.

Two days later she went into a bookstore and impulsively bought a novel, Malcolm Lowry's *Under the Volcano*. While thumbing through it at home, she came across this passage: "The leaves of cacti attracted with their freshness; green trees shot by *evening sunlight* might have been weeping willows tossing in the *gusty wind* which had sprung up; *a lake of yellow sunlight* disappeared in the distance . . . But there was *something baleful* now about the evening. *Black clouds* plunged up to the south. *The sun poured molten glass* on the fields . . ." (italics mine). Thus the dreamer saw with an artist's eye what she would later read.

An actor or actress would be more inclined to dramatize what he or she psychically pre-views from books, newspaper articles, or moving pictures. Sometimes they act out in their dreams the roles they will later play, even when such parts are at the time completely unfamiliar to them. Priestley tells about a girl in a London drama group who had such a dream. The director had announced that the next play would be by the Italian dramatist Pirandello. The girl had never heard of Pirandello or seen any of his plays.

That night she dreamed she was in Italy, a country she had never visited, and found herself in a "long, narrow room with arches along one side, leading into a rose garden." Men and women in medieval dress were seated at a table, eating. She walked toward the rose garden, where a bat flew toward her. She caught the bat and held it in her hand. The next morning the actress went to the library and took out a volume of Pirandello's plays. In the very first one she read, there was a description of the scene she had dreamed about. One of the stage directions was for a bat to fly into the scene.

Even more striking were the dreams of Mrs. M, the actress-psychic who had had premonitions of the trouble on *Gemini VI* and of the flash fire that killed three astronauts in January, 1967. It will be recalled that she worked these premonitions into a dream-sequence in which her daughter was a girl astronaut, a role the young lady was later given in a television series. Mrs. M was also psychically sensitive to her own work as an actress and had many dreams of parts she would play later.

AN ACTRESS DREAMS OF FUTURE ROLES

From 1954 to 1965 Mrs. M had 1,300 precognitive dreams, which were studied by Professor Hans Bender of the University of Freiburg in Germany. Among these were several in which she dramatized scenes from a film she was to act in two years later. At this time she had no knowledge of such a film and what her part would be in it. Dr. Bender described these dreams in an article about the "Gotenhafen Case," which appeared in the October, 1966 issue of *International Journal of Psychiatry*.

The film, *Night Fell Upon Gotenhafen,* went into production late in 1959. In the movie a group of farm women fought their way to a ship in the seaport of Gotenhafen, near Danzig, during World War II. The ship was hit by Russian torpedoes in the Baltic Sea, and most of the refugees were drowned.

On September 15, 1957, two years before the first scenes of the film were shot—and before the script was even written—Mrs. M had what Dr. Bender calls her "baby" dream. In this dream she was swimming with several women and their babies when one of the babies swam underwater, and Mrs. M was afraid the child would die. In a scene from the picture filmed two years later, the farm woman played by Mrs. M had a newborn child. The baby died during the torpedoing, and Mrs. M then jumped from a lifeboat into the water.

On October 10, 1957, Mrs. M had her "swimming" dream. A cameraman was trying to photograph her as she swam but she refused, thinking, "It is not worth it." In the actual film, two years later, the character played by Mrs. M was drowned when she leaped into the water during the torpedoing. As Mrs. M sank beneath the surface, pulled down by a diver outside camera range, an underwater camera recorded her descent. This sequence was filmed three times, leaving the actress in a state of exhaustion. The scene was later cut from the film, and the dream had correctly predicted that Mrs. M's effort was indeed "not worth it."

On April 29, 1958—about a year and a half before the first scenes were shot—Mrs. M had her "ship's cook" dream. In the dream it was early evening and she was on a small ocean steamer. The passengers were resting in deck chairs, and she was having a "pleasant and animated" conversation with the ship's cook.

One evening in September, 1959, during the filming at sea, Mrs. M was reminded of this dream. It was very hot, and the actors and crew were lying on deck chairs on the steamer, which was actually a chartered fishing boat. Mrs. M sat next to an actor who had recently introduced her to a friend of his, the ship's cook. The latter was a kindly man who attended to Mrs. M whenever she would come on the boat exhausted after hours of swimming in the sea.

The fishing boat itself appeared in a dream on May 22, 1959. The dreamer was on a "very old, dirty steamer" which was difficult to maneuver and took hours to get out of port. The crew was "unkempt" and "somewhat drunk." In the film the actual fishing boat, loaded with coal, was very old and dirty. The members of the real-life crew drank continually. And it was several hours before the boat finally got out of Bremerhaven to begin its film journey.

In February and July, 1958, Mrs. M dreamed about a "gigantic lobster with huge claws which was eaten at a great feast, a party with many people." During the filming the divers, hired for the shipwreck scenes, caught a large lobster weighing almost twelve pounds. Mrs. M prepared a lobster dinner for "a party with many people."

One of the divers, a girl, appeared earlier in Mrs. M's dreams. On January 3, 1959, Mrs. M dreamed of "protective asbestos suits," "a crater filled with a white chalky substance," and a picture of a woman with flowing hair painted by Eve Hagemann, a Hamburg artist.

Each element of this dream came true during the filming. On the first day after the company's arrival in Heligoland, the actors tried a new type of protective asbestos suit to prevent drowning. A "crater lake" composed of "a white, chalky substance" had been formed along the jetty of Heligoland. One of the divers, an attractive girl named Evelyn, with flowing hair, bore a striking resemblance to the girl in the dream-portrait.

Bear in mind that the script had not yet been written when Mrs. M began dreaming about the film and her role in it. Nor was it even certain what scenes would be filmed. At the time of the "boat" dream, three months before the filming began, there was no plan to charter a fishing boat.

A question arises: What connection was there between the dreams of Mrs. M and the ideas of the future scriptwriter and director? Did the dream-dramatist send suggestions to the creative part of the writer's mind? Did the dream of the dirty fishing boat plant the suggestion in the director's mind to charter the actual boat that was used? Did many of these vivid dream-scenes find their way into the as yet dormant minds of the writer and director?

Perhaps Mrs. M in a sense helped to "create" the future in her dream-pictures and at the same time got feedback from the future she had created.

CHAPTER SIXTEEN

Creating the Future

Did Jules Verne know more than a hundred years ago that *Apollo XI* would land on the moon in July, 1969? Was he, subliminally if not consciously, getting "feedback" from the future when in 1865 he wrote his novel *From the Earth to the Moon*—and in 1870 *Round the Moon*—feedback from ideas that he himself may have projected into the next century and that set in motion a chain of events leading to the successful moon landing?

The correspondence between what happens in the two novels and the circumstances surrounding the moon shot is quite striking. Consider these coincidences: There were three men in Verne's spacecraft and three astronauts in *Apollo XI* and *XII*. Verne's imaginary launching area was in Cape Town in Florida, close to the present Cape Kennedy. Verne's spaceship, named the *Columbiad*, was cone-shaped, similar in appearance to the *Apollo XI* command module, named the *Columbia*.

Verne calculated that the *Columbiad*, travelling 7 miles a second —about 25,000 miles an hour—would reach the moon in slightly over 4 days, a time span of 97 hours, 13 minutes, and 20 seconds. *Apollo XI*, travelling more than 24,000 miles an hour when pulling away from the earth, got to the moon in 4 days, 6 hours, and 46 minutes. Total flight time for the entire trip was 195 hours, 18 minutes, and

35 seconds—*an average of 97 hours and slightly over 39 minutes each way.* As with the modern Apollos, the *Columbiad* was equipped with rockets to jolt it out of lunar orbit and to slow down its reentry into the earth's atmosphere.

In Verne's story, the computations of the space shot—angle of fire, flight time, and flight trajectory—were made by the Cambridge Observatory in England. A hundred years later, calculations of American and Russian satellite and space flights were being made at the Smithsonian Astrophysical Laboratory—in Cambridge.

Verne must have known also, at least subliminally, that the Soviets would first send up dogs before their cosmonauts went into space. Two dogs accompanied the men in the *Columbiad*.

Just as modern astronauts and cosmonauts take along food capsules to conserve cabin space, the crew of the *Columbiad* ate meat and vegetables "reduced by strong hydraulic pressure to the smallest possible dimensions."

It is worth noting also that Verne, a Frenchman, picked neither France nor England, dominant powers of his time, as the countries that would first explore space. Rather, he chose the United States, a relatively new nation just getting over the trauma of the Civil War.

Yet, prophetic as the two novels were of the flights of *Apollo XI* and *XII*, in some respects they presaged even more dramatically the near-fatal journey of *Apollo XIII*. Although the *Columbiad* intended to land on the moon, it was unable to. Instead, it went into lunar orbit and the three men were fearful, as were the *Apollo XIII* astronauts, that they might either stay forever in orbit or crash into the moon itself. However, as in the case of *Apollo XIII*, Verne's spacemen were able to fire their rockets to get out of orbit and head back to earth.

One of the most astonishing links to the future in Verne's book was the trouble that developed in the *Columbiad* when oxygen began to escape on the way to the moon. Just as the *Apollo XIII* astronauts were in jeopardy following the explosion of the oxygen tank in the service module, Verne's space travelers were in danger of asphyxiation and of freezing to death because of heat loss. Moreover, the *Columbiad* paralleled the return journey of *Apollo XIII* by safely reentering the earth's atmosphere and falling into the Pacific, where the three men were rescued by a U.S. vessel.

It should also be noted that *Round the Moon,* which described the peril in space of the *Columbiad,* was written exactly one hundred years before the flight of *Apollo XIII* in April, 1970.

Was it mere coincidence that so many events in space came to pass in the twentieth century long after Verne's narrative prophecies were written? Verne himself said, "What one man can imagine another man can do." The first "other man" who thought he might do what Verne had imagined was the Russian schoolteacher Tsiolkovsky, who was a boy at the time Verne dreamed up his *Columbiad.*

Tsiolkovsky, called "the father of astronautics," was the first man to work out the mathematical calculations of spaceflight. Suggesting that the rocket principle be used to allow craft to escape from the earth's atmosphere, he revealed that his inspiration was Jules Verne, who directed his thinking "along certain channels." With Tsiolkovsky's scientific and romantic imagination fired by reading *From the Earth to the Moon,* he also wrote science fiction, in which he emphasized the theme of man's conquest of space.

It was a remarkable journey of ideas, from Verne the Frenchman to Tsiolkovsky the Russian, and forward in time to an American, Robert Hutchings Goddard, "the father of modern rocketry." What Verne had imagined, what Tsiolkovsky had worked out in blueprints, Goddard developed in practice by launching the first liquid-propellant rocket in March, 1926. The next human link in the chain was a German, Hermann Oberth, who advanced rocketry to its highest point—the thrust to the moon.

In a sense, then, Jules Verne not only predicted the future but also helped shape it with his ideas. *From the Earth to the Moon* visualized the end-result of an original concept of space technology and was itself perhaps shaped by feedback from the future.

FROM SPACE FICTION TO REALITY—AND BACK

But even Jules Verne was not the first science fiction writer to help "create" the future in space exploration. Verne himself may have been influenced by a writer called Cyrano de Bergerac (not the fictional hero of Rostand's play) who wrote *Voyage to the Moon* in 1656. Writer-scientist Arthur C. Clarke believes that de Bergerac must be given credit for anticipating rocket propulsion.

After Verne science fiction became a popular form of writing, and many space-prophets sprang from its ranks. Clarke, Robert Heinlein, Isaac Asimov, Hugo Gernsback, and others followed the lead of de Bergerac and Verne in predicting the kind of space technology that has actually come into being. In 1946 Clarke conceived the idea of "synchronous orbit." Years later, in 1963, a communications satellite using this principle was born—Syncom II—to be followed by others of its type and eventually Comsat, which boosts communication between NASA ground crews and spaceships.

Even writers who were not science-minded seemed to have their eyes on the heavens and "saw" objects in space that were only discovered much later. The satirist Jonathan Swift inserted a paragraph in *Gulliver's Travels* that has had scientists shaking their heads ever since. His astronomers in the imaginary land of Laputa discovered "Deimos" and "Phobos," two moons revolving about Mars, one going faster than the other—hardly appropriate behavior for a planet's satellites.

Swift couldn't have known, when he wrote the book in 1726, that the red planet had even one moon, let alone two. The astronomers of that period could see no such moons through their telescopes. The moons were not spotted until 150 years later, in 1877, by the American astronomer Asaph Hall. Were the moons there in 1726, sensed clairvoyantly by Swift?

One daring school of thought believes that at least Phobos, the faster-moving satellite, may not have been in existence at the time, that it is an artificial body, perhaps a hollow sphere, put into orbit later by intelligent beings on Mars. The opponents of this theory, who represent the majority of scientists, are convinced that there is no intelligent life on Mars and that the moons were created by natural forces.

Swift did not limit himself to mention of the moons and the unusual speed of Phobos. A description of their orbits, which was verified by astronomers in the following century, was also given: "The innermost [satellite] is distant from the center of the primary planet exactly three of his diameters, and the outermost five; the former revolves in the space of ten hours, and the latter in twenty-one and a half; so that the squares of their periodical times are very near in the same proportion with the cubes of their distance from the center of Mars, which evidently shows them to be governed by the same law of gravitation that influences the other heavenly bodies."

Pretty heavy stuff for a nonscientist on a fictional journey to an imaginary land—but accurate. Phobos orbits Mars in the same direction that planet rotates but in less than one-third the time, so that it appears to rise in the west and set in the east. This is the only known body in the universe that revolves around a central body *faster* than that central body's rotation, and so would support the theory that Phobos is an artificial satellite.

Gordon H. Evans in the June, 1964 issue of *Fate* magazine points out that Phobos' orbit has been shrinking and that it may be within its last one percent of life, a fact which further supports the theory of recent origin. If so, Phobos may not have been in existence when *Gulliver's Travels* was written, but in his subliminal mind Swift knew it would be there in 1877 when Hall looked through his telescope.

Martin Gardner, in his *Fads and Fallacies,* attempts to debunk such "nonsense" as precognition and clairvoyance, and he calls Swift's description of the Martian moons a "lucky guess." However, the story of precognition is full of such "lucky guesses," and writers who cannot find a more reasonable alternative are as unscientific as they accuse psychic researchers of being.

Let's carry this "guessing game" further. Perhaps some superior individual on Mars, reading *Gulliver's Travels* in 1726, thought what a neat trick it would be to design and launch Phobos according to the Laputan specifications. Whereupon he strolled into his laboratory and built the satellite.

"HE WILL DISCOVER A NEW WORLD"

Astronomer Percival Lowell was less a prophet than a scientist when he surmised in 1905 that an unseen "Planet X" was orbiting beyond Neptune, thought at the time to be the outermost planet in the solar system. In 1930 his calculations were confirmed by the young astronomer Clyde Tombaugh, who discovered the planet Pluto.

So far purely science. If we go back a bit in time, however, we find that a minor prophet had predicted in Dr. Tombaugh's high school yearbook that "he will discover a new world."

HOW TO DREAM UP A COMET

Charles L. Tweedale awakened one morning at 4 A.M., in the year 1886, from a wonderful dream in a state of great excitement. In his dream he had looked up into the heavens just before sunrise and had seen a comet in the eastern sky. Dressing quickly, Tweedale went into another room where he had a telescope and peered into it. It was just before dawn and, true to his dream, he saw the comet rise in the east. It was not visible to the naked eye.

Tweedale ran breathlessly to the telegraph office, which was not yet open, to send out news to the world of his great discovery. But as the sun came up, a newspaper boy walked by shouting out the headlines. Tweedale bought a paper, which contained the news that a comet had been discovered by the astronomers Barnard and Hartwig.

In his dream did Tweedale "see" himself "seeing" the comet just before sunrise? Or was he getting psychic feedback from the dis- covery by the two astronomers? Or did his dream-scenarist, know- ing what was going to be in the morning newspapers, write the sequence which he later acted out? Did Tweedale's dream "create" the future and—in circular fashion—did the future "create" his dream?

CHARIOTS WITHOUT ANIMALS, MACHINES LIKE BIRDS

Many imaginative and creative minds not only foresaw the future of vehicles in the air, on the ground, and beneath the sea, but may have generated ideas that were picked up by future scientists and inventors.

That versatile genius Leonardo da Vinci made numerous diagrams of aircraft and added a drawing of a "tent-roof" parachute. Centuries later his ideas were incorporated into functional airplanes and para- chutes. Nostradamus wrote of balloons and flying machines. But even further back—in the thirteenth century—there was technologi- cal feedback from the distant future. Roger Bacon, an English monk who discovered gunpowder, had visions of twentieth-century ships, airplanes, and automobiles:

> Instruments may be made by which the largest ships, with only one man guiding them, will be carried with greater velocity than if they were full of sailors. Chariots may be constructed that will move with

incredible rapidity without the help of animals. Instruments of flying may be formed in which a man, sitting at his ease and meditating on any subject, may beat the air with his artificial wings after the manner of birds . . . as also machines which will enable men to walk at the bottom of the sea . . .

But Jules Verne, again, gave the most detailed blueprints of future moving vehicles. Along with trips to the moon, he "created" a future of airplanes, dirigibles, helicopters, submarines, and balloons. Like Tsiolkovsky in the area of rocketry, later scientists, inventors, and even explorers credited Verne with directing their thinking "along certain channels."

Admiral Byrd, famous polar explorer, said that Jules Verne had been his guide. Simon Lake, father of the modern submarine, drew his inspiration from the *Nautilus,* the fictional submarine of *Twenty Thousand Leagues Under the Sea,* and called Verne the "director-general of my life." The Verne *Nautilus* was strikingly similar to the contemporary atomic submarine called the *Nautilus,* and anticipated ballistic missiles.

Writing such books as *Five Weeks in a Balloon* and *The Albatross,* Verne visualized helicopters half a century before the Wright brothers, dirigibles well before the *Zeppelin,* and of course airplanes. In addition, Verne's "airscanner," conceived at least eighty years before the Palomar Observatory was built, had a reflector with almost the same dimensions as the modern telescope. Verne foresaw television, neon lights, air-conditioning, moving sidewalks, guided missiles, and tanks. As Marshal Lyautey of France once told the Chamber of Deputies in Paris, modern science was simply putting into practice what Verne had described in words.

"YOU WILL DIE BY THE SPEAR"

At times the dream-play becomes a psychodrama that will somehow work out a solution to a problem that has been bothering the waking mind. The dream has often presented ideas to inventors, artists, and writers that had impact on the life of their time. Thus the future may be "created" as the mind sleeps.

For years inventor Elias Howe had tried, without success, to perfect the sewing machine. Then one night he dreamed that he had been captured by savages who dragged him before their king. The king issued an ultimatum: If within twenty-four hours Howe did not produce a machine that would sew, he would die by the spear. In the dream, Howe racked his brains, but no solution would come. The deadline passed, and now the savages were approaching. Clutching their gleaming spears, they stood over him menacingly. Slowly they raised the spears, then he saw the points come down at him.

Suddenly he forgot his fear in the dream as he stared at the tips of the descending spears: each had eye-shaped holes. Howe immediately awakened and realized that for his sewing machine, the eye of the needle should be near the point, not at the top or in the middle. Getting hastily out of bed, he ran to his laboratory, filed a needle to the proper size, drilled a hole near its tip, and inserted it in the machine. The problem was solved. Did Howe's dream-play with its far-seeing savages thus "create" the future of the sewing machine?

James Watt also had a problem that was taken over by the timeless mind that sees the future. The standard process for making lead shot for shotguns was to cut and chop metal, a costly procedure, and Watt thought a simpler method might be found. One night he had a dream that returned several times. He was walking through a storm but instead of rain, he was showered with tiny lead pellets. Awakening, he realized that molten lead, falling through the air, would harden into small spheres.

Watt went to a near-by church which had a water-filled moat at its base. Here he melted several pounds of lead and flung it from the bell tower. Then he ran downstairs and scooped the tiny lead pellets from the bottom of the moat. The dream had dramatized the future of the lead shot industry, which was revolutionized by the process.

In the case of the naturalist Louis Agassiz, the dreaming mind became an artist who sketched on one canvas a scene from past and future. Agassiz had for two weeks studied the impression of a fossil fish on a stone slab, but the image was so blurred that he could not decipher it. He finally abandoned the project, but a few nights later he dreamed that he saw a sketch of the entire fossilized fish. He rushed to the museum but the impression faded and the fossil was as indistinct as before. The following night the dream-artist again drew for him a clear picture of the restored fossil, but once more it faded from his mind when he awakened.

The next night, before retiring, Agassiz placed paper and pencil at his bedside. At dawn the dream-artist returned and again drew a sketch of the fish. Agassiz woke up and immediately traced the image as he had seen it in his dream. Then he went back to sleep, and in the morning examined the sketch he had made. It had clearly defined features he had not thought possible in the fossil. He hurried over to the Jardin des Plantes and began to chisel on the surface of the stone, with his drawing as guide. The layer of stone fell loose, revealing the fossil in excellent condition and identical to the one he had seen in his dream.

THE "LITTLE PEOPLE" FROM THE FUTURE

If a composer hears a new melody in his dream, is the dream "re-creating" a scene in the future when the composition will be written and performed? Musicians such as Beethoven and Mozart had the unusual ability to hear whole symphonies in their mental ear which they later wrote down. Were they hearing the orchestra playing the completed work before an audience?

In the eighteenth century Giuseppe Tartini dreamed one night that he had concluded a deal with the Devil, who promised to give him aid and comfort at all times. Having made their pact, Tartini decided to test Lucifer's musicianship and handed him a violin. The Evil One then played a melody "so singularly beautiful, and executed with such taste and precision, that it surpassed all that he had ever heard or conceived in his life."

When Tartini awakened, he leaped out of bed, grabbed his violin and tried to play what he had heard in his dream. But all he could remember, to his chagrin, was a repeated trill. Using this as a theme, Tartini later composed his best work, "The Devil's Trill."

The dream or dream-like state has served poets and writers well. Thomas de Quincey took opium, and in his drug-induced state he wrote such literary gems as *Confessions of an English Opium Eater*. De Quincey wrote of his psychedelic fantasies: "A theatre seemed suddenly opened and lighted within my brain, which presented nightly spectacles of more than earthly splendour."

Coleridge, who tasted the delights of the same drug, fell asleep in his chair one day in 1797 just after reading the following sentence in

Purchas's Pilgrimage: "Here the Khan Kubla commanded a palace to be built, and a stately garden thereunto. And thus ten miles of fertile ground were inclosed with a wall." Coleridge slept profoundly for three hours, and in his dream composed two to three hundred lines based on the words he had read. Later he wrote his famous poem "Kubla Khan."

Robert Louis Stevenson invited his characters from the future to visit him in dreams and tell him what to write. His dream-plays were filled with "little people" who each evening provided him with "truncheons of tales upon their lighted theatre." One of his dreams was of a beast-like criminal who was pursued by the police but was able to elude them by drinking a potion and changing his appearance. This character became the two-sided Dr. Jekyll and Mr. Hyde.

STRICTLY FOR THE BIRDS

A short story by Daphne du Maurier may well have been the most startling and gruesome literary example of "creating" the future. Alfred Hitchcock, the film and television producer, adapted the story into a movie, *The Birds,* in which flocks of birds attack and kill human beings.

The setting of du Maurier's story was the west coast of England. In May, 1960, some time after the release of the film, a group of schoolchildren in Leicestershire, England, were at play when out of the sky came screaming magpies, just as in the film and the book. The children received deep gashes in their heads, hands, and ears before the birds were finally driven away. Since magpies are considered harmless creatures, their behavior was inexplicable.

Did the emotional impact of the movie somehow create psychic vibrations that affected the birds and changed their behavior pattern for that one day? Or, since the incident took place on the west coast of England, did the psychic vibrations come from du Maurier's story?

Did both du Maurier and Hitchcock in the book and the film "create" a future reality in which the magpies went mad and attacked the children? Or did the author and later the producer sense in the depth of their minds what was going to happen and then dramatize this incident from the future?

CHAPTER SEVENTEEN

Forecasting in the Laboratory

In the last decade perhaps the most meaningful experiments in extrasensory perception have been those at the Dream Laboratory at the Maimonides Medical Center in Brooklyn, New York. The experiments, supervised by Dr. Montague Ullman, head of the psychiatry department at Maimonides, and psychologist Stanley Krippner, were designed to influence dreams through telepathy and clairvoyance.

A person with potential psychic ability would be invited to spend the night in a soundproof room at the Laboratory. As he slept, electrodes attached to his head would send his brain wave patterns to an electroencephalograph (EEG) in the separate control room. Here an "experimenter" would sit during the night and watch for an REM pattern—rapid eye movements—which would indicate dreaming. The experimenter would then awaken the sleeper over the intercom and ask him to describe his dreams.

Meanwhile, just after the sleeper had retired for the night, a third person, the "agent" or "sender," would select one envelope from a number of sealed envelopes, each containing the print of a famous painting. He would then go to a third room at the other end of the building and stay there all night, concentrating on the painting. From time to time he would write down his feelings about the picture and try to "send" his impressions of it to the sleeping subject.

After the night of dreaming, the "dream review" would begin. The experimenter would ask the subject to retell each dream and give his associations to it. Then the dreamer would be shown the prints of twelve paintings, one of them the "target" picture for the night, and asked which one matched his dreams. This procedure would be followed on eleven other nights with different persons as subjects and a different painting used each night. At the end of the twelve-night series, three professional judges would evaluate the success of each subject by comparing his dreams with the twelve paintings.

The results were often quite striking. One of the target paintings was *Animals* by Tamayo, showing two dogs eating pieces of meat, a huge black rock in the background. The subject that night dreamed about "that mermaid from Black Rock" and about a banquet where she was eating "rib steak." Another night the picture was *Zapatistas* by Oroco, depicting a group of Mexican revolutionaries on the move, with clouds and mountains in the background. The subject, a psychologist, dreamed of "New Mexico," "Indians," "heavy clouds and mountains," and "a DeMille supertype colossal production."

Another target painting was Gaugin's *The Moon and the Earth* featuring a naked, dark-skinned girl by a stream of water. The sleeper, a secretary, dreamed three times about "scantily clad girls." She pictured herself in a bathing suit and in one dream saw "a dancing girl" with "dark, tan shoulders." On another night, when the painting was of an elderly rabbi sitting at a table reading a book, the sleeper dreamed of "an older man, a minister or priest," who was "reading from a book."

Ullman and Krippner noticed that often the sleeper seemed to dream of a target picture that was used on a later night, indicating not telepathy but precognition. One subject, an actor, dreamed of "a Negro man on a boat being tossed by waves." Homer's *The Gulf Stream,* the target some weeks later, depicted a black man on a raft with a hurricane in the background. And after many such dream-experiments over a period of several years, Ullman and Krippner decided to try a different kind of test, involving possible precognition. In 1969 the talented young psychic, Malcolm Bessent, was brought over from England as the subject for these tests.

On eight different nights in the precognition series, Malcolm would go to sleep in the soundproof room while the experimenter in the control room watched his brain-wave patterns for signs of dreaming. But this time there was no "sender" in the third room because the picture would not be selected until the following morning, after the night of dreaming was over. Malcolm's only instructions were to try to dream about what would happen in the morning when the picture would be chosen and a sequence of actions worked out that were based on the theme of the picture.

No one else in the Laboratory knew the content of Malcolm's dreams except the experimenter. In the morning staff members would choose at random a series of numbers that would lead to a specific page and one of 1200 key words in a book of dream descriptions. Dr. Krippner would then find a painting in the Dream Laboratory files that matched the target word or phrase. For example, after the first night of dreams, the target word picked was "corridor." The painting that matched it was Van Gogh's *Corridor of the St. Paul Hospital*.

Dr. Krippner then created for Malcolm what he called a "multi-sensory environment"—a series of actions dramatizing the target word and theme of the painting and involving each of the five senses. The purpose of this dramatization was, hopefully, to create an emotional and sensory impact from the future which might affect Malcolm's dreams.

But, extraordinarily, the stimulus would be given in the morning, the response made the night before.

The sleeper tossed restlessly on his bed. In his dream he was in a mental hospital, surrounded by people who were drinking out of glasses, while doctors and psychiatrists wandered through the scene. A female patient on the second floor broke loose and ran down the corridor toward an archway. The dreamer sensed a feeling of hostility in the atmosphere. Suddenly he was thinking of an airplane trip to Canada.

"Malcolm, wake up."

The voice came over the intercom from the control room. The dreamer stirred and the fog of sleep began to dissipate.

"I'm awake."

The young lady who was watching the electroencephalograph knew from the movements of the needle that Malcolm had been dreaming.

"Please tell me what is going on in your mind."

"I saw a large concrete building . . . a patient escaping from upstairs . . . she had a white coat on, like a doctor's coat, and people were arguing with her in the street . . . medical people . . . white cups on a tray . . ."

"Anything else?"

"A whole collection of people . . . some of them drinking . . . coffee and toast, biscuits, breakfast . . . on a tray and rattled as they were carried . . ."

"All right, you can go back to sleep now."

Several times during the night Malcolm was awakened and asked to describe his dreams. Late in the morning he woke up for the last time. Diane Schneider, the experimenter in the control room, spoke to him again.

"About how many dreams do you think you had during the night?"

"I don't know—about twenty."

Malcolm had had just four dreams—the average dreamer has four to six. Then he was asked to recall what had happened in his four dreams. Once more he told Diane about a large concrete building, doctors and psychologists, a mental patient escaping from the hospital disguised as a doctor, a feeling of hostility. And, incongruously, the desire to take an airplane trip to Canada.

The door of Malcolm's room opened and two grim-faced men wearing white hospital uniforms walked in. They slipped a tight-fitting jacket over his head, gripped his arms firmly and guided him out into the corridor. No lights were on, and he could hardly see as he stumbled down the hall. He wondered sleepily if he were in a strait jacket.

In the distance he heard a man laughing hysterically, while the music of "Spellbound" played on a phonograph. The laughing grew louder, more bizarre as the men took Malcolm into an office. Seated behind the desk was Dr. Stanley Krippner, director of the Dream Laboratory, a wild look in his eyes as he roared with laughter. A picture was hanging on the wall—Van Gogh's *Corridor of the St. Paul Hospital*.

Malcolm blinked at the picture and thought, "My God—that's my dream." He wondered uneasily how Krippner knew what he had dreamed about. He had communicated only with Diane, the experimenter, and she was pledged to secrecy.

"How do you do, Mr. Van Gogh?" said Dr. Krippner, grinning. He told Malcolm to be seated, handed him a pill with a glass of water, and ordered him to swallow it. Then he dipped a cotton swab into a jar of acetone and wiped the young man's face with it. He explained that this was a precautionary measure—Malcolm must be disinfected.

While the theremin played the eerie, whining "Spellbound" theme, Dr. Krippner turned out the light and showed slides of very weird drawings. He told Malcolm they were the work of mental patients in the psychiatric ward. As each drawing flashed on the wall, Krippner giggled.

Had Dr. Krippner gone mad? An uneasy thought came to Malcolm—was he too a mental patient, captive in an out-of-this-world hospital run by an insane Dr. Krippner? Or was he still dreaming, expecting to be awakened at any moment?

Malcolm's reactions to the dramatization of the picture indicated how closely Van Gogh's *Corridor of the St. Paul Hospital* and the target word "corridor" were matched by his dreams the night before —the first night of the experiments. And yet when Krippner devised the late morning drama with himself and Malcolm as the leading characters, he hadn't the faintest idea what the psychic had dreamed about. To insure that there would be no contact with the dreamer or experimenter, Krippner had slept all night in an isolated room.

Here is how Krippner designed the sense stimulation: sense of movement—Malcolm being led down the darkened corridor, which also represented the target word "corridor"; sense of hearing—the "Spellbound" music, originally composed for a film about a woman psychiatrist and her patient and related to the theme of hospital and mental patients, as was Dr. Krippner's simulated madness; sense of sight—the Van Gogh picture on the wall and the slides presumably of the patients' drawings; sense of taste—Malcolm taking the pill and drinking the glass of water; sense of touch and smell—swabbing the acetone on Malcolm's face.

How did Malcolm's four dreams "pre-view" the target picture and multisensory environment? The dreams were charged with a feeling of hostility characteristic of psychiatric patients. The image of a female patient in doctor's clothes running down the "corridor" may have been inspired by the "Spellbound" theme and its association with the lady psychiatrist in the film. The dream-scene of people drinking was a prevision of Malcolm's drinking the glass of water when he took the pill the next morning. And, of course, the dreams all centered on a mental hospital, doctors, and patients.

Did Malcolm "see" the future in his dreams? It is possible that Krippner picked up Malcolm's dreams telepathically before he devised the multisensory environment. But there is still the problem of selecting the correct page and item numbers in the book of dream-descriptions. If the staff members who made these choices were also linked telepathically with the dreamer's mind, they might then clairvoyantly pick the right numbers. This would imply, of course, a super-psychical gift on the part of Dr. Krippner and his staff.

In the second experiment, which took place about a week later, the dominant theme of the dreams was of discipline and an authoritarian atmosphere. During the night Malcolm kept thinking of a "penal colony" and a "state penitentiary." When he woke up from one of his dreams, he accused experimenter Diane Schneider of making him "feel like a robot." Another dream was about "people finding an answer to a particular question."

How did these dream-images, thoughts, and feelings compare with the experience of the following morning? The picture chosen was Renoir's *Boy Studying,* matching the target word "desk." After the night of dreaming, Dr. Krippner wore a business suit and received Malcolm in his office as if he were a new student in school. Malcolm was seated at a desk and given a written examination, in which he had to "find answers to particular questions."

To improve Malcolm's performance on the test, Krippner hypnotized him while a recording was played, "Deep Relaxation." Whenever Malcolm missed a question, Dr. Krippner was "stern and punitive." Malcolm was reminded of his dreams, in which there had been an "authoritarian atmosphere," he had "felt like a robot," and he had kept thinking of a "penal colony" and a "state penitentiary." He recalled also one of his dreams in which "he did everything he was told and was amazed to find out it was true," suggestive of the teacher-pupil relationship.

Telepathic elements, unrelated to the experiment, seemed to creep into this night of dreams. In one dream Malcolm saw a "big brown bear." It will be recalled that Ann Jensen in Dallas saw a newspaper picture of a "big, brown bear" in her crystal ball. In Malcolm's dream it also "seemed like a picture." Did Malcolm, in some strange way, pick up the "big, brown bear" from Mrs. Jensen's mind? Or was I the catalyst, since I had planned to write about Malcolm, or possibly a mental relay station in the journey of the brown bear from Mrs. Jensen's crystal ball to Malcolm's dream?

In the psychic world all minds seem to converge.

Malcolm scored a bull's-eye during the third night of dreams. The target picture was Cokovsky's *Fruits and Flowers*. One of the visual stimuli was a bowl of fruit. In the morning Malcolm was asked to smell the fruit and to pare, cut, and eat it. When awakened the night before, he had said, "All I can think of is a bowl of fruit." During the morning dream review, he said it was "as if the letters were in mid-air, a 'Bowl of Fruit.'"

The target picture for the fourth night of dreaming was *People Soup,* a collage. After one of Malcolm's dreams, he remarked, "I had the idea I would make a collage." He also dreamed of a soup-like image: "There were very shallow pools of water . . . a really beautiful golden color."

The main feeling-tone of this dream-series was of spirituality, relating to several elements in the post-dreaming environment. One of the faces in the target picture was that of Christ, while the record played the next morning was "Mass in F Minor" by the Electric Prunes. In Malcolm's dreams Dr. Krippner became a Christ-like figure. There was ". . . awareness . . . enlightenment . . . I was at a light-collecting farm . . . a natural harmony and knowledge . . . People were perfectly aware and in possession of themselves and their environment . . . rays of light coming from his [Dr. Krippner's] hands . . ."

For the fifth night the key word was "Parka hood" and the target picture was *Walrus Hunter* by Akpaliapik. The visual stimulus consisted of white northern lights from a color organ and sheets draped over furniture to resemble ice and snow. Cold water and ice were applied to Malcolm's face and back and several fans blew air on him. His dreams had emphasized the theme of whiteness: "I was just standing in a room, surrounded by white. Every imaginable thing in the room was white . . . the light was very bright . . . predominant colors were pale and ice blues and whites . . ."

The sixth dream-series is of special significance because the target theme touched a personal problem of Malcolm's. This emotional link stimulated precognition not only of the picture but also of a future situation in Malcom's life when his problem was solved.

The target picture was *The Spinal Column* by Netter, matching the target words "body back." In the post-dreaming environment Malcolm was given a back massage while "Dry Bones" was played on the phonograph. Malcolm had dreamed of a "device" to be used in "a larger psychic operation; some kind of power house or energy center which would be tapped in some way . . . like a generating force . . . used as a healing force . . . a natural polarity healing . . . suddenly I can relax . . ."

Along with the "power house or energy center" theme, Malcolm dreamed about the house of a friend he was going to visit later in Canada: "Very big house . . . white pillars outside." Malcolm had never been to Canada and had no idea what his friend's house looked like. Yet the "white pillars" seemed to be related to the "spinal column" or "body back" theme.

When Malcolm went to Toronto the following month, the big house with the "white pillars" was there but, strangely enough, it was a recent purchase and had not yet been bought or even seen when Malcolm had his dream. As for Malcolm's personal problem, all his life he had suffered with backache, although he did not know the cause. While he was in Toronto, his host told him one day that an osteopath was coming over to give a massage and he asked Malcolm if he would like one. The osteopath discovered that Malcolm had a dislocated pelvis that was causing his pain. After the massage, Malcolm had no more backaches.

The seventh night of dreaming was notable for the striking correspondence to the next morning's target picture and sensory environment, and also because my "old black car" appeared in Malcolm's dreams. Significant elements below are italicized.

The target picture was *Blue Grey Gnatcatcher* by Malick. The visual stimulus consisted of *two plants with leaves* surrounding the picture. To stimulate his olfactory sense, Malcolm was asked to smell the flowers and leaves. Movement was brought into the post-dreaming scene when Malcolm was taken by *car* across the *Verazzano Narrows Bridge* connecting Brooklyn with Staten Island. On the Island he roamed through the *Grymes Hill woods,* found a *number of leaves,* put them in a *basket,* and brought them back to the Dream Laboratory. As taste "feedback" *he sampled one of these leaves.*

For aural stimulation selections from Whitman's *Leaves of Grass* were read to Malcolm, while "Autumn Leaves" and "Wild Flowers" were playing on the phonograph. One of the lines from Whitman's poems was: "What is known I strip away; I launch all men and women forward with me into the unknown."

Dialogue between Malcolm and Diane during the dream-sessions the night before:

"I was dreaming of *traffic.*"

"What about traffic, Malcolm?"

"*Heavy traffic* . . . outdoors . . ."

"Were you in a vehicle?"

"Yes."

"That's all?"

"I'm thinking of being in the *country* . . . *Green colors* . . . a *bridge* . . . It was a misty early morning . . . *trees* and stuff . . . *driving over the bridge* . . . the *bridge* has some significance . . . a *large basket* . . . there was a terrific hassle to get through the *traffic* . . ."

"Was it a residential area or an area where you usually expect to see heavy traffic?"

"I think it was as New York is—residential area and business all thrown together . . . *very heavy traffic* . . . thinking about the *country* and hearing *crickets* . . . *dew on the grass* . . . *birds singing* . . . *a lot of trees* . . . the river didn't seem to need such *a big bridge* . . . it may involve eating—*a special type of eating.*"

Several elements in the dreams related to the "movement" experience—going across the bridge, picking flowers, etc. "A special type of eating" anticipated Malcolm's later tasting the leaves. Another dream-image was suggestive of the line "I launch all men and women forward into the unknown" in one Whitman poem: "I began thinking about taking off on a rocket ship. One of the scenes from *2001*. . ."

At one point my car came into the dream-scene. "I thought about Canada and then I thought of this old (black) car and then I was thinking I was going to be driving there." I, too, had been thinking of driving to Canada in my "old black car," although Malcolm didn't know it at the time and had not yet seen my car.

Themes in the sleeper's own life keep weaving through precognitive dreams. During the first series of dreams Malcolm had thought about an airplane trip to Canada. In a later series he saw the "white pillars" of his friend's home. Now the "old black car" was in the dream. It was obvious throughout the eight nights of the experiment that Malcolm had emotional links to Canada, and wherever possible they would be combined with the target pictures and the post-dreaming multisensory environments. The desire to go to Canada evidently provided a strong psychic link between Malcolm and me. The "old black car" crept once again into his eighth and last series of dreams.

I have left out many thoughts, images, feelings in the eight dream-series that were closely related to the target word and picture and the sensory environment created by Dr. Krippner on each morning following the dreams. There was also much material, as is true of all dreams, that showed little or no correspondence with the targets. With a little digging, however, such unrelated feelings and images might prove to have significance in the life of the dreamer.

An interesting sidelight of these dreams was that some of the material on certain nights pre-viewed not the targets of the following morning but those for later experiments. In the third dream-series, for example, on the night of July 31, 1969, Malcolm dreamed that he had "a big white towel" around his neck "instead of a scarf." Almost a month later, on the morning following the fifth dream-series, a parka made of a towel was put on Malcolm's head.

At the end of the eight nights of experiments, a panel of judges not connected with the Dream Laboratory was asked to examine the dreams and see how closely they corresponded with the targets. The results were positive and were judged "statistically significant."

One of the aims of the Central Premonitions Registry is to send persons to the Dream Laboratory who have shown ability to predict the future. Here they will be tested for precognition under controlled or laboratory conditions. Already two psychics who send premonitions to the Registry—Malcolm Bessent and Alan Vaughan—have taken part in experiments at Maimonides. Robert Nelson, director of the Central Premonitions Registry, has acted as "sender" in the experiments in dream-clairvoyance.

SEEING THE FUTURE IN THE WITCH'S CRADLE

It is like a swing, except that it has a larger platform and is used not by children but by adults. The subject, strapped in and blindfolded, stands on the platform. Soon it begins to move, imperceptibly, then swings in wider and wider arcs. The subject, already deprived of the sense of sight, feels himself gradually drifting out of contact with the everyday world. He is going into a trance-state in which the mind may wander away from present time and space.

Its technical name is ASCID (Altered States of Consciousness Induction Device), but it is also known as the Witch's Cradle. (In medieval times witches often took "trips" to visit the Devil by swinging in a bag suspended from a tree.) The ASCID was designed by R. E. L. Masters and is now beginning to be used for psychotherapy and research. There is one in the Foundation for Mind Research in New York City, run by Masters and his wife, philosopher Jean Houston. Masters and Houston formerly investigated the influence of psychedelic drugs on mental behavior, but today they are employing the ASCID and other devices to induce "trips" without the aid of drugs.

The "trips" are not just for thrills. The object is to explore the mind in its depths and to evoke a wide range of extraordinary experiences, including religious, mystical, and peak experiences so rare in Western culture. Extrasensory happenings may occur as a byproduct of the experiments. In at least one case a psychic "saw" the future in the ASCID.

Alan Vaughan visited the Foundation one day and was strapped into the Witch's Cradle. He wondered if the premonitions that came to him during meditation and at other times, some of them mentioned in earlier chapters of this book, might be repeated under experimental conditions. As the Cradle swung back and forth and around in a circle, Vaughan went into a light trance. Bob Masters asked him questions about the future. The answers, listed below, were sent to the Central Premonitions Registry on December 5, 1969.

Jacqueline Kennedy will be estranged from Onassis by her son John and will take up permanent residence in the United States.

Ethel Kennedy will not remarry.

Ted Kennedy will suffer more tragedies in the next few years, but by overcoming them, will gain the confidence of the American public and will be elected President in 1976.

A madman will attack the Pope and attempt to kill him early next year. (A would-be assassin did try to kill the Pope in November, 1970. He was described by the newspapers as a "madman.")

The Vietnam War will be substantially over in 18 months. Only a small token force of U.S. troops will then remain.

By 1972–73 severe flooding will affect the Eastern Coast of the United States. This will gradually worsen in some areas, particularly New Jersey.

Although most of these predictions were new, the last about "severe flooding" reaffirmed Vaughan's premonition about a rising water level around New York City, a prediction also voiced by Malcolm Bessent and on file with the Central Premonitions Registry.

THE COMPUTER SEES THE FUTURE

Douglas Dean of the Newark College of Engineering believes that successful businessmen make decisions based more on hunches than on logical thinking. He has put the theory to test by devising a precognition experiment in which executives predict the future actions of a computer.

The computer doesn't make conscious moves, of course. It is equipped with a device which allows it to make a random choice of numbers after the businessmen, using their intuition, punch numbers they believe will be matched by the machine. Neither the computer, Dean, nor the businessmen know in advance which numbers the machine will pick.

First the executives are handed IBM cards with 100 columns of numbers from 0 to 9, and asked to punch the number in each row they think the computer will generate later. The odds are 10 to 1 against the executives' selecting the right number in each column. 10

correct guesses in 100 rows would give a "chance" result. Scores above 16 and below 4 would be statistically significant.

The executives' performance seems to depend on two factors that are related and are tested by both clairvoyance and precognition. If the businessmen believe strongly in the possibility of ESP (and so far there has been a ratio of three to one in favor of belief among those tested), they tend to score above chance in the clairvoyance test where the target numbers are generated *before* they make their guesses. If they are "dynamic" rather than "slow" personalities, a quality determined before the test, they also tend to make significant scores on the precognition test when the target is generated *after* they make their guesses. "Slows" score below chance on this test.

The "dynamic" high scorers are generally outstanding in their business life, the low-scoring "slows" not so successful in running their companies. The "dynamics" try to accomplish as much work in a day as is humanly possible. The "slows" are more passive on the job and more inclined to put off their tasks. The "dynamics" rely mostly on intuition in making business decisions, the "slows" go by the book and what is supposed to be the logic of a business situation.

For example, a "dynamic" executive, debating where to build a new plant for his company, would first look over all the objective facts, which might point to Oregon as the preferred location of the plant. But at the last moment his inner voice might say "No" and recommend Wisconsin. The executive discards the data compiled by his experts and builds in Wisconsin. His choice generally proves to be the right one.

One of the men tested is the president of a large steel company. He believes that intuition is nine-tenths of his job and that the successful executive must be a generalist who does not spend too much time listening to the advice or considering the factual data offered by his specialists. "The final step," he says, "is that the intuition will flow through me."

In one of the computer tests, the executives were divided into two groups, one made up of those who had at least doubled their company's profits over the previous five years, and the other those who had failed to do so. The first group scored significantly higher, the second significantly lower than chance.

Dean believes that the computer-precognition tests may prove extremely valuable in the future in picking men for top executive jobs.

THE MAN IN THE EMPTY CHAIR

Many laboratory experiments in precognition, particularly in Europe, are based on the psychic genius of one man. Outstanding among such seers is Gerard Croiset, the protégé of Dr. W. H. C. Tenhaeff of the University of Utrecht in Holland. For twenty-five years he has been rigidly tested by psychologists and parapsychologists from all over the world.

Possibly Croiset's most amazing precognitive feat is the "chair test," in which he describes a person who will be at a meeting to take place some time in the future. A chair is pointed out to him, and although no one yet knows who will sit in it, including its eventual occupant, Croiset correctly describes the appearance of this person and many events in his life.

March, 1948. Croiset is taken to a hall, where the second seat from the right in the fifth row is pointed out to him, and he is asked to visualize who will sit in it. He "sees" a man who years before was strolling near a large villa on a hill. The man came across an unconscious woman wearing a light dress, and he summoned help for her. When the meeting finally takes place, the man who sits in that seat verifies all the details of Croiset's vision. Twelve years before his wife was hit by an automobile. When he found her, she was unconscious and he held her in his arms after calling an ambulance.

In other chair tests, Croiset visualized a young man who had almost lost a finger in an electric saw, a drug manufacturer whose sister had had polio as a child, and a police inspector who had a leaking fountain pen. Each person visualized appeared later and verified what Croiset had seen.

In one test that took place in Italy, the members of the audience had not even been invited when Croiset got his impressions. The psychic had an image of a young girl wearing "a dark dress and light-colored blouse." This detail and others were confirmed later when the girl sat in the chair. Croiset had also seen a dead animal falling at the girl's feet. She admitted that a few days before, when she was walking past a butcher shop, a dead chicken fell in front of her.

But perhaps Croiset's most startling prediction was of an unoccupied chair. There was to be a meeting four days later in Rotterdam. Who would be in chair number 18?

"I see nothing."

"Are you sure?"

"Absolutely."

There were thirty chairs in all, and thirty persons had been invited. But on the night of the meeting, there was a heavy snowfall. Twenty-nine persons showed up and took their seats at random. There was one empty chair—number eighteen.

In January, 1969, a film was made in Holland of Croiset as he described a man and woman unknown to him who would appear at a gathering in Denver, Colorado, a few weeks later. Of the woman he said: "She has had an emotional experience dealing with page 64 of a book she was reading." He described the man as wearing "a coat with green spots, made by a chemical from his work in a scientific laboratory."

The second part of the film was shot at the Denver gathering, where men and women were handed forms on which they answered questions about themselves. One of the women said that she had recently read a book on cats and was upset by an item discussing the problem of putting a cat to sleep. The item was found to be on page 64 of the book. One of the men questioned admitted that he had a coat answering Croiset's description, with green spots that came from a chemical.

The film was shown later by Dr. Jule Eisenbud at an ESP symposium at the University of California at Los Angeles.

Croiset also sees the future in other situations. A young man who had been a failure in his business life once visited the psychic for a reading. Croiset felt that the boy would be very successful in the future, but along with this impression came the apparently irrelevant image of a black chicken. The chicken meant nothing to the young man. Later, however, he became a successful salesman for a liqueur called the "Black Chicken."

Precognition experiments, started by Rhine at Duke University, Soal in England, and other parapsychologists, are now going on in laboratories all over the world. Card-guessing has been replaced by more intriguing and ingenious experiments such as those at the Dream Laboratory and the computer tests of Douglas Dean. Experiments are even under way to predict the action of electrons in the subatomic realm.

CHAPTER EIGHTEEN

Diary of a Swedish Seer

What do all the cases previously discussed, particularly the psychic experiences of ordinary people, have to do with the idea of premonitions bureaus? The London Bureau and the Central Premonitions Registry in New York City hope to develop amateur seers who will learn to separate mere fanciful impressions from true premonitions. Perhaps the overall picture of the psychic dimension given in this book, together with hints about meditation and other techniques and the "dream-catching" suggestions at the end of this chapter, will help the neophyte understand and evaluate his own dreams and visions, especially as they relate to newsworthy events.

No better model for an analytical approach to premonitions can be studied than the Swedish seer Eva Hellström. Mrs. Hellström, founder of the Swedish Society for Psychical Research, records her psychic impressions in a diary and judges them by the following criteria: Are they accompanied by a strong conviction, that vivid "here-and-now" feeling? Are the dreams and visions in color (a positive sign) or black and white? Do they dramatize realistically the events of the future or are they symbolic? Do the premonitions appear as dreams, as images seen or voices heard between the states of sleeping and waking, or as daytime experiences? Are the visions "stills" or moving pictures?

If she feels that the impression is truly premonitory, Mrs. Hellström has it verified by witnesses, and watches the newspapers for corroborating articles and photos. Sometimes she will sketch maps or other important visual matter involved. These are later compared with police reports and with real objects and scenes that were previsioned.

The following cases have been culled from Mrs. Hellström's diary and were confirmed by her husband, Bo Hellström (now deceased) and other witnesses, and by later newspaper articles and police reports. They illustrate many categories of special interest to the Central Premonitions Bureau—natural catastrophes, accidents, wars, deaths, previsions of newspaper articles, etc. In keeping with one of the themes of this book, I have tried to discover the emotional link in each case between Mrs. Hellström and the event she forecast.

A book about Mrs. Hellström's psychic experiences will be published soon, written in collaboration with Dr. Rolf Ejvegaard, who teaches psychology and philosophy at the University of Stockholm. Mrs. Hellström has translated the contents of her diary for use in this chapter and is aware that some of the English constructions may be awkward.

A LANDSLIDE OF CLAY

On September 16-17, 1950, Mrs. Hellström had a dream that was "so realistic," she immediately recorded it in her diary. Her daughter-in-law and her maid witnessed her entry in the morning. She notes that the dream came in symbolic form. (In the quoted material that follows, all italics are the author's.)

> I dreamed last night that my husband received a letter written by hand with ink . . . something about an accident—16 people killed. I remember thinking: "Since they write Bo about it, I suppose it must be some *catastrophe* at a dam-construction or similar site. [Mr. Hellström was an engineer.] Or somebody close to him was killed . . ." The letter came from *Göteborg*.
>
> (Signed) Eva Hellström
>
> I have been told the above dream, which I herewith verify.
>
> Sept. 17, 1950
Anna Britta Hellström
>
> Also undersigned September 20th, 1950.
>
> Helga Eriksson

12 days later, on September 29, a landslide of clay deposits swept over a village outside Göteborg, Sweden, and poured into the Göta Alv River. 35 houses were demolished, leaving 300 people homeless, while 20 persons were hurt and 1 died. A Swedish newspaper called it the greatest natural catastrophe in the history of Sweden.

Mrs. Hellström writes that of seven premonitions of natural catastrophes, this was the only one in symbolic form. It would appear from the dream that she was emotionally linked with Göteborg and the Göta Alv River by her husband's work as a consulting engineer and by her residence there at the beginning of her married life.

TRAPPED IN A "KILN"

On November 5, 1951, Mrs. Hellström dreamed in color of an explosion with "such a strong character of reality" that she was certain it was a precognitive dream.

> I was travelling on a train toward Saltsjöbaden . . . At the station, where I stepped off, there was a crowd and there had been an accident. Something was burning, which looked like a *kind of kiln* . . . *It smoked and glowed.* They said that *a laborer had been trapped in the kiln.* After awhile I saw some workmen coming past carrying a stretcher with a wounded man . . . I think he had something covering him. I wondered if he was dead. The dream was in color. I remember the *red glow* and it was dark, so it must have been late in the evening or at night.

On December 11, 1951, this entry in Mrs. Hellström's diary was witnessed by a prominent physician in Stockholm who prefers to remain anonymous:

> The above record of a dream was told me by Mrs. Hellström. The details I do not remember so clearly, but this written record have I read this day.

On Thursday, November 20, 1952—after Mrs. Hellström had pondered her dream for a year—she clipped an article from her morning newspaper about an explosion in a tunnel under a building at Nacka, a station on the railway line she had dreamed about. The headlines in the evening newspapers of November 19 read:

> Tunnel Disaster at Nacka. *Laborer Trapped Behind the Rocks.* Workmen Try to Save Doomed Man.

Explosion in Rocks at Nacka. *Laborer Killed in Tunnel.*
Severely Injured Men Crawl Out of *Sea of Fire.*

The explosion was caused by a charge of blasting powder that had
gone off too soon. A news article stated: "To the very last one hoped
to find him (the laborer) alive behind the stone barrier. Oxygen was
pumped in between the stones to make it easier for him to breathe."
Mrs. Hellström writes: "This seems to be the moment—in the dream
—when I came into the story."

The article further states that "there was *a thick, almost impene-
trable smoke* filling the tunnel . . . During the rescue work the violent blows with the spits on the walls in the rock produced *small
intense flashes*"—calling to mind Mrs. Hellström's dream about a
"kind of kiln," "smoke," and a *"red glow."* She had assumed that
it was night. Although the actual accident happened in the middle
of the day, the electric lines had been destroyed and the explosion
occurred in the darkest part of the tunnel.

Mrs. Hellström wonders if she pre-viewed the details of the accident from newspaper accounts rather than the actual scene. She
writes, however, that she had a "strong feeling of being present on
the spot after travelling on the train." In the dream she caught a
glimpse of a friend who was living in the area and who may have
been her emotional link to the disaster.

A MAN FLOATING IN AIR

This dream of a fatal accident was so vivid that when Mrs. Hellström woke up she had an immediate feeling that it was precognitive.

> August 5, 1952. I dreamed that I was walking on something that
> looked like a *flat roof,* perhaps with *a low barrier. I saw a man fall
> down from the roof.* Saw him floating in the air. *He died. The building
> was high, made of stone.*
> Wasn't quite sure but I imagined that there was somebody else . . .
> who perhaps may have pushed him down. . .

Mrs. Hellström's husband, to whom she showed her entry in the
diary, then added:

> Correctly copied from the diary, we certify:
>   Bo Hellström

On December 8, 1952, five months later, Mrs. Hellström learned that a man had fallen from a high roof at the gasworks at Värtan, a harbor in Stockholm, and was so badly injured it was doubtful that he would recover. The curate asked Mrs. Hellström to lead prayers for the man's recovery. He died the next morning.

The police report said that "the roof of the coke-conveyor was *flat*" as in the dream. A kind of scaffolding was visible in the picture of the building, similar to the *"low barrier"* in the dream. The picture also showed that the building was a brickhouse about twenty meters or sixty-five feet high.

Although Mrs. Hellström had a feeling in the dream that the man was pushed, the police report said that he had struck his head on the roof and as he fell, a board fell on top of his body. As in the case of the man who dreamed about Air Marshal Goddard's "death" in an airplane, Mrs. Hellström made the wrong inference as she watched the man fall in her dream.

There was an emotional link that may have motivated the dream. Although Mrs. Hellström had never seen or heard of the man before, the curate who asked her to lead prayers for him knew the parish nurse to whom he was engaged. And Mrs. Hellström may have sensed that she would be asked to lead the prayers.

THE GREEN TRAIN AND TROLLEY #4

One of the most striking cases in Mrs. Hellström's diary is her dream of an accident between a street-car and a railroad train. Mrs. Hellström was so impressed with the many unusual aspects of the case that she sent a description of it to two Swedish scientists and to Dr. J. B. Rhine at Duke University.

March 26, 1954. I dreamed this morning about a street-car accident. The dream had the character of precognition and was in color. But I can't understand how it can come true because it was *a collision between a street-car and a green railway car.* . .

I had the feeling that Bo and I were flying over Stockholm. I looked down and thought we were somewhere in the neighborhood of Kungsträdgarden [a park] . . . I said to myself, "The green one ran into #4 from the back. There was a motorcar and it was his fault." I saw an ordinary blue tram of the #4 type, and a green train . . . run into the tram. . .

In the dream the green railway car was "driven to one side by the impact and came to rest at right angles to tram #4." Mrs. Hellström thought that a careless automobile driver had caused the accident and told this to a policeman. When she awoke, she made a sketch of the accident.

Mrs. Hellström was puzzled by the green railway car, as all the train carriages were painted in different shades of brown. However, in June of the same year she visited a friend and noted with surprise that the train included a new green car, the first she had ever seen on this line. The conductor told her that the railroad had ordered five or six such green cars, better equipped and more modern than the brown ones.

"I feel almost sure," she then wrote in her diary, "that the accident will happen when the train from Djursholm [a suburb of Stockholm] and the #4 trolley meet at Valhallavägen [a street in Stockholm]. This is a place where there have been accidents between autos and trains but so far as I know, *never with a trolley,* and in any case, never with a *green Djursholm car.*"

Just as Mrs. Hellström had predicted, on March 4, 1956, there was a collision at Valhallavägen between a train with green cars from Djursholm and a #4 trolley. Accidents involving a street-car and a train were so rare that a railway employee who had been working for the company thirty-three years had never known of one:

I herewith confirm that the train from Djursholm, since I started working for the Stockholm-Djursholm Railway Company in the year 1923, has not been involved in a collision with a tram until the accident of March 4th, 1956. . .
Djursholm, September 12th, 1958

                              Eric Panzar, Stationmaster

Another significant detail was that the dream had specifically shown tram #4, as distinguished from other street-cars, in the accident. A further correspondence between the dream and the reality was that the vehicles came to rest at right angles to each other. The sketch of the accident made by the police was almost identical to that drawn by Mrs. Hellström after her dream.

The fifth item of interest, one that was very puzzling to Mrs. Hellström, was the appearance of the auto in the dream and her anxiety to inform the police that the driver had caused the dream-accident.

Although there was no auto involved in the real accident. Mrs. Hellström recalled that about twenty-five years before, she had been made uneasy by a drunken driver just ahead of her car on a London road. The other driver's car turned over on its side, and Mrs. Hellström had gone to an English policeman and offered to be a witness against the man.

I herewith confirm that her (Mrs. Hellström's) reports and statements concerning the car accident in London at the beginning of 1930 are in accordance with the actual facts.

(signed) Bo Hellström

The dream thus combined events of the past with those of the future accident. The seer's emotional link to the past accident stirred precognition of another accident involving the trolley and the train. As a thoughtful observer of her premonitory dreams, she noticed that, in such a dream, "the details at the beginning very often are right when the happening occurs. At the end of the dream, however, when the conscious mind gradually returns, the details sometimes become vague and indistinct and will very likely turn out to be wrong."

THE SOUND OF EGYPTIAN DRUMS

In 1952 Mrs. Hellström took a trip through Egypt. One afternoon in Aswan, she had a very striking vision while awake. It appeared in the form of a moving picture, in color, and was symbolic rather than realistic. It was accompanied by a "strong conviction" that there would be a future war between England and Egypt.

February 17, 1952. Today after lunch I was so tired that I had a pain in the throat. I lay for half an hour trying in vain to sleep. Then I saw a vision. Not very clear—I believe it was a riot or turmoil of some kind. Then I saw a bridge that collapsed or went to pieces. People were hanging on the iron beams . . . amongst them was a Scotsman in a kilt, which I believe symbolizes that the English are in it.

In this vision bits of the past are woven into the fabric of the future. Mrs. Hellström later learned that there had once been fighting in the area and that people, having retreated to the bridge, hung on the iron beams to save themselves. She felt strongly that the vision sym-

bolized something terrible that was going to happen—*something
which would sever all relations between Britain and Egypt.*

War between Britain and Egypt broke out on October 31, 1956.
Mrs. Hellström wondered why she had seen a Scotsman in kilts. She
wrote, "If I had seen an ordinary Englishman in an ordinary suit, he
could have belonged to any nation. Because I saw the Scotsman with
his typical kilt, I understood that it concerned Britain."

Admittedly, it is much more difficult to interpret a symbolic dream
than one in which the facts are laid out graphically. Many persons
allow symbolic dreams of the future to slip away, even though they
are accompanied by strong undefined feelings of apprehension. In
such cases, it is best to think about the dream, note the images that
are associated with it, and perhaps the subliminal message will
emerge. By keeping a record of every dream and reviewing it from
time to time, the meaning may become clear as the subconscious
mind works it through.

Was there an emotional link between Mrs. Hellström, a Swede, and
the 1956 war between Britain and Egypt? Chances are that vibrations
of the future were caught by Mrs. Hellström from the Egyptian setting in which she was travelling.

THE RUNAWAY WHITE HORSE

On the lighter side, Mrs. Hellström often dreams of scenes in plays
or films she will see in the future. One day she had what she calls a
"combined dream and vision." It was in color and accompanied by
a strong conviction that it would come true.

> November 22nd, 1952. Yesterday, while I was resting, I saw a vision
> or had a dream or both combined . . . I think it had to do with a lot
> of white horses in a cluster doing something. I was there with them.
> Then all of a sudden . . . a big white horse ran along the road at full
> gallop or ran away with a flying mane. But he swayed to and fro on the
> road like this. [She made a sketch showing the horse running forward
> in a zigzag pattern.] It was very beautiful. It ran away from me.

The next afternoon Mrs. Hellström and her daughter decided to
see a movie, *Viva Zapata*. She suspected that the "runaway horse"
might appear and when the scene came on, she nudged her daughter and cried out, "There is my horse!" As a conscientious psychic

and researcher, Mrs. Hellström took her daughter back home and showed her the diary with the sketch in it. Both Mr. Hellström and the daughter signed statements as witnesses.

Although the cases mentioned earlier are all newsworthy events that would be of significance to premonitions registries—the laborer trapped in the tunnel, the man who fell from the brickhouse, the trolley and the train, and the vision of a future war—the white horse incident was of purely personal interest. But as an example of the precognition of a film, play, or newspaper article, it should be noted down along with other dreams and visions.

The would-be seer should follow Mrs. Hellström's lead in keeping a record of every dream, no matter how trivial, that seems to be extrasensory. (It is better, in fact, to record *all* dreams until the psychic ones can be separated from the everyday variety.) After her first precognitive dream, the Swedish seer says that she began "writing notes of everything and collecting verifications, snapshots, and newspaper clippings and putting everything in big casebooks . . . *I have written down everything, including small unimportant cases.* I have not sorted out the good ones and left out the minor ones."

Special attention should be paid to something that seems likely to get into the newspapers. Note if the premonition is auditory or visual, whether the "here-and-now" conviction is strong, whether the scene is stationary or moving, in color or black and white. Mrs. Hellström also comments: "In my ordinary dreams I am the center; in my ESP dreams I am the spectator and I am not emotionally engaged in the event. There are very few exceptions." Mrs. Hellström gets many premonitions during the hypnagogic state when she is falling asleep, or in the hypnopompic state when she is beginning to wake up.

Keep a diary and, as soon as possible, write down the details of the dream. If it seems to be precognitive, get the signature of at least two witnesses. If it concerns a public event or personality, send a copy to either the British Premonitions Bureau or the Central Premonitions Registry. After that, keep thinking about your dream-experience and if it is symbolic rather than realistic, try to understand what the symbols mean to you.

After each dream or vision of an earthquake, plane crash, assassination, or happy event that may be in the news, listen to the radio or television or watch the newspapers for verification. Clip out the news article that is pertinent and send it to the premonitions bureau that has your prediction on record.

HOW TO "CATCH" YOUR DREAMS

Here is a list of suggestions on the art of "dream-catching" sent to each would-be psychic who contacts the Central Premonitions Registry:

1 Before you go to sleep, tell yourself that you are going to remember your dreams. If there is something specific that you would like to dream about, concentrate on it before you fall asleep.

2 Keep a pen and pad under the pillow or at the bedside. A pen with a built-in flashlight is especially recommended.

3 When you awaken, before you open your eyes, begin remembering what you were dreaming about. If you cannot recall any images, try to remember what you were feeling or thinking about. As soon as you get "something" reach for your pen and notebook.

4 If it's still dark, turn on a soft light and jot down the image, or a list of incidents that you remember. As soon as you write down one image, you will probably find yourself recalling others. Write one word, or so, for each incident.

5 Now, working with your simple outline, write out each incident as fully as you can, providing as many details as possible.

6 Later in the day, re-read your dream notes and if anything appears regarding some well-known person, or event of national or international consequence—and you feel it might relate to the future—write it in a letter to the Registry.

You will find that the more practice you get at this, the better you will become at recalling your dreams. Scientific studies show that most people dream four or five times a night, and that one is more likely to remember a dream if one awakens while the dream is still in progress. If you cannot recall any dreams for several consecutive nights, try setting your alarm for half an hour earlier. Experimenting in this fashion should produce some dreams.

MORE HINTS FOR THE NEW PSYCHIC

Possibly the most important technique for developing into a seer is meditation. Arthur Ford, one of America's famous psychics, suggested sitting quietly for at least twenty minutes or half an hour each day. "Each beginner should find a place where it is quiet as it is possible to be in this noisy world. He should shut out as much light as possible and sit in the most comfortable position he can." Different kinds of meditation are described in books on yoga or Zen disciplines, as well as in general books on the subject. Perhaps the most important first step before meditating is to relax body and mind.

If you find it difficult to meditate by yourself, find a meditation circle in your community, particularly one that meets for the purpose of developing ESP powers. The prophets of the Aquarian Age are all meditators, either alone or in group sessions which they may lead. The American Society for Psychical Research in New York City has groups that meet regularly and meditate prior to testing for extrasensory perception.

CHAPTER NINETEEN

What's Going On Down There?

The time has come to ask what time itself is all about. If we are able to visualize scenes that will not take place until some time in the future, we may be mistaken in our comfortable notion that the world is as we see it, or as it has been explained to us by scientists, historians, and other scholars. Do our senses mislead us into thinking that the universe is one of cause and effect, of one happening leading logically to another, of one day connected by a natural sequence of events to the next?

Or is the universe as we know it an illusion? Is time itself an illusion? Is there an "eternal now," with all that has happened and will happen going on alongside the present? If that thought startles you, take another look at your conventional ideas of time, with its neat division into days, months, years, and centuries. Try to imagine that eons and eons ago, before our solar system was formed, when the universe was a huge ball of gas, time had a beginning out of nothingness. Immediately the finite mind asks, but what went before? The average person cannot conceive of time starting at a given point without another time preceding it. And when time ends—then what?

Or perhaps our waking life is really a dream, and the dream itself, with its crazy-quilt mixture of past, present, and future, is the true reality. Philosophers in the East can handle this kind of question better than those of us in the West, who want definite, common-sense answers. Twenty-five hundred years ago a Chinese gentleman named Chuang Tzu awoke from a dream in which he had been a butterfly. The thoughtful Chuang mused to himself: Did I, Chuang Tzu, dream that I was a butterfly or am I a butterfly who is now dreaming that he is Chuang Tzu?

St. Augustine in his *Confessions* voiced the dilemma of the average person, who is not concerned with the nature of time until he is required to think about it: "What then is time? If no one asks me, I know; if I want to explain it to a questioner, I do not know."

"THE ETERNAL NOW"

Serious writers on premonitions and precognition, aware that seeing the future violates well-entrenched laws of an orderly universe, feel compelled to find an explanation for this curious phenomenon. Writers J. W. Dunne, H. F. Saltmarsh, J. B. Priestley, and many more from the ranks of literary men, parapsychologists, philosophers, physicists, and engineers have worked out intricate theories about time, giving them such labels as "the eternal now," "the serial universe," "the specious present," "circular time," "two-dimensional time," "four-dimensional space," etc.—most of them based on the idea that past and future in some way coexist with the present.

It is not necessary to dwell too long on these theories, because they seem to bring up more problems than they solve. Many of them are fascinating and thought provoking, but when one is through considering them, he is still apt to say, "Yes, but what is time?" It is almost impossible to conceive of the future already existing and the past continuing to exist. Only the cagey Jung has come up with a theory the average man can live with—synchronicity. Jung points out that since we are confronted with strange coincidences in time and space for which there is no apparent cause-and-effect relationship, there must be an "a-causal principle" at work. In other words, stop breaking your head trying to figure this thing out; just accept the truth that the universe is not what it seems to be.

Some of the time-concepts are not without value, however. J. W. Dunne, a thoughtful scientist and engineer, kept a careful record of his dreams and discovered that some of the dream-images related to events just past and an equal number to those in the near future.

This would be an astonishing discovery in itself, but Dunne wouldn't let well enough alone. He devised an intricate theory about the nature of time, which can be only touched upon here.

Time, said Dunne, is a dimension which also has length and under certain circumstances can be observed as occupying space. A person in his conscious life can glimpse only what is taking place in the present, three-dimensional world, in which space is space and time is time. But on a deeper level of the mind, another part of the personality sees time as space—that is, the events that take place in time are spread out so that he can view portions of past, present, and future at a glance. So what is "time" to the conscious personality becomes "space" for the unconscious self.

Another student of precognition, H. F. Saltmarsh, hit upon the ingenious idea of spreading out the "now" so that the present moment, which he calls the "specious present," may be of short duration for the conscious mind and longer for the deeper-level mind. The subliminal mind thus gets a wider view of the "now," which includes part of the future not yet experienced by the conscious mind.

Saltmarsh's theory does have some psychological validity. One's experience of the flow of time differs according to his mood, feelings, and concentration. Sometimes his specious present, his "now," passes quickly. At other times, particularly in emotional states when other levels of the mind may be involved, time may be stretched out to include what are called premonitions. However, Saltmarsh is honest enough to admit that "the phenomenon of precognition is itself so odd and so out of parallel with all our normal experience, that we must not be surprised if any hypothesis to account for it be bizarre and fantastic."

The theory of "eternal recurrence," advanced by the philosopher Ouspensky, is easy enough to grasp in its essentials but practically impossible to accept. Ouspensky believes that, with some exceptions, when we die we are immediately born into the circumstances of our previous birth and relive that same life in all its details. This boring repetition goes on and will go on indefinitely. Nostradamus, for example, can see clearly what will happen in five hundred years because it has already happened an infinite number of times, and in each of his infinite number of lives, he has made the same prediction of events that have already taken place.

Are you "out there," Nostradamus?

In *The Future Is Now,* the Australian writer Arthur W. Osborn sets forth an appealing theory that has its base in Eastern philosophy. He believes that events of the future are preceded by "thought-forms" existing in a Cosmic Mind and experienced in the minds of individuals: "The images which impress themselves upon outer consciousness are reflections of inner events." Every happening starts out as an idea which later takes on objective form.

Mrs. Milden, for example, has a vision of the little boy with the long fringe of hair. This thought-form then materializes on the television screen two days later. Thought-forms give some validity to the notion that the mind may help create the future.

THE THEORY OF SUBLIMINAL COMPUTERS

While I was talking over this chapter with a friend who is knowledgeable in all aspects of psychic phenomena, he said, "Why bother to discuss time or invent new theories about it? The mystery of precognition is fascinating in itself. Let it remain a mystery." But since the itch to throw light on the problem by coming up with my own neat, all-embracing theory is very strong, however, I will first repeat Saltmarsh's warning that "we must not be surprised if any hypothesis to account for it (precognition) be bizarre and fantastic."

I believe, however, that my theory of "subliminal computers" is easier to digest, if difficult in some of its aspects, than the concept of an "eternal now." Philosophically considered, time may be an illusion. But for the sake of sanity, let us try to fit it into the framework of our daily lives and see how precognition can be reconciled with it.

Many students of psychic phenomena believe that all minds may come together in a vast "etheric pool," where the totality of knowledge—every fact about the universe past and present—is stored. How does the mind tap and use this knowledge? Perhaps in the same way that computers are used in our technological culture. When there is a problem involving a multitude of details, of facts and figures that may take months to correlate, a programmer feeds all the data into a computer, and the giant mechanical brain quickly assimilates it and gives back an answer.

It may be that in our minds, also, at very deep levels there is a kind of computer that clairvoyantly scans the etheric pool, makes rapid calculations, then extrapolates an event that will occur later. When there are only a few facts to consider, our conscious minds can make inferences about the future. But as the situation grows more and more complicated, the conscious mind simply cannot cope with the problem. Down below, however, the subliminal computer gathers all data about the present which will lead to a future happening, then signals a prediction to the top layer of consciousness.

Charles Richet, the physiologist, once said, "If we knew the totality of things in the present, we should know the totality of things to come. Our ignorance of the future is the result of our ignorance of the present." But our ignorance may be only on a conscious level. "Down there" where the subliminal computer operates, we may know the "totality of things" in the present that gives us a blueprint of the future.

What kind of data must be available in this "totality of things"? It is easy to conceive of changes in the physical world that will bring predictable results. Dealing with man and his vagaries is a more difficult matter. Yet even Immanuel Kant, the philosopher, has observed: ". . . if we could penetrate into the soul of a man so that it will reveal itself by acts internal as well as external, if we could understand all the motives, even the slightest, and at the same time all the external influences, we could calculate the future conduct of this man with all the certainty of an eclipse of the sun or of the moon."

Let's go back to the *Titanic*. The mental computer needs information about the ship—every detail of its construction, where it is built, the date and hour when it will sail, its route through the ocean. It must be aware of the movement of currents, the amount of rainfall and other climatic changes that will influence the direction and velocity of the iceberg, and where the iceberg will be at the exact moment the ship strikes it. These are the "external influences." But it must also have information about the minds and motives, "even the slightest," of all persons involved in the project—the officials of the White Star line, the construction crew, the crew of the ship, the captain. It must take into account the swiftly moving internal events, how minds and motives may shift from day to day, even from minute to minute. It must consider, as a psychiatrist would, the subtleties of each personality and its flaws, such as the pride of Captain Smith in his "indestructible" liner.

The mental computer, knowing all these facts and their logical consequences through clairvoyance, processes them. After an astronomical number of calculations, it sends up this prediction: on April 14, 1912, at precisely the hour of 11:40 P.M., the iceberg will be in such-and-such a position in mid-Atlantic, so many degrees latitude and longitude, and the *Titanic* will be on a collision course with it.

When Mrs. Milden had her vision of the boy with the long fringe of hair, a mass of details had to be processed before she could see what would take place on the television screen. Her subliminal computer had to know where the boy was at the time of the vision, then follow him into the future—scan his every action for the next two days and fix his exact position on the television screen. It had to trace the activities and thoughts of the camera crew and the director until the cameras were set up at just the angles that would reproduce the picture first seen in Mrs. Milden's mind.

When Malcolm Bessent dreamed about a mental hospital, his subliminal computer first had to know which numbers the staff members would choose "at random" leading to the page and item in the book of dream-descriptions. Then the sleeping Malcolm had to scan Dr. Krippner's mind hours before Krippner created the multisensory environment based on the target word and picture.

For thousands of years, mental computers have been processing material from the etheric pool and making predictions. Hundreds, perhaps thousands of persons came to the subliminal conclusion that the *Titanic* would sink on its maiden voyage. Two hundred or more human seismographs received signals from "down below" that a mountain of coal slag would descend on the town of Aberfan. At this very moment there may be millions of such computers in minds all over the world flashing news to the "upper story" of events good and bad that will soon occur.

THE DRAMATIC SENSE TAKES OVER

Why doesn't the computer just send up a simple "headline" message of what is going to happen? This is too prosaic for the mind of man, especially on its deeper levels. Man must take his raw, factual materials and "create" a meaningful experience out of them. He must see the event in emotional and theatrical terms. So now the playwright mind intercepts the message from the computer mind and dramatizes it.

The play that is created is both personal and predictive. Referring to premonitions of disaster, Dr. Eisenbud writes: "Behind each one of them possibly some psychological drama was being played out whose finale, or third act resolution, as it were, called for just such a stage effect as the phenomenon of 'precognition' itself."

The playwright mind chooses one of a number of dramatic forms in which to make its presentation. Just as there are writers who see the stage in either representational or symbolic terms, the dream-or-vision playwright sometimes projects the future graphically, other times in expressionistic or surrealistic images. J. Connon Middleton, for example, not only visualizes the *Titanic* sinking but adds the symbolic detail of himself floating a little above the wreck. An analytic level of the mind makes the interpretation: Middleton will be spared.

EMOTIONS AND INTERNAL MOTIVATIONS

Why is one particular future event dramatized and not another? According to Dr. Ian Stevenson, "Precognition seems to occur in just those situations where our emotions are most strongly aroused —threats to the well-being of ourselves and those we love."

This is especially true of death-portents. The link, however, may not be a direct one. Eva Hellström dreams of a clay landslide that devastates a village, presumably because her husband was an engineer who once worked in the area and because she lived there at the start of her married life. The link extends to public figures. Innumerable persons sense that President Kennedy will be shot because of their close personal bond to the presidency.

This happens not only in the case of "threats" but of "good things." Jung's patient dreams about the scarab because she needs a breakthrough in her analysis. Malcolm Bessent, suffering from a bad back, is strongly motivated to dream of the "dry bones" environment created the next morning by Dr. Krippner, and also of a future situation in which his ailment will be cured.

Another motivation for the drama of the future is one's life-style. Alan Vaughan, with a strong interest in science and a career in science-editing, gets vivid feelings about the fate of the astronauts.

Morgan Robertson, fascinated by the sea, writes a book in which he unconsciously predicts the sinking of the *Titanic*. Gerard Croiset, because of his own stormy childhood, scores his greatest successes in locating lost children.

Geography also plays a part. A psychic is especially sensitive to "something terrible" that will happen in his own country or a place he may be visiting. Those who dreamed of the Aberfan coal slide lived in England, not far from the scene of the tragedy. The Central Premonitions Registry reported no advance notice of the earthquake in Peru or the cyclone in Pakistan, possibly because other continents were involved. Yet there must have been thousands of South Americans and Pakistanis who sensed what was coming.

What of the time factor in relation to premonitions? Generally, we have noticed that when a disaster is about to strike (e.g., the *Titanic* and Aberfan cases), the premonitions increase in number and intensity as the event nears. Yet there have been striking examples of premonitions that came many years before—for example, the mother who sensed that her child would be buried in the sand during World War II first dreamed of it twenty-seven years earlier.

Time and space shrink when the emotional link is strong, as it is between mother and child. Dr. Karlis Osis, director of research at the American Society for Psychical Research, has conducted many experiments in long-distance clairvoyance and has found that test scores seem to fall off as the distance increases. There are, however, variables that may change this pattern, and the most dynamic is probably the emotional link between sender and receiver.

Emotion may also be a significant variable in cases of precognition. Although premonitions do seem to gather force as the future event comes closer, there are times when the mental computer makes a great leap forward. That is why a mother's vision could reach across twenty-seven years to the scene which her subliminal mind and emotions have re-created. Time contracts or expands for us depending on our emotional relationship to an event.

AN INFINITE NUMBER OF FUTURES

We come, then, to the inevitable question—free will or determinism? If our subliminal computers consider all the factors that will lead to what seems to be an inescapable result, the determinists would appear to win the argument. But we have many cases that point the other way.

It will be recalled, for example, that Lady Varden dreamed that her coachman became ill while driving and fell on his head in the street. When the dream-scene was about to come true, however, she jumped out of the brougham and hailed a policeman, who caught the driver before he fell. Was the computer wrong, or did it carelessly leave out one or more facts that would change the result?

There have been a number of instances given in which at least one fact was different from those in the dream or vision. J. Connon Middleton saw the keel of the *Titanic* floating upwards rather than in its down position. All the facts in the dream of Air Marshal Goddard's flight and crash came true except the most important one—he and his passengers survived. Madame de Ferriëm thought the mine explosion would occur during the Christmas season, whereas the month was October. Was the subliminal computer wrong in each case?

The writer conjectured earlier that each psychic, perhaps seeing the future scene as it would have been physically in the present, may have made assumptions based on this observation in the dream or vision. Another possibility, illustrated by the Goddard case, is that the dream may in some way alter the course of events it has depicted. Perhaps just the fact that Goddard was told about the dream changed the outcome.

There seems to be room in the future for both "internal motivations" and "external events" that interrupt the sequence. It could be an act of intervention on the part of the psychic. At the time of Lady Varden's dream, her thought-form—to use Osborn's term—was of the coachman falling on his head. But by calling the policeman, she was able to change the future that seemed fated when the computer reached its conclusion. Yet sometimes even this will not work, as the Samarra cases have shown.

At any given moment in time, there are an infinite number of possibilities. When a psychic has a dream or vision, he sees the computerized result *as of that moment*. Premonitions of events outside human control, such as natural disasters, apparently point to an irreversible fate. An important variable in all cases of premonition, however—perhaps the most important—is man himself, with his ability to think about the future and his will to change it. There is also a certain activity in the unconscious mind of the person marked by fate that may somehow direct him away from his peril.

Take the case of law student Brown in which three persons had the same dream of a man's murder. Perhaps, according to all the subliminal computer calculations at the time, the murder was fated to happen. The vividness of the three identical dreams suggests that somewhere a bushy-headed, unkempt killer was lurking and that he might at some point in the future meet the young man and slit open his head with a hatchet blow. But something happened to prevent this confrontation. Perhaps the three dreams themselves or even the discussion between the law student and the other dreamers broke the chain of events that was leading to the murder.

The analogy of the drama comes in again. We may all be characters in a cosmic play, with our fates known only to the celestial playwright who has plotted our actions. Occasionally, however, while we are still performing in the first act, we get glimpses—dramatic flashes—of what will happen in the second or third act. Perhaps the play is only in the planning or rehearsal stage, and the playwright decides to rewrite some scenes. The dramatist "out there" who conceived of the murder may have decided on a kinder fate for the young law student. Or he may have abandoned the project altogether.

Or—and this is where the possibility of free will comes in more emphatically—a strong-minded character in the play may decide to direct his own fate, and he browbeats the playwright into revising the script. Every writer knows that his characters sometimes have a will of their own, with motivations so strong that the writer must often give in to them. A sense of awe at the refusal of their characters to follow a preconceived plan was felt by Goethe, Blake, Poe, Dante, and a host of other writers.

In real-life situations the same thing may happen. The more passive characters, those who shrug their shoulders and bow to what appears to be inevitable, accept the future they may see in their dreams and visions. Willful souls, like the lady who was concerned about her coachman, demand that the cosmic playwright, if there is one, rewrite his script closer to their heart's desire. The more determined characters in reality, like many on the stage, improvise their life-scripts rather than meekly follow the dialogue and stage directions assigned to them. Thus they may not only change the future but help to create it.

In each given moment the computer can foresee possibilities that the actions of man can avert. If human beings, concerned about their fate and the fate of others, have an option to change the future, there is valid reason for the existence of premonitions registries. The concerted action of some two hundred persons who had premonitions of the Aberfan tragedy, for example, could have pressured the British government into removing the coal slag before it roared down the mountain. Unfortunately, there was no London Premonitions Bureau at the time to sound an alert.

RECAPITULATION

Let's try to draw it all together.

We start out with the theory that all minds converge somewhere "out there," and exchange information, and that every mind knows subliminally what is going on in every other mind and in the inanimate world.

Next comes "feedback" from the future—the presentiment of an event that is somehow tied to our emotional needs. Our subliminal computer scans the etheric pool for information and selects the facts that will lead to this event, then sends up its prediction.

Now the playwright mind takes over and directs a psychodrama, in which the characters rehearse a scene out of their future and at the same time work through our personal problems. This happens on many mental stages—in dreams or visions, perhaps in hunches or undefined feelings that "something terrible" is going to happen.

The premonitions are sometimes of disasters involving ourselves or our relatives or friends. Young children to whom we all have some kind of link may be the future victims. Sometimes one or two facts are wrong, either because we make an assumption from our own viewpoint as we would in the present, or because in some way the future does change slightly. It may be the very fact of seeing a future disaster that helps to prevent or change it.

As we see the future, we may be helping to create it at the same time. Perhaps the thought-form of Dr. Eisenbud's patient in some way influenced the explosion in the Pennsylvania Hotel, so that the dreamer not only helped to create the future but also got feedback from it—all in the service of his neurosis. In a more exalted sphere, Jules Verne "dreamed up" a technology of the future in the form of spaceships, helicopters, airplanes, television sets, and so forth. We know that later scientists and inventors acknowledged their debt to him.

A word of caution. When large-scale events are foreseen, such as monumental natural disasters, wars, sweeping political and social changes, hysteria and bias may get in the way and completely distort our picture of the future.

One more point. In meditation or any other kind of collective experience in which the emotions, thoughts, or will of a group may operate, the effect is more powerful than when one's individual mental and emotional forces are working alone. When not one, but several persons get strong feelings that "something terrible" is about to happen, the combined will to act may prevent the disaster.

Can we change the future? Practicing psychics and human seismographs, not only in England and America but also Russia and other countries, may in time alert premonitions bureaus all over the world to a natural disaster, an assassination, or other newsworthy events, good and bad. Let's see what the prophets of the Aquarian Age predict for the next thirty years and what, if anything, can be done about it.

CHAPTER TWENTY

The Next Thirty Years—
A Sneak Preview

Prophecy is a delicate art that requires self-analysis and detachment from the psychic experience as well as involvement in it. In addition to being director and often star performer in the subliminal drama, the seer must also be spectator and critic. He must ask himself if he is witnessing actual scenes from the future or if the playwright mind, perhaps stimulated by bias or an overheated imagination, has been carried away by its sense of the dramatic.

The seer should be especially on his guard when asked to predict what will happen in the far future in politics, economics, international relations, and other large-scale—but non-personal—areas. Jeane Dixon, for one, continues to scan the world of tomorrow with her psychic eye, making prognoses that are startling but also suspect. Because of her religious orientation, Mrs. Dixon sees the future as a battlefield on which the forces of good and evil will contend. Evil will have its way at first, but good will triumph in the denouement.

The end of the century, says Mrs. Dixon, will witness the climax of this battle, at least until holy warfare breaks out again in the twenty-first century. Just as 999, the last year of the first millennium, was believed to mark the end of the world, Mrs. Dixon pictures 1999 as the year of cosmic upheavals in war and religion. In the year 2000

Oriental hordes will invade the Middle East and Israel will be in great peril. When things look darkest, however, a Cross will light the eastern sky, the Lord will intervene on the side of the righteous, and the Israelis will then "finally accept Jesus Christ as the son of God." Curtain.

Mrs. Dixon is firmly convinced that the Anti-Christ, whose coming has been predicted since biblical times, will finally appear and cause terrible suffering before he is routed. The seeress had a vision in 1952 in which she saw the symbol of a "false prophet" who would herald the coming of a Christ-like figure. The latter appeared in another vision ten years later, and Mrs. Dixon at first accepted him as a genuine Messiah but later changed her mind, deciding that he would be a pretender who would mask his evil purpose with simulated goodness. Mrs. Dixon warns that this enemy of mankind, born at the time of her 1962 vision, is now growing up somewhere in the Arab world.

Mrs. Dixon's change of heart has caused some confusion among professional psychics. Daniel Logan also stated that a child "born in Egypt in 1962" would "lead many to recognize the truth." Although his appearance would not be the Second Coming, Logan does not see the Arab leader as the Anti-Christ.

The Anti-Christ theme is not a new one, and Mrs. Dixon has apparently been influenced by prophets of the last two thousand years. In 380 A.D. St. Martin, Bishop of Tours, announced that the Anti-Christ had been born and was growing to maturity under the watchful eye of the Devil. Again in 1080 another bishop warned that the evil child had been born. A preacher was so disturbed by his vision in 1412 that he wrote to Pope Benedict XIII, with the information that the Anti-Christ was then nine years old.

According to one view, there would be three Anti-Christs who would wage war for twenty-seven years. And a more modern prophetess, Josephine Lamartine, almost hit the target when she predicted in 1850 that the true Anti-Christ would be born in 1900, missing Hitler's birthdate by eleven years. Mrs. Dixon may also be familiar with the prediction of St. Hildegarde who said in 1100 that the Anti-Christ would appear "at the end of the time of the Gentiles," and would fulfill a biblical prophecy.

In choosing 1999 as the fateful year, Mrs. Dixon may be following

Nostradamus, who said that "in the seventh month" of that year a terrible Arab prince would come out of the sky and destroy Paris. The seeress, with a nervous look at Mao and other potential leaders in Southeast Asia, also predicts an invasion by Mongol armies, but their connection with the Arab conqueror is not clear. Although Nostradamus named Paris as the scene of the holocaust, Mrs. Dixon sees the whole world engulfed in war at that time, with the center of the fighting in Jerusalem.

Natural disasters will add to the general chaos. Edgar Cayce, the modern prophet's prophet, also pinpointed 1999 and foresaw the shifting of the poles between 1998–2000. Mrs. Dixon, without giving a date, predicts a devastating earthquake in Jerusalem that will influence political events, but she doesn't say how. After the dramatic appearance of the Cross in the sky (the Bible predicted that "the sign of the Son of Man" would appear in the heavens) peace will reign. The devil will stir up new troubles later but since our cutoff date is 2000, we won't look into Mrs. Dixon's predictions for the next century.

When Mrs. Dixon and other prophets put aside their religious apprehensions, the future they envision seems a bit more reasonable, although still threatened by the violent acts of man and nature. In the 1980s, for example, Mrs. Dixon sees a comet hitting the earth and causing great havoc—cataclysmic earthquakes and giant tidal waves. She claims to know the exact spot where the comet will strike, but refuses to be pinned down at this time.

WHAT THE PSYCHICS PREDICT

Many other prophets and prophetesses, including those mentioned earlier, have made forecasts for the next thirty years. Among them are some of the star performers of the Central Premonitions Registry, including Malcolm Bessent and Alan Vaughan. Strangely, Lorna Middleton, whose astonishing predictions make up a good part of the Registry's "hits," doesn't care to predict much for the far future. She is more temperamentally suited to impressions of events good and bad that are about to occur.

Let's see what the consensus is among the seers for many of the categories used by the Central Premonitions Registry:

ECONOMICS: Financially, says Mrs. Dixon, the country is in for more trouble, with a possible panic that will follow a sharp increase in gold prices. To compound our problems, Japan will rise to the top economically, and this will have an impact on the labor movement in America. Daniel Logan also sees Japan as the foremost industrial nation in the next thirty years, and he predicts a depression in the United States during the early 1970s that will ruin many small businessmen.

Adrienne Coulter believes that Spain will rise once more to economic prominence. Germany, says Malcolm Bessent, will be economically dominant in Europe by 1974 and will have a trade war with France that will draw in Belgium. Ann Jensen forecasts vast changes in world marketing during the 1980s, with a possible return to the barter system in some areas of the world in the 1990s.

STOCK MARKET: Mrs. Jensen sees the stock market in serious trouble for the next five years, with a low point dangerously close to the bottom level of the 1929 crash. During this time many "paper millionaires" will lose much of their assets. In the 1980s there will be a radical change in the way the market operates.

POLITICS: Mrs. Jensen thinks that the year 1976 will bring back "the spirit of the other '76." Jeanne Gardner sees the same year as the starting point of good government in the United States until a "bad event" occurs in 1982. The late English psychic Pendragon foresaw a powerful figure arising in the United States, possibly a Virginian, who would unite the country and probably end the Vietnam war. Jeane Dixon predicts that five new Supreme Court justices will be appointed during the Nixon administration, also that before 1980 the two-party system will vanish from the American scene.

Bessent believes that the next five years will be very trying for the United States and that the country will be about to "explode," particularly New York City. In 1969 he predicted that an American Indian leader would emerge in the next five years who would unite the tribes and that there might be a land settlement for all the Indians. As this book goes to press, there has been a strong movement toward unity and activism among the Indians in 1970 and 1971. Indian rights are receiving greater attention in Washington, and "aboriginal titles" to vast acreage taken from the Indians have been awarded to many tribes, including the Seminoles and Navajos.

For the ladies two women psychics offer a special treat. Mrs. Dixon promises a woman president in the 1980s, possibly arriving at the same time as the comet. In a trance prediction, Mrs. Jensen foresaw a world government in the 1990s, headed by a woman.

WAR AND INTERNATIONAL RELATIONS: Most prophets lean in the direction of trouble with Red China, while Russia and the United States will draw closer together. Pendragon envisioned the expansion of China through conquest—the invasion of Laos, Thailand, Cambodia, then southward to Sumatra, Borneo, New Guinea, and Australia. He promised that Japan and possibly India would be our allies in a conflict with China, the Soviets remaining neutral.

Both Pendragon and Mrs. Jensen believe that in the 1970s and 1980s there will be greater cooperation between the United States and Russia. Daniel Logan also thinks that Russia and the U.S. will become allies and will eventually fight against the real menace, China. In an earlier book Mrs. Dixon predicted that we would be aligned with Russia in a war with China during the 1980s. In her latest book, however, she speaks of Russian plans for world conquest which will be interrupted by a natural phenomenon in 1985 (the comet?).

Vaughan predicts war with China about 1981, Bessent in 1979. Ann Jensen, on the other hand, sees no world wars in the next thirty years, only local skirmishes, small uprisings. Jeanne Gardner is one of the few seers who believe that we will have good relations with China. She warns, however that America will face danger on five fronts, the result of a plot by foreign powers to thin out our forces and weaken the country. There will be a "fireball" dropped over New York City—a bomb that will go astray.

According to Mrs. Dixon, the war with China will result from our involvement in Vietnam and Korea. The consensus seems to be that the Vietnam war will go on for many years. Ann Jensen sees it finally petering out at the end of the decade, but for Logan it will grow in intensity. The Middle East, in Pendragon's view, is not as menacing as the Far East, but there will be a conflict between Iran and Egypt, with Iran winning. An earlier prophet, Cheiro, joins Mrs. Dixon and others in seeing Armageddon beginning in Palestine.

NATURAL DISASTERS: Pendragon foretold great devastation in the United States, with many eastern cities—Boston, New York, Philadelphia, Pittsburgh—wiped out. Echoing the predictions of Bessent and Vaughan, but on a much more frightening scale, Pendragon visualized many cities underwater. However, most of the inland cities will be spared.

Daniel Logan believes that New York City will no longer exist by the twenty-first century, a prediction shared by Cayce and other earlier prophets who saw the doom of world capitals. Logan thinks that the earth has been moved off its axis by the detonation of atomic weapons, and that in the future there will be devastating earthquakes on the East and West Coast and in the Middle East, where thousands will die.

Jeanne Gardner predicts that the Russians will test a 100-megaton bomb in the Alaskan area, causing the sinking of glaciers and the inundation of California. Adrienne Coulter, in common with Edgar Cayce, sees a shifting of the poles, causing disturbances in an area covering Alaska, the West Coast, Hawaii, and as far west as Japan. She also foresees trouble for Louisiana, which may go under water. Vaughan predicts a major earthquake for California in fifteen to twenty years but not a separation of the state from the mainland.

Ann Jensen sees no important natural disasters in the next twenty or thirty years. California will not "slide into the ocean."

THE SPACE RACE: Both Logan and Mrs. Jensen believe there will be calamities in outer space. Vaughan predicts greater cooperation between the United States and Russia in the space program. Vaughan and Adrienne Coulter also foresee new technical advances during the '70s. In a trance-prediction, Mrs. Jensen envisioned man-made islands in space, and the discovery of a new planet with "trees, water, vegetation, strange fruits and vegetables."

SCIENCE AND HEALTH: Several psychics believe there will soon be a cure for cancer, with cures for other diseases to follow. According to Mrs. Jensen, there will be serious health problems in the Far East, with people "dying in the streets" from cholera, malaria, and other such diseases. For the rest of the world, however, there will be discoveries of new plants and oils with nutritional uses. Life

will be extended, the aging process slowed down, and human beings will be "treated and patched up, and sent on their way as good as
new."

RELIGION (under MISCELLANEOUS): Alan Vaughan sees a
new religion coming into being toward the end of the century that
will combine elements of other religions, including those of Christi-
anity. The "sun" will be involved. Mrs. Jensen also sees a united
religion, with a revival of awareness and spirituality, and a "kinder
spirit everywhere."

WHAT THE HUMAN SEISMOGRAPHS FORECAST

The following predictions are culled from those sent by potential
human seismographs to the Central Premonitions Registry:

POLITICS: There will be two political upheavals coming in the
1970s. In 1975 the Soviet Union will be controlled by a trio of man-
agers who are pro-production and anti-military.

The capital of the United States will be moved from Washington,
D.C. to the Midwest.

There will be a big scandal in Washington involving an oil deal.
Several politicians will be implicated.

WAR AND INTERNATIONAL RELATIONS: The Israeli-
Arab war will be over in June, 1973.

An "abysmal tyrant" will arise who will dominate the eastern and
middle regions of Africa.

THE SPACE RACE: A new small planet will be discovered in the
vicinity of Mars.

A new kind of animal will appear in space.

SCIENCE AND HEALTH: Within ten years it will be discovered
that preservatives are responsible for cancer because they destroy
cells. [Author's note: This prediction may be one of those based on
hysteria. It was sent in right after the cyclamate scare.]

During the 1970s it will be possible to prevent brain-damage in
children.

PROMINENT PERSONALITIES—DEATH AND INJURY: In 1971 a major political figure in Russia will be assassinated.

An assassination attempt will be made on the life of a prominent American governor, but it will probably not be successful.

A well-known political figure will die in an auto accident. Two children in the car will escape death.

THE KENNEDYS: Ethel Kennedy will marry Andy Williams.

MISCELLANEOUS: A respected scientist will make an extreme statement on the possibility of time travel.

A new form of theater will arise in 1971, focusing on the commentator who will serve as guide on stage. The success of the play will depend on the calibre of the commentator. Entertainers such as Johnny Carson will prove very popular in this form.

News content in newspapers will be minimal, but there will be computerized information service. Newspapers will be made up in magazine style and owned by television networks.

Architectural styles will give way to a new concept featuring the use of decks.

New islands will rise in the Pacific, starting in 1971.

In 1999 people will be living underwater in cities.

"STRANGE, BRAINLESS CHILDREN . . ."

Early in 1970 Ann Jensen of Dallas, Texas, made a tape recording of her forecast for the next thirty years, assisted by two friends, Jeanne Coffin and Jean Fowler. After Mrs. Coffin hypnotized her, she made her prophecies in trance and was not aware of what she had said until she woke up and played back the tape.

Mrs. Jensen's predictions were sent to the author and filed with the Central Premonitions Registry. Here are a few excerpts from the tape. Mrs. Coffin asks the questions:

What do you see for the 1970–1980 period?

"There will be another assassination. A very fine man, a Lincoln-like figure, but not someone in the upper echelons of government. It will be hard for the people to take. There will be much bitterness and changes that might bring on civil clashes and disorders. It will be a very trying time in the White House. It will need a steady hand and a steadier brain. This will come some time before 1976.

"But '76 will bring back some of the spirit of the other '76. 1977 will bring a cosmic upheaval, nothing to be frightened of if one has foresight, knowledge of what is coming . . . Some of the things the hippie children are talking about will materialize but in a much different way than they have expected . . .

"For those who have ruined their minds with drugs there will be compounds before the next five years have passed, places of treatment for these strange, brainless children that we have ruined. There is no hope, for what they have destroyed will never be replaced."

What do you see for the 1980s?

"The '80s will bring hope for a much better world, a better understanding, a demand of the world and of each other that if we can get together and make rules for war, then we can also get together and make rules for peace. This will come into being in some form at the beginning of the '80s, after periods of ups and downs during the '70s."

Will the war in Vietnam be over?

"The war is slowly dragging its way out. It will be some time before we are completely out. It may take all of this decade, but this was a hopeless situation from the first . . . The people of the West are tired, very tired of war, of having to take their very best and expend it. It is time we must protect our own and restore our own."

Will there be any natural disasters in the 1980s such as earthquakes?

"Nothing of any large importance. Only minor disturbances. Mount Pelée will act up but not to any great extent."

Will California continue to slide into the ocean?

"I don't think California will slide into any ocean. I see no catastrophe there."

What about the spiritual outlook for our country?

"There will be a revival in 1980. A great revival lifted into a much higher awareness. This started back in the '60s. This is the glimmer that the hippie children saw but they didn't take time to grow into it. This is the thing that is beckoning to everyone in one way or another, and in the '80s we will see the fruit . . . Some of the ugliness of the present, some of the vulgarities will linger like skeletons in a closet, and we will shudder that we let this happen."

Will the hippies have any future in the '80s?

"Some of them will be grandfathers by then and very stable, those who only indulged in the hair and the freedom. But those who have overindulged in the pills and the drugs will be behind fences."

Will they still turn toward the East for religion or will they come back to Western religions?

"The Cross will always be there, but there will be a united religion, a coming to understand that God is God, regardless of what we call Him, and some Eastern countries would naturally see a God of slant eyes, with yellow skin. The human heart responds as a human heart, no matter where, and the human soul is the same, no matter what body it inhabits."

"PEOPLE DYING IN THE STREETS . . ."

Let's move to 1990—from 1990 to 2000. What do you see here for the political situation?

"I see a woman at the head of a world government. I see satellite governments around the world government. I see that as the states bow down to the federal government in this country, so will the countries of the world bow down to the world government. We will still have states' rights and federal rights, but there will also be a world right. And this will usher in the year 2000.

"It will be a time of rapid communication, rapid travel, much exploring, much visionary communication without mechanizations of any sort. Life will be extended, but life will also be made much kinder. The aging process will be slowed down. As we preserve trees now, we will find that humans can be treated and patched up, and sent on as good as new. There will be cures for many of the diseases that haunt us now. There will be new things, though, to contend with."

Is starvation going to be a big problem?

"I see new methods of getting and supplying food. There will be new discoveries of vital, life-giving plants that have been ignored. There will be oils we haven't dreamed of using before. More consumption of chickens, turkeys, guineas—especially the guinea hens, ducks. All of these will be produced more than cattle. Cattle are expensive.

"Air-conditioning will be one thing we are going to have to come to terms with. Why? I can't get more on this. What is air-conditioning doing? Why was I told this? This is strange. Air-conditioning has been a life-saver for so many of us."

Will we have a major war between 1990–2000?

"No world war. It will be almost family to family—small uprisings, not in our country nor in South America or in this part of the world, but in the East—the Far East. There will be epidemics where there is overcrowding. Cholera, malaria, all the things that take them off in such great hordes. These are things I don't like to see—people dying in the streets, people stricken and going so fast, it's too fast to bury them. This will not happen in any country where there is sanitation. I see the water contaminated."

"THE SECOND COMING OF LOVE . . ."

What about our exploration of the planets? Will we find people on any of them?

"I don't see it."

Any form of life?

"Yes. We will find one planet that is very beautiful. It has trees, water, vegetation, strange fruits and vegetables. There will be a form of life—animal life. Like a jungle, a dream jungle. The pictures brought back from this planet are so beautiful. I see a tangle of blooming vines—beautiful, colorful. The trees, the oceans, the water covers.

"It will be a long time before it could be settled. A long time. But we will have islands, man-made islands built in space. Our grandchildren will land there. All this will come to pass."

Are we going to lose some spacemen in this venture?

"The thing I push away from me will be the calamities in outer space. This sickens me. I don't like to see it."

This international government you talk about, where will its head-quarters be?

"This will depend on the country that is elected. It will be a shifting thing. I see an island where the government can be set up, but it will shift from one country to another."

Will it be peaceful or warlike?

"Very peaceful. It will be because—this may sound like utopia and it is—because everyone everywhere will be touched in some way."

Do the American people and the people of the world have the insight to carry through these next thirty years to come out the way you see it should spiritually and economically?

"We have children with visions and dreams, little children between ten and twelve who know so much, who are being told and instructed by their own innermost nature. They want something . . . I see the coming of a better understanding, of a keener sense of responsibility. It will be almost an idealistic state of being when every man loves and every man is aware and every man is ready to help . . . when mother will go back to her rightful position, when father will no longer be afraid or too indifferent to speak, when sex will be some-thing to be enjoyed as love and not a commodity to be exploited, when the home will be a center and not a prison to escape from . . .

"These are things we will find as the year 2000 approaches. It will be the second coming, so to speak, of love."

Will man really love his neighbor?

"Yes, man will love his neighbor."

(End of tape.)

AN IMAGINATIVE LEAP FORWARD

It is the year 2000. There is peace throughout the world, follow-ing a series of frightful wars centering in the Middle East. Many religious persons all over the world claim that they saw a Cross appear in the sky on the last day of December, 1999, and that the peace which followed was a direct consequence of this divine sign. Others, particularly scientists, scoff at this, insisting that a natural phenomenon was responsible—a temperature inversion layer in the atmosphere or possibly ball lightning. There is genuine relief, however, that wars have ceased, at least for the time being, and that the United Nations with a less belligerent China as a member is now much stronger and is respected by all nations.

Although there have been many Arab leaders in the past thirty years, not one of them stood out above the others and none who could be identified as the Anti-Christ. The Israelis—and Jews throughout the world—still have not accepted Jesus as their Savior, but they are kindly disposed toward him and his followers. There is, in fact, more cooperation among all religious groups and more understanding of the common truth that inspires them.

There is now a cure for most diseases, including the dread cancer, and much less malnutrition on earth with the new techniques of creating proteins and other food elements in the laboratory. Russia and the United States, now cooperating in outer space, sent a fleet of space ships to Mars in 1989, powered by the new electromagnetic drive. Although no life was found on the red planet, Daniel Logan believes that the Martians have gone underground. Phobos, the Martian satellite, has mysteriously disappeared, much to the bewilderment of astronomers. In the political sphere, a woman was elected president of the United States in 1992, who had a baby while in office.

Although many cultists predicted the end of the world in 1999, January 1, 2000, dawned bright and clear. In 1997 New York City was mysteriously inundated by water that ruined a good deal of the city and its buildings, but its inhabitants were safely evacuated. This gave the city planners a chance to redesign and rebuild Manhattan, making it livable for those who moved back when the water receded. Seers who had predicted that the metropolis would be flooded were accused by other psychics of having "created" the floods through the release of thought-forms into the ether. The consensus now is that it is better to think of good things and release positive vibrations into the world.

A few gloomy souls keep warning that the Anti-Christ has finally been born, but the feeling is general that the world is in the midst of a spiritual rebirth. Possibly the most amazing phenomenon has been the almost universal psychic ability of the young generation. Nearly every government in the world now accepts the reality of psychic experience, and degrees in parapsychology are granted at most universities. Many nations, including the United States and Russia, have installed official oracles, who are consulted on matters of politics and war. One reason there is peace may be the fear of world leaders that oracles from other countries can move in psychically and pick their brains.

Parapsychology has received a tremendous lift from the great success of the London and New York premonitions agencies in recent years. Their most spectacular triumph was the warning about the comet that made an unheralded appearance in 1984 and caused devastation everywhere. Hundreds of letters and phone calls had been received in London and New York telling of dreams and visions of the comet and what it would do. Again in 1992 a disaster was averted in a Welsh town when people all over England and in some other countries had frightening dreams of a coal slide. The British Premonitions Bureau, after processing these premonitions in a computer, issued an early warning alert, adults and children were removed to a safe area, and the coal slide took place as predicted.

There are now premonitions registries in most capitals of the world—New York, London, Moscow, Peking, Stockholm, Oslo, Tel Aviv, etc. All are interconnected through the "psychic hot line"—phone, radio, cable, and Comsat, even some purely mental transmission from registry to registry. With the new psychic sensitivity in people everywhere, human seismographs are commonplace. Through meditation and other techniques, they can now respond to events about to happen in remote corners of the earth, not just in their own geographical area.

And now in May, 2000, the premonitions begin to pour in—warning of another earthquake in Peru as great in scope as South America's worst quake on May 31, 1970. The switchboards in premonitions registries all over the world are buzzing with calls pinpointing certain mountain villages once more as the location of the impending disaster. The calls are in different languages:

"An earthquake is coming in Peru!"
"Ein Erdbeben in Peru!"
"Jordbävning in Peru!"
"Tremblement de terre!"
"Tremblor de tierra!"
"Terremoto!"

The warnings are processed in a "central premonitions computer" that serves the registries, and the prognosis is for a terrible quake, fully as destructive as the 1970 one. An early warning alert is sounded and the registry at Bogota, Colombia, is reached through the psychic hot line. Lima does not have a registry and Bogota is the nearest geographically.

The Bogota registry contacts the authorities in Peru with the computerized information. Evacuation begins immediately. Thousands are saved, before another earthquake devastates the Peruvian villages. This time the world is ready to help. Money, food, and clothing are promptly channeled through the United Nations and the Red Cross, using the air services of many countries. The towns are miraculously rebuilt almost overnight with prefabricated housing, and the happy Peruvians go back to their way of life, almost as if nothing had happened.

A reporter, interviewing many of the evacuees, discovers that there had been many intimations of disaster among them, too—in dreams, visions, uneasy feelings, even voices warning them to leave immediately. One woman swore that the Virgin Mary appeared and showed her a vision of the destruction that would follow. A small child had dreamed of the earthquake but she told her mother that she was not afraid, for this time they would all be saved. The villagers also recount stories handed down by their fathers and grandfathers of warnings given by the old men and women of the village before the great disaster of 1970.

After the quake a premonitions registry is set up in Lima, and the villagers are instructed how to contact it when they anticipate another disaster.

Perhaps the world of tomorrow will be as described above, perhaps not. But as we enter the Age of Aquarius, there are signs everywhere of an awakening interest in religion and psychic phenomena.

In time psychics and seers will probably be far more commonplace than they are today, as the average person becomes aware of the treasures stored in his subliminal computer. Perhaps in the year 2000 every man will be a human seismograph with his psychic ear tuned to coming events.

Perhaps, best of all, there truly will be a "second coming of love."

"More Things in Heaven and Earth"

Today, in the year 1971, certain countries are beginning to take an official interest in psychic phenomena. From the Ostrander-Schroeder book *Psychic Discoveries Behind the Iron Curtain* and other sources we learn that Russian scientists, with government approval, are actively investigating telepathy and precognition. An astrophysicist, Nikolai Kozyrev, has theorized that time is a form of energy that is "thin near the sender . . . denser around the receiver." Kozyrev believes that "thoughts may change the density of time." Creating the future?

The Ostrander-Schroeder book hints that a premonitions bureau may be operating somewhere in Russia. Soviet scientists, according to this story, have offered money to peasants if they send in predictions. And in Bulgaria, a blind woman named Vanga Dimitrova is an official seer who receives a salary. Soviet parapsychologists, in keeping with the Marxist determination to find a physical cause for everything, are studying the energy field around her.

Although the Russians would not put it in these terms, they evidently believe, with Shakespeare, that there are "more things in heaven and earth" than can be detected by the senses or laboratory instruments. "Heaven" is presumably being studied as a suitable environment for ESP during space flights. A Russian newspaper states that cosmonauts have had telepathic experiences with each other while in orbit, and implies that conditions beyond earth gravity may make it possible.

Along with their regular training, says this newspaper, cosmonauts are being trained to develop telepathy and precognition. If mechanical equipment such as radio should fail, they may be able to communicate mentally with ground crews through a coded message using the Morse system. Another purpose of this training program is to avoid dangers in space by sensing what may happen. A Russian biologist has said that because space ships travel so fast, their occupants may "literally be able to see the future."

What of the United States? If our government is interested in exploring the psychic world, it has made no public announcements. But there are signs of a breakthrough. The work with the dolphins in Florida and elsewhere may include testing for ESP as well as communication through sounds. (The Russians are also experimenting with ways of communicating with dolphins in the Crimea.) There is also some evidence that the U.S. Army has shown an interest in the potential use of ESP in wartime. About a decade ago, an Army medical research unit sent a camera crew to photograph and evaluate the Rhine experiments at Duke University.

Dr. Thelma Moss, a psychologist at the University of California at Los Angeles, recently described a long-distance ESP experiment between the campus and the Air Force Academy in Colorado Springs, Colorado. The U.C.L.A. students looked at color slides and tried to transmit mentally the scenes along with their emotional reactions. One slide was of the North Pole, and a "receiver" in Colorado had an impression of howling winds and bitter cold. Dr. Moss writes that "the government had nothing to do with the experiment," yet the fact that the Air Force Academy participated may suggest increasing interest in government circles.

What is the attitude of those who run the NASA program? Are they open to the idea of developing telepathy and precognition in the astronauts to avert dangers in outer space and for communication with ground crews? So far there is no indication that NASA plans to test and train astronauts in ESP.

My feeling, however, is that before long, there will be a greater willingness on the part of NASA and other government agencies to explore the practical possibilities of extrasensory perception. This will happen if only because the United States will not allow Russia to get too far ahead in any aspect of the space or other programs.

One of NASA's own spacemen decided not to wait for an official test. On February 9, 1971, just after the safe return to earth of the *Apollo XIV* astronauts, it was revealed that Edgar D. Mitchell had conducted his own psi-experiments while in flight. Concentrating on the five cards used by Dr. Rhine in the telepathy experiments at Duke University, Mitchell tried to communicate mentally with four persons on earth.

Just after the launching of *Apollo XIV* the *New York Times* of February 1, 1971 said of Mitchell: "It is also his nature to wonder and ponder over things that he, and other men, cannot understand. Commander Mitchell is fascinated, primarily as a scientist (he has a degree in astronautics) by the phenomenon of extrasensory perception . . ."

Is Mitchell the prototype of the new spaceman, one who looks beyond technology to the mysterious forces recorded not on instruments but in the depths of the mind and soul? It is tempting to think so. Before his Apollo 14 flight, Mitchell, who practices meditation, had readings with the late medium, Arthur Ford. Ford claimed that several of those now in the NASA program belong to Spiritual Frontiers Fellowship. Also, a glance at the Biographical Dictionary of Parapsychology reveals names of astrophysicists and space-rocket technologists who study the paranormal.

The unmanned missile probes have sent back unusual data to "ponder over." A NASA news release of May 15, 1970, states that Phobos, the fast-moving Martian satellite described by Jonathan Swift 150 years before it was seen through a telescope, has a very unusual shape—like a potato. "Phobos, the larger of the two Martian moons," says the release, "appeared lopsided—considerably longer than it is wide—in a photograph taken 86,000 miles from Mars by Mariner 7." Another strange fact is that Phobos "appears to be the darkest body of any size yet observed in our solar system."

This doesn't prove, of course, that Phobos is an artificial satellite, but it does make one wonder what was stirring in Jonathan Swift's subliminal mind when he wrote *Gulliver's Travels*.

What about the new generation growing up in the Aquarian Age? Is it so fanciful to believe that most of them may be practicing psychics in the year 2000? Ann Jensen, during her trance-predictions, saw "children with visions and dreams, little children between ten and twelve who know so much, who are being told and instructed by their inner nature . . ." Adrienne Coulter has predicted that the children of the hippie generation will be psychically and spiritually oriented.

Paul Neary, a New York psychic who was recommended to me by Arthur Ford, says that psychics among the very young are practically "coming out of the woodwork." Neary believes that a new breed of psychic is emerging who will demonstrate powers far beyond those of today's more mature sensitives and will use "four hundred to five hundred per cent more of their minds than the average person." The youthful seer, says Neary, is the prototype of a newly emerging kind of man.

Neary sees a spiritual rebirth by the year 2000, with extrasensory perception and mental healing commonplace by 1990. But first there will be a tremendous upheaval in nature, probably in 1974–75, that will devastate one-third of the globe and include the United States. He points to the Peru disaster of 1970, one of the worst in history, and the Pakistani cyclone that took an estimated 200,000 to a million lives as forerunners of an even greater catastrophe.

In a recent meeting of psychics using the crystal ball as a focus of attention, Neary and the other sensitives witnessed scenes of this catastrophe: ". . . a great stillness in New York . . . the earth with one piece missing . . . a new map of the world . . ." Neary also predicts a world-wide famine in 1974–76. After a period of suffering, however, the awakening will begin, people will change, and "loving kindness" will be the rule in human relationships.

One of Neary's predictions in the political realm is tied to this disaster and is echoed in part by the predictions of other psychics. Democracy as we know it, says Neary, will end with Nixon as the last president. Jeane Dixon believes that before 1980 "the two-party system will vanish from the American scene." Malcolm Bessent thinks the country may "explode" in the next five years, and "a new political structure will come into being."

The position of the author is that forecasts of cosmic disasters must be viewed with a certain amount of skepticism. In evaluating the predictions of psychics for the next thirty years—some of which dovetail while others are at variance—I believe that the odds are against a worldwide cataclysm. It must be borne in mind, however, that the United States may be just as vulnerable to catastrophe as Peru, Pakistan, and other areas that have been hit in recent years by large-scale natural disasters.

As I write this, in February, 1971, word has just come of a near-major earthquake in Los Angeles, with more than 60 known dead and over 1,000 injured. This was the worst quake in the Los Angeles area since the Long Beach quake of 1933 that killed 115 persons. It is not, however, the "one bad quake" of the decade or even of the next thirty years forecast by Dr. William T. Pecora of the U.S. Geological Survey. The San Andreas fault, where the "big" quake is expected, was not involved. And the severity of the quake, as measured by the Richter scale, was 6.6, below the minimum 7 required of a major earthquake.

A severe natural disaster—yes; a cosmic cataclysm—no.

As for the new psychics of the Aquarian Age, I believe there is considerable evidence that they are already here. I have met quite a few very young and talented psychics, some of them with "strange eyes" (Paul Neary's phrase), others with a cooler look.

The year 2000 seems closer in another respect—the interest of governments in psychic phenomena. To my knowledge there is as yet no official seer on the federal payroll, but it may be coming. Although it is not publicized, Washington politicians make regular trips to psychics. The late Senator Mendel Rivers frequently had readings from Arthur Ford.

In 1971, as this is being written, interest in telepathy, clairvoyance, precognition and other forms of "psi" is becoming universal. Scientists such as marine biologist Sir Alister Hardy (past president of the British Society for Psychical Research) and the late Chester F. Carlson, inventor of the Xerox copying process, have been actively associated with parapsychological organizations. In a lecture forum given by the American Society for Psychical Research on December 4, 1968, to honor Carlson's memory, his wife told the audience of many telepathic experiences she shared with her husband.

Businessmen, doctors, lawyers, housewives, wage-earners—ordinary persons throughout the world—are testing their capacity as human seismographs and sending predictions to the British Premonitions Bureau and the Central Premonitions Registry. Meanwhile, new registries are being activated, including one in Toronto, Canada. It is not unrealistic to believe that in the year 2000 there will be a network of such bureaus throughout the world.

With the mushrooming of human seismographs, more and more mail is coming to the Central Premonitions Registry, including letters from countries as distant as Venezuela, Germany, and Switzerland. Following a recent early morning television broadcast in which Robert Nelson spoke about the Registry, 2,700 letters and phone calls came from "ordinary people," all eager to learn how they might develop their psychic sense. From a statistical point of view, the more predictions received, the larger will be the percentage of "hits."

Each reader who holds this book in his hand is a potential human seismograph or psychic. In time, using such techniques as meditation and dream analysis, he may be able to sense the vibrations of natural and mechanical disasters about to happen. An important step on the road to becoming a practicing seer is to send such impressions to either the British Premonitions Bureau or the Central Premonitions Registry. Here are their addresses:

THE CENTRAL PREMONITIONS REGISTRY
BOX 482
TIMES SQUARE STATION
NEW YORK, N.Y. 10036

BRITISH PREMONITIONS BUREAU
T.V. TIMES
247 TOTTENHAM COURT ROAD
LONDON, W1P OAU

The following is a questionnaire now being sent by the Central Premonitions Registry to persons who have demonstrated psychic ability. The object is to discover, if possible, common factors in precognitive experience.

QUESTIONNAIRE FOR PSI PROFILE

1. Name ....
2. Age at which PSI first discovered, and nature of phenomena ....
....
....
3. Date of Birth ....
4. Father's Occupation ....
5. Parents' Religion ....
   (If Mother's religion different from Father, enter here) ....
....
6. Your Religion or Beliefs ....
....
....
7. Relationship with Parents (e.g. closest to mother, etc.) ....
....
....
8. Family History: a) Number of Brothers .... b) Sisters
   .... c) Your family rank (e.g. oldest, etc.) ....
....
9. Education ....
....
10. Occupation ....
....
11. PSI Experienced in Dreams: a) Do you dream in color ....
....
   b) Describe kind of psi, e.g. Telepathy, precognition ....
....
   c) Are any particular colors more intense ....
   d) What colors ....
   e) How do your psychic dreams differ from ordinary dreams ....
....
....
   f) Are you usually an observer or a participant ....
....
   g) Are you aware of the passage of time ....
....
   h) Do you experience any particular sense of goodness or evil in
   trance state ....
....

    i) Are your dreams familiar, as if you've already experienced them
....

....

12. PSI experienced through Meditation: a) Are you aware of the passage
of time ....
b) Do you experience any particular sense of goodness or evil ......
....

....
c) Do you ever feel as if you are "out of your body" ....
....

13. Have you ever felt that an arm or some part of your body was moving
when you knew it actually was not ....
....

14. Have you ever experienced a sense of "oneness with Nature," or the
Universe .... a) When, and under what conditions
....
....
....

15. Comments: ....
....
....
....
....

RETURN TO:

Robert D. Nelson, Director
Central Premonitions Registry
Box 482, Times Sq. Sta.
New York, N.Y. 10036

INDEX

ABOUT THE AUTHOR

HERBERT B. GREENHOUSE was born in Chicago, educated at Northwestern University and the University of Southern California, and served in the Army during World War II. He has been an advertising copywriter, a playwright for stage, radio, and television, and is a pianist and composer. An avid investigator of psychic phenomena, Mr. Greenhouse is a member of the American Society for Psychical Research and has participated in many ESP laboratory experiments. He is the author of *In Defense of Ghosts, Thoughts of the Imitation of Christ,* and *How to Double Your Vocabulary.* He lives in New Jersey and has a retreat in the Berkshires.